Girls Write Now is a terrific mento
anthology proves its importance a
blazes with the talent, insight, and
giving us all cause to celebrate and

HILMA WOLITZER, *AN AVAILABLE MAN*

I can't think of an organization that does more for young women's self-esteem than Girls Write Now. Within a nurturing community of women writers, these teenage girls from across New York's five boroughs flourish—creating the sparkling, honest, poetic writing you see within these pages. What an inspiration!

CHRISTINA BAKER KLINE, *ORPHAN TRAIN*

There is something amazing about witnessing the process of a young person recognizing herself, discovering her voice, and realizing that she has something valuable to say. *New Worlds* features page after page of these powerful moments, with poets and storytellers, memoirists and humorists, fantasists and chroniclers all writing themselves into being—through the daring act of sharing their voices and using their words.

ANDI BUCHANAN, *THE DARING BOOK FOR GIRLS*

Writers are surprisingly good talkers, if only to ourselves. We tell ourselves that if we show what we write, people will think we're stupid, or lame, or crazy. Are girls particularly vulnerable to those voices? I don't know. I just know I was. That's why I pick up the annual Girls Write Now anthology with such eagerness. There is courage, will, and heart on every page.

JUDY BLUNDELL, *WHAT I SAW AND HOW I LIED*

An intriguing collection of writing by some remarkable young women. They are all confronting their lives through their poetry and prose.

PATRICIA BOSWORTH, *JANE FONDA*

The struggling to bloom in this book is palpable. These are girls in the process of being changed by the world. Reading their thoughts on such an intimate level is an honor, and a privilege.

VANESSA GRIGORIADIS, *NATIONAL MAGAZINE AWARD WINNER*

What's so important about this anthology is how each writer has learned to bravely ask and answer some of the big questions about growing up as a woman in these times. It is inspiring to experience these proud, original voices.

JULIE METZ, *PERFECTION*

GIRLS WRITE NOW
2013 ANTHOLOGY

ANTHOLOGY EDITORIAL COMMITTEE

Shea'la Finch
Managing Editor

Laura Barlament

Wendy Caster

Vivian Conan

Kristen Demaline

Jillian Gallagher

Heather M. Graham

Whitney Jacoby

Kathleen Kraft

Kirsten Reach

Cherise Wolas

Laura Cheung
Communications Coordinator

Rebecca Haverson
Program Coordinator

Laura Stenson Wynne
Director of Programs

Maya Nussbaum
Founder & Executive Director

DESIGNER

Jenifer Carter

COPY EDITOR

Hannah Sheldon-Dean

PHOTOGRAPHER

Aehee Asano

ABOUT THE ANTHOLOGY

After guiding each mentee through so many of the rites of the writer's life—creation, revision, submission, public presentation—the Girls Write Now Mentoring Program culminates with our annual anthology, in which each student and mentor showcases their best original work. Structured around this year's overarching curricular theme, *New Worlds*, the 2013 Anthology is composed of stories that celebrate the incredible diversity and creative fearlessness of our intergenerational community—including poetry, fiction, memoir, and more—that surprise us and stretch our understanding of the world, and ourselves.

The Girls Write Now anthology has been recognized as Outstanding Book of the Year by the Independent Publisher Book Awards, and has earned additional honors from the International Book Awards, the National Indie Excellence Awards, the Next Generation Indie Book Awards, and the New York Book Festival.

ABOUT GIRLS WRITE NOW

Distinguished as one of the top 15 after-school arts and culture programs in the nation by The President's Committee on Arts & Humanities, Girls Write Now is New York's first and only organization with a writing and mentoring model for girls. Now celebrating our 15th anniversary, Girls Write Now is a community of women writers dedicated to providing guidance, support and opportunities for high school girls to develop their creative, independent voices, and write their way to a better future. We do this work through our flagship Mentoring Program, which matches professional women writers with underserved high school girls for a one- to four-year mentorship; the Girls College Bound Program, which helps New York City girls successfully navigate the college essay and application process; and our Digital Media Mentoring Program, in partnership with Parsons The New School for Design and with leadership support from the MacArthur Foundation-funded Hive Digital Learning Fund in the New York Community Trust.

2012-13 LITERARY PARTNERS

Algonquin Books

Alliance for Young Artists & Writers

Book Riot

Bust Magazine

Dramatics Play Service, Inc.

Girl Be Heard

Hive Learning Network NYC

Jane Austen Society of North America

Mary Jo Bang & Bread Loaf Writers' Conference

McNally Jackson

Mentoring Partnership of New York

Middlebury College Press

Open Road Integrated Media

Parsons The New School for Design

Penguin Group USA

People StyleWatch

Poet-Linc at Lincoln Center

Poetry Society

Poets Out Loud at Fordham University

Random House Children's Books

Scholastic

Story Bundle

Travel + Leisure Magazine

Ugly Duckling Presse

Wave Books

Writers House, LLC

Young to Publishing Group

CELEBRATING 15 YEARS

More than 4,500 high-need high school girls served (90% girls of color, 90% high-need, and 20% immigrants)

Distinguished twice by the White House in two years

Won Youth, I.N.C. Innovator Award for being one of New York City's most enterprising non-profits

Featured by *The New York Times* and *NBC Nightly News*, and as a top place to volunteer by both *Great Non-Profits* and *Time Out New York*

Annual network of 150 high-level active volunteers, with mentors alone donating over 10,000 hours of service each year

Mentees have won hundreds of medals from the Scholastic Art & Writing Awards

100% of Mentoring Program seniors graduate from high school—with portfolios, awards, scholarships, new skills, and a sense of confidence

ANTHOLOGY SUPPORTERS

We are grateful to the countless institutions and individuals who have supported our work through their generous contributions. Visit our website at www.girlswritenow.org to view the full list or download our most recent Annual Report.

Girls Write Now would like to thank Amazon.com, which provided the charitable contribution that made possible this year's anthology.

amazon.com

The anthology is supported, in part, by public funds from the National Endowment for the Arts; the New York State Council on the Arts, a State Agency; and the New York City Department of Cultural Affairs, in partnership with the City Council.

New Worlds: The Girls Write Now 2013 Anthology, 15th Anniversary Edition

Girls Write Now, Inc.

247 West 37 Street, Suite 1800

New York, NY 10018

info@girlswritenow.org

www.girlswritenow.org

Printed in the United States

ISBN 978-0-615-81827-6

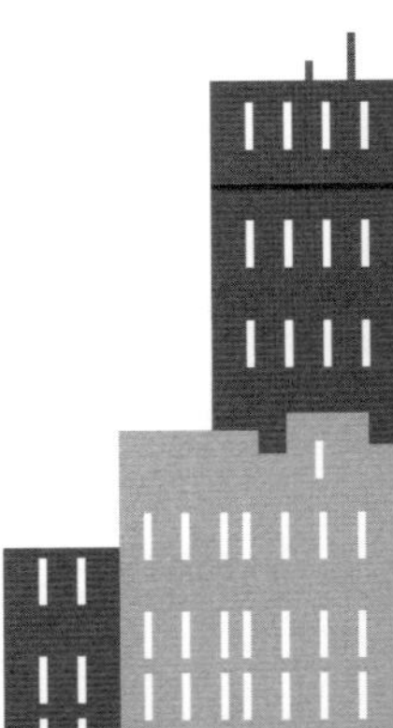

girls write now

NEW worlds

2013 ANTHOLOGY

15 YEARS

foreword

Girls Write Now! Could there be three more on-point words to describe this wonderful group? So imagine my happiness in being asked to introduce these voices by way of an anthology that celebrates fifteen years of this balance—of process, of friendship, of vision—between the young mentee and seasoned writer. In a perfect pairing, we cheer the writer just out of the gate, fueled by youthful energy and purpose, as we appreciate the empathy of that mentor, who has chosen to put out her hand in thoughtful sisterhood, with knowledge that she can help define the strength of our future.

This year's *New Worlds* theme was particularly resonant for me, as a former "Army brat" who grew up all over the world, with no one particular home, and yet in place of permanent roots, a lifelong curiosity for far-flung places and diversity of cultures. Wherever we'd landed, my mother had reached out to community theater as a way to anchor herself to her own constant love of the performing arts. In doing so, she gave me my mentors, my babysitters: a rotating cast of young women who were involved in local theater productions and who shone bright lights of creativity into my life.

My own mentors defined themselves via the drama of improvisation, rehearsal, set design, costumes, and opening night. Even today, almost twenty years and twenty-odd books into my career as a novelist, I'm bound to an education in the theater. Whether in a book's three-act structure, in the snap of dialogue, or in my desire to read my drafts out loud, as I "rehearse" all my words for a final performance before I show them to my editor.

These pages also mark a final performance, and the many rooms in the house of this anthology are a bristling intrigue. Whether in fiction or fantasy, in essays of humor or personal heartbreak, in free verse or dialogue, it is a compilation of work that calls us to pay attention. By cutting the ribbon on *New Worlds: The Girls Write Now 2013 Anthology*, we celebrate both the basis of the Girls Write Now community and the hard-shine polish of the written word as it has been altered, expanded, reworked, cut, and perfected on the page. With each sentence set, each word placed for maximum impact of voice, style, tone, and form, it is now your turn, as a member of the reading audience, to lose yourself to the thrill of being transported somewhere else.

ADELE GRIFFIN

MAY 2013

Terra incognita: unknown or unexplored territory. We know it as the blank space on maps from when the world was still being defined. A distant cry from the maps of today, always at our fingertips, updated in real-time as roads shift and boundaries are redirected.

Where is the *terra incognita*—the new worlds—of today? A new world can be a place, a sensation, or a different perspective. It's as subtle as a shift in expectation, or as concrete as a college application. You prepare for it your whole life—or it can happen overnight.

This year, a new world opened up for Girls Write Now as we marked our 15th anniversary—an extraordinary coming-of-age moment felt not only by the organization, but by the girls we serve, who were born around the same time our movement was.

Through pair sessions, workshops, portfolio building, readings, and publication, teens suited up with skills for the next stage of life, while the organization that supports them prepared to share this honed model with new audiences on a larger scale. Together we developed the strength and savvy required to thrive in unexplored territories.

Within these pages, you have 150 new worlds to discover, the culmination of a year of exploration from 75 pairs built upon a history of infinitely rich community writing. In the form of poetry, prose, fan fiction, essays, and more, you will hear our mentees and mentors reporting on the *terra incognita* of new experiences, as well as the echos of our alumnae reflecting on coming of age as artists at their own crucial 15 year point.

Begin by meeting our intrepid authors in the profiles section *(p. 2)*. Continue on to the chapters *(p. 77)*, which have been sorted by the themes of the new worlds they investigate. Conclude with a behind-the-scenes glimpse of our 2013 workshop experience *(p. 297)*. And on your travels, use the icons located throughout the book as your compass:

Found next to every piece in the main body, this icon will lead you to the work of the author's mentor or mentee.

Found in the main body, this icon will locate the profile of the author and her mentor/mentee partner.

Found in the profiles section, follow this icon to read the author's work.

We hope this anthology will inspire you to continue seeking and examining new worlds, to join our explorers, and to add your voice to reshaping the map.

2013 ANTHOLOGY
EDITORIAL COMMITTEE

To celebrate Girls Write Now's 15th anniversary, we invited our alumnae to reflect on their relationship to writing when they turned fifteen—also the average age of our current mentees. Mentors and mentees from years past share their voices below, and throughout this book.

Fifteen is a plateau, a high dive. When it was my turn I was too terrified to jump, so I put everything I needed in my notebook—song lyrics, poetry, declarations, ideas. Moons, stars, planets, hearts. Writing became my second skin, my big sister. When sixteen rolled around, I closed my eyes and leapt.
MORGAN BADEN, MENTOR 2007-2010

Every word and every bit of it was a treasure—something I left behind to be found again. Emotions and thoughts were just leaking out of my pores and filling in empty spaces. Being fifteen, writing was everything.
XIAO HONG ZHANG, MENTEE 2006-2007

At fifteen there was so much I wanted to say but didn't know how. So I hopped from full sentences to stanzas. The images, white space, and rhythm of small poems could hold all the big questions and large feelings. I was writing love letters to myself and the world.
SARAH HERRINGTON, MENTOR 2006-2007

Writing at fifteen felt forbidden because it was. Not writing, but wanting only to write. I hid to write, and hid my writing; told everyone I would be an obstetrician-gynecologist. I always spoke the full, hyphenated profession, loving the syllabic cadence. It wasn't an aspiration; it was a character.
NANA EKUA BREW-HAMMOND, MENTOR 2004-2008

Wow, fifteen years already! I still remember when I read for the ten year anniversary. Fifteen was nothing but first relationships and questions in sight. It's as if I was walking the same dark cloud every day; like a bad dream. Writing was the window for escaping past all the fuzziness. And over time, the only fuzzies left were warm.
CARMEN LI, MENTEE 2005-2008

follow to author's mentor / mentee piece

follow to the author's profile

follow to the author's work

CHENELLE AGNEW

YEARS AS MENTEE: *1*

GRADE: *10*

HIGH SCHOOL: *High School of Telecommunication Arts and Technology*

BORN: *NY, NY*

LIVES: *Brooklyn, NY*

PUBLICATIONS AND RECOGNITIONS: *Scholastic Art & Writing Award Honorable Mention in Poetry*

EHMONIE HAINEY

YEARS AS MENTOR: *1*

OCCUPATION: *Fashion and Beauty Writer*

PUBLICATIONS AND RECOGNITIONS: *Bella Online, Examiner.com, HandbagDuJour.com, Shecky's, WhatsHaute.com*

CHENELLE SAYS: My relationship with Ehmonie has opened me up to different perspectives and new ways to approach challenges. Recently, my mentor has been helping me better prepare myself for college and job applications, which will be very useful in the future. My mentor teaches me something new every time we meet that always leaves an impact on me and makes me mindful of other things in my surroundings.

 *p. 167*

EHMONIE SAYS: Chenelle and I first wrote pieces relating to the civil rights movement for the historical fiction workshop, and we decided to explore this theme again. When we meet each week, we often discuss our perspectives of the world as it is now, and how it was back then, and we also like to share our insights on political issues, current world events, and what's happening in our communities. Chenelle has a very mature and unique perspective on things, and I find that I am always learning something new when I talk to her.

 *p. 169*

TATYANA ALEXANDER

YEARS AS MENTEE: *3*

GRADE: *12*

HIGH SCHOOL: *Academy for Conservation and the Environment*

BORN: *NY, NY*

LIVES: *Brooklyn, NY*

PUBLICATIONS AND RECOGNITIONS: *Scholastic Art & Writing Award Honorable Mention in Senior Writing Portfolio*

TATYANA SAYS: The relationship Jillian and I have has opened the new worlds of cafes and hot chocolate, of having deep conversations about the curiosities of life and the morals in between. Our conversations teach me that every stage of life has transitions, and no matter how serious they are there is always room to take a deep breath and laugh.

 *p. 244*

JILLIAN GALLAGHER

YEARS AS MENTOR: *2*

OCCUPATION: *Senior Writer, FutureBrand*

JILLIAN SAYS: What did I learn about new worlds this year from Tatyana? Sometimes you don't have to go far to find a new world. It can live in an existing relationship—returning back to the same topics, but with a deeper understanding of the person you're talking to. Seeing someone you know well making progress. And knowing you have a friend, where there used to just be a mentee.

 *p. 247*

NISHAT ANJUM

YEARS AS MENTEE: *1*

GRADE: *11*

HIGH SCHOOL: *Susan E. Wagner High School*

BORN: *Bangladesh*

LIVES: *Staten Island, NY*

PUBLICATIONS AND RECOGNITIONS: *Scholastic Art & Writing Award Silver Key in Short Story*

NISHAT SAYS: Being a teenager is about developing your own identity and finding your place in the world. While I haven't discovered what the universe wants me to do, I wouldn't have realized my potential as a writer if I weren't paired with Julie. Meeting Julie was like opening my eyes to the world beyond my island. I learned that sometimes the best story you can tell is your own, and that fewer words can have more significance. By encouraging me to reach past my comfort zones, Julie has given me a better perspective of who I am.

 *p. 144*

JULIE SALAMON

YEARS AS MENTOR: *1*

OCCUPATION: *Author; Journalist*

PUBLICATIONS AND RECOGNITIONS: *Wendy and the Lost Boys, Hospital, The Devil's Candy, Facing the Wind, The Net of Dreams, The Christmas Tree, Rambam's Ladder; The New York Times, The New Yorker, Vanity Fair, Vogue, The Wall Street Journal*

JULIE SAYS: I've explored many cultures, and had close relationships with people from all kinds of backgrounds. These have included Muslims, but never someone who chose to wear a hijab. Through Nishat I have examined my preconceptions about what wearing a headscarf signifies, and learned what it actually means to her. Most satisfying has been discovering a person and writer who feels so familiar yet comes from a different generation, culture, experience. Our work, especially the conversations surrounding it, is true pleasure. It's inspiring and thought-provoking, but also a lot of fun. When I think of Nishat, I smile.

 *p. 143*

MAXINE ARMSTRONG

YEARS AS MENTEE: *1*

GRADE: *10*

HIGH SCHOOL: *Brooklyn Collaborative Studies*

BORN: *NY, NY*

LIVES: *Brooklyn, NY*

PUBLICATIONS AND RECOGNITIONS: *Scholastic Art & Writing Award Honorable Mention in Short Story*

MAXINE SAYS: We went to see the dress rehearsal of the play *Hollow Roots* by Christina Anderson, and we read stories together from *The Book of Fantasy*. We met at a different coffee shop every week until we found one we loved.

 *p. 116*

HANNA PYLVÄINEN

YEARS AS MENTOR: *1*

OCCUPATION: *Novelist*

PUBLICATIONS AND RECOGNITIONS: *We Sinners*

HANNA SAYS: Although I grew up reading science fiction, I always write realism. Reading and writing literary fantasy and magical realism with Maxine has brought me back to some old authors and new ones. It's also raised the strange and difficult question of how to write fantastical events in a way that is not "genre."

 *p. 118*

ANDREINA AVALOS

YEARS AS MENTEE: *2*

GRADE: *12*

HIGH SCHOOL: *Urban Assembly School for Law and Justice*

BORN: *NY, NY*

LIVES: *Brooklyn, NY*

COLLEGE: *New York City College of Technology*

HEATHER GRAHAM

YEARS AS MENTOR: *3*

OCCUPATION: *Deputy Health Editor, iVillage, NBC Universal*

PUBLICATIONS AND RECOGNITIONS: *DailyGlow.com, EverydayHealth.com, Lifescript.com, Mediabistro.com, New York Moves*

ANDREINA SAYS: Heather is always there when I need her to support me. We have a strong bond. Her voice saying, "Don't fall in love with your words," always pops in my head when I struggle with editing my own work. She has taught me if something doesn't work out then you must go with another idea. This is my second and last year with her. I will truly miss our time together, but I know we will still keep in touch!

 *p. 105*

HEATHER SAYS: This is our second year together and our bond is even stronger. We even wrote a piece together for the CHAPTERS reading series, which was really fun. I'll be sad to see Andreina go off to college in the fall, but I'm so proud of her and know she'll do well.

 *p. 107*

MARIAH TERESA AVILES

YEARS AS MENTEE: *4*

GRADE: *12*

HIGH SCHOOL: *Young Women's Leadership School of East Harlem*

BORN: *NY, NY*

LIVES: *Bronx, NY*

PUBLICATIONS AND RECOGNITIONS: *GWN Poetry Ambassador, Poet-Linc Poetry Slam at Lincoln Center, Poets Out Loud at Fordham University*

MARIAH SAYS: I remember the first time we met, and it determined the next three years of our future. Although we've worked independently on different things over the years, we shared the same writing struggles and achievements. Now we're reaching our last chapter only to start another book together. Even if distance tries to creep in, the pages will be tightly bound.

 *p. 179*

ALLISON ADAIR ALBERTS

YEARS AS MENTOR: *3*

OCCUPATION: *PhD Student, Fordham University*

PUBLICATIONS AND RECOGNITIONS: *Rhetorikos: Excellence in Student Writing*

ALLISON SAYS: Over the past three years, Riah and I have explored genres, vocabulary, structures, writing techniques, editing, and each other's friendship.

 *p. 98*

KAADIANA BARNES

YEARS AS MENTEE: *1*

GRADE: *12*

HIGH SCHOOL: *The Young Women's Leadership School of East Harlem*

BORN: *NY, NY*

LIVES: *NY, NY*

PUBLICATIONS AND RECOGNITIONS: *Scholastic Art & Writing Award Honorable Mention in Poetry; Xavier Scholarship*

COLLEGE: *Fairfield University*

KATHRYN O'DELL

YEARS AS MENTOR: *1*

OCCUPATION: *Education Editor*

KAADIANA SAYS: I've created great memories with Kathryn throughout the year. We had multiple meetings a week to work on different assignments, like my college essay, Scholastic writing piece, writing prompts, and much more. My favorite memory of spending time with Kathryn is when I prepared my performance for the Urban Word Teen Slam in a recording studio in her home.

 *p. 271*

KATHRYN SAYS: Kaadiana, earning her black belt in karate this year, approaches her writing much like I imagine she approaches a karate tournament. She is silent, strong, and fearless. The blank page is her opponent, and it doesn't stand a chance. As soon as we begin a writing exercise (and sometimes before), Kaadiana's pen attacks the paper. Soon the paper is filled with Kaadiana's words—about her life, her neighborhood, her thoughts, her feelings. The tournament is over. The paper loses; Kaadiana wins. Kaadiana's voracious approach to writing has inspired me to attack that blank page!

 *p. 141*

SWATI BARUA

YEARS AS MENTEE: *1*

GRADE: *12*

HIGH SCHOOL: *Susan E. Wagner High School*

BORN: *Bangladesh*

LIVES: *Staten Island, NY*

PUBLICATIONS AND RECOGNITIONS: *Scholastic Art & Writing Award Honorable Mention in Personal Essay/Memoir*

COLLEGE: *Polytechnic Institute of New York University*

LAURA BARLAMENT

YEARS AS MENTOR: *1*

OCCUPATION: *Associate Director of Communications and Marketing, Wagner College*

PUBLICATIONS AND RECOGNITIONS: *Wagner Magazine*

SWATI SAYS: I had stopped writing for a period of time before joining Girls Write Now, but it sounded so exciting that I applied on a whim. It was like being reintroduced to my Old World. Together with Laura, I explored this world that that was within me all along. For the life of me, I hope I won't have to leave it any time soon.

 *p. 193*

LAURA SAYS: The first new world where Swati took me was our meeting place: the Todt Hill-Westerleigh Library. I had passed it many times without ever noticing that it was a library! This awkwardly named branch of the New York Public Library system looks like a generic office building filled with tax accountants and insurance brokers. But Swati knew its true identity: a magical place of adventure and discovery, a place where vast resources of inspiration and creativity were at our disposal, a place where new relationships develop, new skills are learned, and new aspects of ourselves blossom.

 *p. 224*

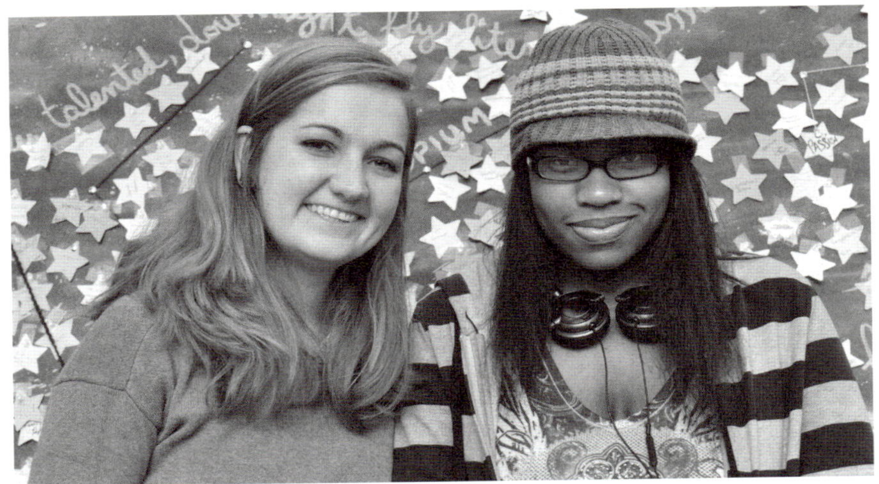

JENNIFER BEAN

YEARS AS MENTEE: *1*

GRADE: *10*

HIGH SCHOOL: *Democracy Prep Charter High School*

BORN: *NY, NY*

LIVES: *NY, NY*

JENNIFER SAYS: Thanks my mentor, I have experience with new genres that did not interest me before. We have written poetry, historical fiction, nonfiction, and fantasy. Christy has helped me with essays for school; she has pushed me to fully explain my ideas and put my thoughts on paper in an orderly way. Also, she is helping me bring together my fantasy series, *My Life*, which will hopefully be a book trilogy someday.

 *p. 110*

CHRISTY POTTROFF

YEARS AS MENTOR: *1*

OCCUPATION: *PhD student, Fordham University*

CHRISTY SAYS: I can set my clock by it: at 6:00PM on Wednesday, Jennifer and I will talk movies, books, friends, school—and challenge one another to be better writers. Jennifer's thoughtful criticism has made me more aware of tone in my academic writing. She's a poet and fantasy writer, I'm a nonfiction enthusiast. Together, we've found balance. Instead of writing in our comfort zones, we are exploring genre, prose style, language, and form.

 *p. 191*

TUHFA BEGUM

YEARS AS MENTEE: *2*

GRADE: *11*

HIGH SCHOOL: *Vanguard High School*

BORN: *Bangladesh*

LIVES: *Bronx, NY*

PUBLICATIONS AND RECOGNITIONS: *Scholastic Art & Writing Award Silver Key in Personal Essay/Memoir*

JOSLEEN WILSON

YEARS AS MENTOR: *5*

OCCUPATION: *Consultant, Sparks Fly Up Creative Solutions*

PUBLICATIONS AND RECOGNITIONS: *Woman: Your Body, Your Health, Good Health for African Americans, Surviving Family Life, Own Your Own Future*

TUFHA SAYS: On July 20, 1969, Neil Armstrong stepped onto the surface of the moon, boldly proclaiming, "This is one small step for man, one giant leap for mankind." Armstrong did more than enter uncharted territory; he literally entered a new world. Despite my lack of moon-landing experience, I feel like I step into a new world every time I have a pair session with my mentor Josleen. We talk about everything, from monsters to writing to human rights issues. We start unaware of where we are heading; every meeting is an adventure of its own.

 *p. 174*

JOSLEEN SAYS: "Do you know who Charlie Chaplin is?" I randomly ask, trying to start us off. "Silent movie star," Tuhfa answers. How does she know this stuff? She's sixteen and Chaplin's been dead for decades.

"OK, so who's Alexander the Great?"

"You mean Alexander who fought monsters in India and told Aristotle about them? We're studying him in Monsterology class." Thus begins our weekly journey.

"Is your class really called Monsterology?"

"Don't be so silly."

 *p. 286*

BRENDA BOTA

YEARS AS MENTEE: *1*

GRADE: *10*

HIGH SCHOOL: *Bronx Career and College Preparatory School*

BORN: *Yonkers, NY*

LIVES: *Bronx, NY*

PUBLICATIONS AND RECOGNITIONS: *Scholastic Art & Writing Award Honorable Mention in Poetry*

BRENDA SAYS: I was born in Yonkers. I went to Ghana when I was one and came back at the age of five. I'm a radiant person, there's a lot to live and be happy for. I started to realize my love for writing when I was in fifth grade. We were asked to write a three-page short story; I wrote eight pages front and back, and I still wasn't anywhere close to finishing. I have a couple of goals for my future: be a psychologist, write for the beauty and fashion section of magazines (influenced by my awesome mentor Maddy), and publish a book of poetry.

 *p. 94*

MADELYNE ZOLLO

YEARS AS MENTOR: *1*

OCCUPATION: *Beauty Assistant Editor, People StyleWatch*

PUBLICATIONS AND RECOGNITIONS: *Elle.com, The Orlando Sentinel, Plumtv.com*

MADELYNE SAYS: Brenda and I are both first timers this year at Girls Write Now, but what a fun journey we've had together so far! Her avid interest in poetry has reintroduced me to the genre. I've brought her to my offices to see what it's like to be a magazine editor, and to show her that it is possible to have a career where you write for a living. We both agree that we couldn't have been a better match!

 *p. 93*

CHRISTINA BUTAN

YEARS AS MENTEE: *2*

GRADE: *12*

HIGH SCHOOL: *The Young Women's Leadership School of Astoria*

BORN: *NY, NY*

LIVES: *Queens, NY*

PUBLICATIONS AND RECOGNITIONS: *Scholastic Art & Writing Award Gold Keys in Writing Portfolio, Poetry; Silver Key in Journalism; GWN Poetry Ambassador, Poet-Linc Poetry Slam at Lincoln Center, Poets Out Loud at Fordham University*

COLLEGE: *SUNY Purchase*

AMY DILUNA

YEARS AS MENTOR: *2*

OCCUPATION: *Senior Editor, TODAY.com*

PUBLICATIONS AND RECOGNITIONS: *New York Daily News*

CHRISTINA SAYS: Spotted Thursday, 4:00PM: two longhaired brunettes laughing insanely over the indie tracklist at Starbucks; customers swear that they can still hear their sputtering bursts in the air, even in their absence. Whether we're giggling about animals making bizarre faces or the ridiculous reasons why I can't eat certain soups, there is never a time a smile isn't shared between us. The world Amy showed me is one filled with friendship, encouragement, and hope. I can't imagine how I'll be spending my Thursday afternoons in the far future, other than reminiscing over the times spent with her.

 *p. 102*

AMY SAYS: Oh, the places she'll go. Our friendship was born nowhere exotic: around rickety tables at an Astoria Starbucks, we conjured characters for stories and giggled over tweets. She'll go now, tap away at her computer at another sticky coffee shop table near her next class. Head down, she'll see word counts and margin widths and assignments that are alternately inspiring and confounding. All I see is a horizon that is nothing but expanse. This girl and her skinny laptop are about to take the world by storm, one coffee shop at a time, and I'm pulling up a chair to watch.

 *p. 103*

CINDY CABAN

YEARS AS MENTEE: *4*

GRADE: *12*

HIGH SCHOOL: *Millennium High School*

BORN: *NY, NY*

LIVES: *Brooklyn, NY*

COLLEGE: *Stony Brook University*

CINDY SAYS: A TV fanatic just like me, we instantly made a connection through our love of shows like *How I Met Your Mother* and *One Tree Hill*. Our weekly sessions have given me the strength to open my eyes to new ideas, especially with my short story project that Jeanine pushed me to continue even when I have writer's block. She also guided me with my college applications, which I could not have done without her help. The best part of it all is the understanding and support she has given me this year.

 *p. 156*

JEANINE POGGI

YEARS AS MENTOR: *1*

OCCUPATION: *TV Reporter, Advertising Age*

PUBLICATIONS AND RECOGNITIONS: *Forbes, TheStreet.com, Women's Wear Daily*

JEANINE SAYS: I read Cindy's answer to the pair snapshot after writing my own. We both had nearly identical first sentences. This essentially sums up our relationship. While the similarities between us were immediate, even down to our brown hair and glasses, Cindy's lyrical poetry stands in stark contrast to my journalistic style of writing. Her ability to make the abstract come alive reintroduced me to a form of writing I relished as a teen, but haven't practiced since. It's art on the page that I am honored to have had an opportunity to admire.

 *p. 155*

FANTA CAMARA

YEARS AS MENTEE: *2*

GRADE: *12*

HIGH SCHOOL: *Bronx International High School*

BORN: *Republic of Guinea*

LIVES: *Bronx, NY*

PUBLICATIONS AND RECOGNITIONS: *Albert Shanka Scholarship*

COLLEGE: *Mercy College*

FANTA SAYS: My relationship with Meg led me to new discoveries: belief in myself, hope in everything I'm doing, and hope for my future. She also taught me an important lesson on not overstressing about things beyond my control. She helped me put things into perspective and focus on the world here and now.

 *p. 92*

MEG CASSIDY

YEARS AS MENTOR: *2*

OCCUPATION: *Publicity Manager, Simon & Schuster*

MEG SAYS: Fanta has introduced me to many new worlds over the past two years, both in NYC and through her writing about her childhood in Guinea. Through her vivid descriptions of her experiences, I have grown to admire her daily courage and growth even more. In our meetings, we constantly seek out new shared interests—in writing, food, family experiences, and even the college application process (which was a daunting new world at first, but one we conquered together). I can't wait to see where she ends up next year, and to follow her accomplishments.

 *p. 90*

RACHEL CANDELARIA

YEARS AS MENTEE: *1*

GRADE: *10*

HIGH SCHOOL: *Brooklyn Preparatory High School*

BORN: *NY, NY*

LIVES: *Queens, NY*

PUBLICATIONS AND RECOGNITIONS: *Scholastic Art & Writing Award Silver Key in Flash Fiction*

RACHEL SAYS: Wendy has been a wonderful editor and audience to my writing. She has more than once helped me understand a situation from a point of view other than my own. I have discovered that I should never quit, even when my writing lags, or let personal doubts stop me from trying new things. She's a fantastic mentor.

 *p. 104*

WENDY CASTER

YEARS AS MENTOR: *1*

OCCUPATION: *Writer*

WENDY SAYS: Rachel is amazing, exceptionally smart and talented. Her writing is lyrical and creative. She is also quite funny. I feel grateful that we were matched up as mentor and mentee. I learned a lot from Rachel, and I really enjoy her company.

 *p. 114*

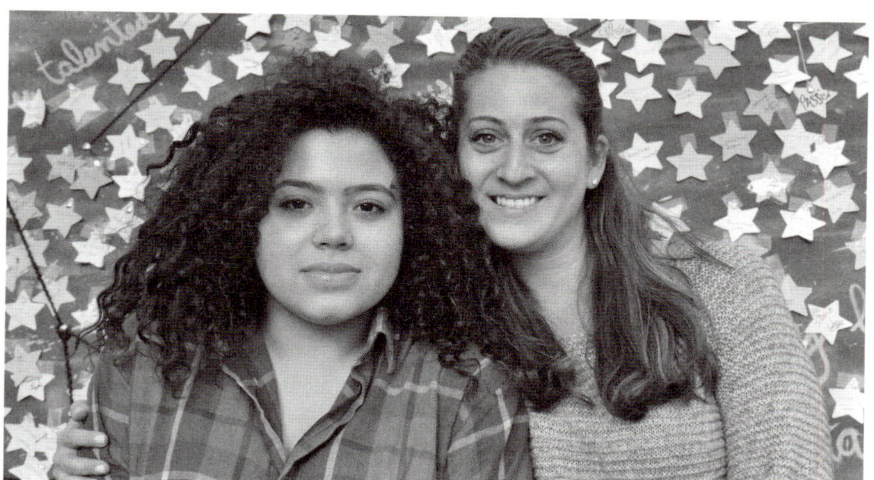

KAYTLIN CARLO

YEARS AS MENTEE: *2*

GRADE: *11*

HIGH SCHOOL: *Pace High School*

BORN: *NY, NY*

LIVES: *Brooklyn, NY*

KAYTLIN SAYS: I have done some things that I would not have done if it weren't for Ashley. For example, we attended a train show at the Bronx Botanical Gardens; it was a surprisingly cool and different experience. The new world that Ashley and I have discovered is the world of blogging. I had wanted to start a blog and she helped me with that.

 *p. 200*

ASHLEY ROSE HOWARD

YEARS AS MENTOR: *2*

OCCUPATION: *Writer; Event Coordinator; Public Relations Professional*

PUBLICATIONS AND RECOGNITIONS: *Life2PointOh.com, NJ.com*

ASHLEY SAYS: This past year with Kaytlin has been an amazing learning experience. During our pair sessions, she has helped me find a healthy balance of unpolished creativity and refined discipline. We've entered new worlds of writing, pitching, and exploring new genres outside of our comfort zone. At times it felt uncomfortable and demanding. But most of our time together became small pockets of creative openness that grew from trust and companionship.

 *p. 201*

SAMANTHA YOUNG CHAN

YEARS AS MENTEE: *3*

GRADE: *12*

HIGH SCHOOL: *Baruch College Campus High School*

BORN: *NY, NY*

LIVES: *NY, NY*

PUBLICATIONS AND RECOGNITIONS: *Sage Scholar; Scholastic Art & Writing Award Silver Key in Science Fiction/Fantasy; Honorable Mentions in Dramatic Script, Short Story*

COLLEGE: *Hunter College*

ALEX BERG

YEARS AS MENTOR: *2*

OCCUPATION: *Associate Producer of Video, Newsweek, The Daily Beast*

PUBLICATIONS AND RECOGNITIONS: *The Huffington Post, iVillage, The New York Times, The Washington Post*

SAMANTHA SAYS: No matter what, Alex is there for me when I need her. When I feel lost in my writing and don't know what to do, she's there to throw ideas at me and never lets me give up. If I'm having a tough week, she encourages me to push forward because things can only get better. Alex helped me with more college applications than I could have ever imagined doing and without her, I surely would have drowned in them. Besides being my mentor, she's a good friend that I can always rely on.

 *p. 198*

ALEX SAYS: My first year mentoring Samantha was a getting-to-know each other period. As her writing evolved, so did our relationship. This year I had the privilege of helping her with her college essays, an experience that built on both her creative abilities and our friendship. Working with Samantha is always heartening. Her approach to writing and her educational pursuits is enthusiastic and unjaded. As she heads off to school, I'm sad we'll see less of each other but thrilled as she embarks on another adventure, carving out a new world for herself.

 *p. 165*

SOPHIA CHAN

YEARS AS MENTEE: *2*

GRADE: *12*

HIGH SCHOOL: *New York City Lab School of Collaborative Studies*

BORN: *NY, NY*

LIVES: *NY, NY*

COLLEGE: *New York University*

PUBLICATIONS AND RECOGNITIONS: *NYU College of Nursing Scholarship*

SIOBHAN BURKE

YEARS AS MENTOR: *2*

OCCUPATION: *Associate Editor, Dance Magazine*

PUBLICATIONS AND RECOGNITIONS: *The Brooklyn Rail, The Columbia Journal of Dance Studies, Dance Teacher, Hyperallergic, The New York Times*

SOPHIA SAYS: Siobhan has introduced me to myself. She has helped me form a personal, unique style. She is the first person to inspire me to think more about who I am. Simple questions like, "What do you think?" make me really think: What do I think? Believe? Want? I am indecisive, but talking to Siobhan leads to concrete decisions, pulled out from my murky consciousness.

 *p. 216*

SIOBHAN SAYS: Before I met Sophia, my writing process was very inward: the final product could be public, but the getting-there was private. As Sophia and I got into the swing of our weekly sessions though, something unexpected happened: I wasn't just learning about her process but sharing my own in a way I never had before. I let her in on my raw, unfinished thoughts. A perceptive writing partner as much as a mentee, she's helped me to appreciate my own false starts and dead ends—to be more accepting and less protective of ideas that don't yet know where they belong.

 *p. 256*

MONICA CHIN

YEARS AS MENTEE: *3*

GRADE: *12*

HIGH SCHOOL: *Baruch College Campus High School*

BORN: *NY, NY*

LIVES: *Manhattan, NY*

PUBLICATIONS AND RECOGNITIONS: *Scholastic Art & Writing Award Silver Keys in Poetry, Flash Fiction; Women in Science and Engineering Honors Program*

COLLEGE: *Stony Brook University*

ELAINE STUART-SHAH

YEARS AS MENTOR: *3*

OCCUPATION: *Writer*

PUBLICATIONS AND RECOGNITIONS: *The Boston Globe, The Brooklyn Rail, Child, Coastal Living, Dance, Modern Bride, The New York Times, The Wall Street Journal*

MONICA SAYS: "xoxo, e" —that is how I will always see Elaine. I cannot explain our relationship; I can only describe the events intertwining our lives that have made us "us." From our meeting three years ago, we have blossomed into a team. She has held my hand and straightened my shoulders. She has spent countless hours with me chatting about school, friendships, guys, and everything in between. She was the first to bring her family to meet mine for brunch, joking that it was like meeting our in-laws. I would never fail to say she is my perfect match.

 *p. 222*

ELAINE SAYS: Three years ago, I sat anxiously next to my shy sophomore mentee at our first-ever pair session, trying to make conversation. A few hours ago, I sat next to Monica outside the Brooklyn Museum, having spent the afternoon discussing art, college, spring break, and prom. In the hundreds of hours we've clocked together, we've investigated crime scenes, climbed Everest, inhabited historical figures,and entered each other's childhood. And talked a lot about boys. My world is so much richer with Monica in it. Words brought us together, and they have bonded us forever.

 *p. 221*

ASHLEY CHRISTIE

YEARS AS MENTEE: *1*

GRADE: *10*

HIGH SCHOOL: *Urban Assembly School for Law and Justice*

BORN: *NY, NY*

LIVES: *Brooklyn, NY*

PUBLICATIONS AND RECOGNITIONS: *Scholastic Art & Writing Award Honorable Mention in Personal Essay/Memoir*

ASHLEY SAYS: I enjoy the company of my mentor because she supports my decisions with everything. She turns my nothings into somethings, gives advice on how to make, then leaves me to take it in, and add my own creativity. She's the best!

 *p. 275*

CHANA PORTER

YEARS AS MENTOR: *1*

OCCUPATION: *Playwright; Theater Artist and Co-Founder, AliveWire Theatrics*

PUBLICATIONS AND RECOGNITIONS: *Leap and the Net Will Appear, Besharet, Animal Hearts, The Dogs of Babel (play adaptation)*

CHANA SAYS: White chocolate fondue and hot apple cider, applications and deadlines, exploring the city together, seeing my own work with new eyes again and again. Everyday she inspires me more.

 *p. 181*

CORRINE CIVIL

YEARS AS MENTEE: *1*

GRADE: *10*

HIGH SCHOOL: *Young Women's Leadership School of East Harlem*

BORN: *NY, NY*

LIVES: *NY, NY*

PUBLICATIONS AND RECOGNITIONS: *Young Writers Workshop at Kenyon College*

ROBIN MARANTZ HENIG

YEARS AS MENTOR: *4*

OCCUPATION: *Journalist*

PUBLICATIONS AND RECOGNITIONS: *Twentysomething: Why Do Young Adults Seem Stuck?*

CORRINE SAYS: I rushed across town in a taxi, the fast merengue music and the driver's constant taps quickening the pace of my heart. Every red light took too long and every green light changed too quickly. I can't be late for our first meeting. Seriously? I had no idea what to expect, and I was nervous about meeting an actual writer one-on-one. The thought of talking in a public cafe seemed too awkward, and my experiences with awkward situations made me skeptical about meeting with Ms. Robin. How should I even address her? Robin? Ms. Henig? Henig?

 *p. 80*

ROBIN SAYS: Corrine arrived a little breathless, worried about keeping me waiting though she was exactly on time. I was upset when she said she'd taken a taxi to get to the cafe near my apartment in Morningside Heights. Corrine lives in East Harlem, and her school is a short walk from home, so she doesn't get over to Amsterdam Avenue in the ordinary course of her day. What had I done? Had I forced her to venture further west than she could go? Was I forgetting how young she was, and how hard it might be to get on a crosstown bus?

 *p. 223*

ALEXUS COLBERT

YEARS AS MENTEE: *1*

GRADE: *10*

HIGH SCHOOL: *Park East High School*

BORN: *NY, NY*

LIVES: *NY, NY*

DAHLMA LLANOS-FIGUEROA

YEARS AS MENTOR: *1*

OCCUPATION: *Novelist*

PUBLICATIONS AND RECOGNITIONS: *Breaking Ground: Anthology of Puerto Rican Women Writers in New York 1980-2012, Daughters of the Stone*

ALEXUS SAYS: "Show, don't tell." This short phrase, taught to me by Dahlma, is a constant reminder of how I can improve my writing. It means illustrating how the character in your story is feeling by exhibiting their actions, expressions, and use of language. This practice has not only improved my writing, but has also improved the relationship between my mentor and myself. Instead of saying to one another, "I am happy to have you as a mentor/ mentee," we talk to each other about problems outside of writing, and we even hug at the beginning and end of every session.

 *p. 289*

DAHLMA SAYS: We used photographs of Chester Higgins, Jr. and Vincent Van Gogh's paintings as triggers for our stories, and turned to Martin Espada, Edna St. Vincent Millay, and Claude McKay for starting points for our poetry. In this way, we were forced to stretch beyond our comfort zones and try something new. Over and over, Alex took in the prompt and made it a part of her own experience. I don't think she will ever say she doesn't know what to write about. All she has to do is open a photography or art or poetry book and dive into the images that jump up to grab her imagination.

 *p. 288*

KARILIS CRUZ

YEARS AS MENTEE: *1*

GRADE: *10*

HIGH SCHOOL: *Urban Assembly School for Media Studies*

BORN: *NY, NY*

LIVES: *NY, NY*

KARILIS SAYS: Lyndsay became my writing partner-in-crime when we joined Girls Write Now. I expected a mentor who would tell me to do this or do that. That's the response I would get from a friend or a teacher about my writing. But Lyndsay understood where I was coming from and worked around it. And that's all I really wanted, but she also became my friend.

 *p. 203*

LYNDSAY FAYE

YEARS AS MENTOR: *1*

OCCUPATION: *Novelist*

PUBLICATIONS AND RECOGNITIONS: *The Gods of Gotham, Dust and Shadow; Best American Mystery Stories 2010; Burning Maiden, Strand Magazine*

LYNDSAY SAYS: I joined Girls Write Now because being a novelist was turning me into a very squirrelly person who sat and stared at a laptop all day, and forgot how to speak English with fellow humans. Now I have a writing friend from my neighborhood who I meet with every week! And she writes just the sort of things I love to read. I'd never have gotten to see her stories if it hadn't been for Girls Write Now.

 *p. 204*

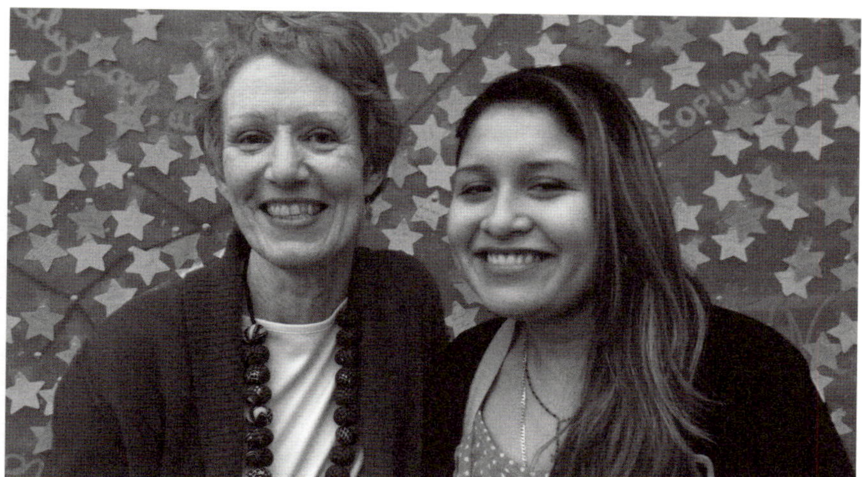

SULEYMA CUELLAR

YEARS AS MENTEE: *2*

GRADE: *12*

HIGH SCHOOL: *St. Jean Baptiste*

BORN: *Mexico*

LIVES: *NY, NY*

COLLEGE: *John Jay College of Criminal Justice*

SULEYMA SAYS: I remember as if it were only yesterday when I was first introduced to Pam. Something told me that I could trust her after our first hello. She became someone important in my life in a short amount of time. I can always count on her for anything I need, and she always knows what to say. Our time together is full of laughter and advice. Pam treats me as a writer, not as a mentee who is learning how to write.

 *p. 230*

PAMELA BAYLESS

YEARS AS MENTOR: *1*

OCCUPATION: *Consultant, Writer*

PUBLICATIONS AND RECOGNITIONS: *The YMCA at 150, The Courage of a Community; Crain's New York Business, Newsweek International, SELF*

PAMELA SAYS: Suleyma reintroduced me to a culture I thought I knew, from a long-ago summer spent living with a family in Mexico City. The culture of Puebla continues to shape her. Her tightly-knit community grounds her in this new world that presents so many different directions. I've been fortunate to witness Suleyma's world through her eyes, which has enlarged my own and reminds me of how much remains to be learned.

 *p. 229*

KRISTASIAH DANIELS

YEARS AS MENTEE: *3*

GRADE: *12*

HIGH SCHOOL: *Brooklyn School for Music and Theatre*

BORN: *NY, NY*

LIVES: *Brooklyn, NY*

PUBLICATIONS AND RECOGNITIONS: *Challenge Grant; 2012-13 Peter Jay Sharp Youth Arts Fellow*

COLLEGE: *University of Bridgeport*

JODI NARDE

YEARS AS MENTOR: *2*

OCCUPATION: *Online Marketing, NYU Press*

PUBLICATIONS AND RECOGNITIONS: *From The Square, New Orleans Review, New York Moves*

KRISTASIAH SAYS: Jodi has been a wonderful mentor, helping me all the way through my college application process. We discovered a new world together by taking a college tour. She also opened my eyes to a new type of writing that I had always tried to avoid before: editing. Now, as it turns out, I love to edit. It has led me to become a better writer and even take a new interest in journalism. We had a lot of fun this year, and now I have memories I will never forget.

 *p. 273*

JODI SAYS: I couldn't contain my excitement when Krissy invited me to her high school talent show this year. I knew I'd be blown away by the performances. Krissy gave an unbelievable singing performance, which left me feeling proud to be a mentor of a young lady with so many talents. As I watched her face light up when she saw me in the audience, I realized I had earned a place in her life as more than her mentor—as her friend.

 *p. 202*

SHANNON DANIELS

YEARS AS MENTEE: *2*

GRADE: *11*

HIGH SCHOOL: *Stuyvesant High School*

BORN: *NY, NY*

LIVES: *NY, NY*

PUBLICATIONS AND RECOGNITIONS: *Scholastic Art & Writing Awards: Gold Key in Poetry; Silver Key in Poetry; Honorable Mention in Personal Essay/Memoir*

WHITNEY JACOBY

YEARS AS MENTOR: *2*

OCCUPATION: *Account Manager, Simon & Schuster*

SHANNON SAYS:
7:37PM, Starbucks on Crosby and Spring:

"Is it even worth-"
"Keep at it; you're on to something here." Whitney and I were reading over the poem I later submitted to the Scholastic Art & Writing Awards. Even though the piece chronicled a very personal story, I knew Whitney was the right person to read it. Having another pair of eyes to look over my grammar and style is a tremendous benefit to my writing, but even more so is talking with someone who will cheer on the completion of every story, no matter how ambitious.

 *p. 132*

WHITNEY SAYS: Everything is different in our second year together. Shannon and I are no longer getting to know each other and building trust—our relationship is now a given, our bond formed. This was a year of exploring new ways of writing, from the fun, environmental video game Shannon developed to the spoken word poem we wrote together. Every meeting with Shannon is a new exciting chapter in our adventure together, each one pushing me to write in ways I never thought possible.

 *p. 134*

GINA DIFRISCO

YEARS AS MENTEE: *4*

GRADE: *12*

HIGH SCHOOL: *Urban Assembly School for Green Careers*

BORN: *NY, NY*

LIVES: *Bronx, NY*

PUBLICATIONS AND RECOGNITIONS: *Full-tuition scholarship to Morrisville State College (SUNY)*

COLLEGE: *Morrisville State College (SUNY)*

KATE TREBUSS

YEARS AS MENTOR: *4*

OCCUPATION: *PhD student, Columbia University*

GINA SAYS: It's not an easy thing to say in only a few words. Doors open every day giving new ideas, options, and opportunities. Talking to Kate is as easy as talking to one of my friends because she is my friend. She knows just what to say when I'm in a bind, and doesn't hesitate to push me to find the solution to any problem on my own. The relationship we have is more than that of a mentor and mentee: it is a true friendship.

 *p. 178*

KATE SAYS: This year will be about old ground not new worlds, I thought, as I prepared to see Gina for our first fall meeting this year. But while the ground we tread in our second year was in some ways familiar, the journey was far richer, more nuanced, less predictable than I could ever have anticipated. Sequels can be formulaic: plots are repeated; characters stumble over the same obstacles and make the same mistakes; heroes defeat new villains using old tactics. Our sequel, though, has been a whole new story.

 *p. 177*

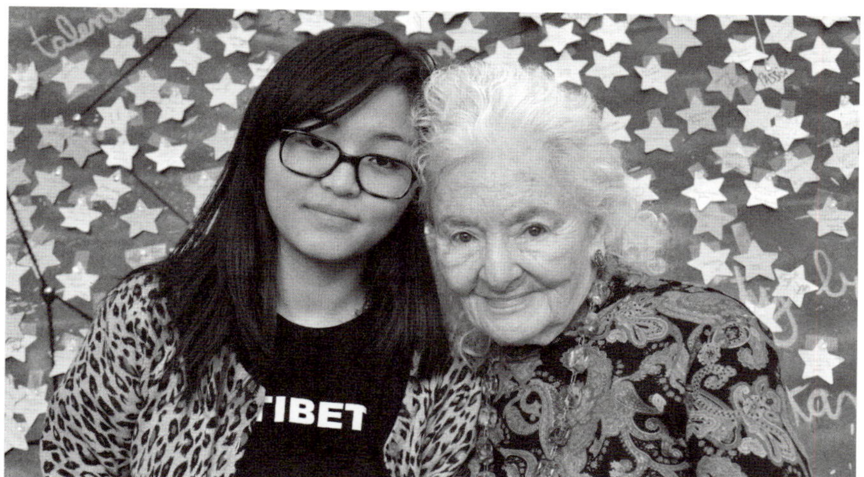

PALDON DOLMA

YEARS AS MENTEE: *1*

GRADE: *11*

HIGH SCHOOL: *Manhattan Hunter Science High School*

BORN: *Tibet*

LIVES: *Bronx, NY*

PALDON SAYS: Alice has not only improved my writing skills, but also increased the positivity, gaiety, and viability of my life. Always guiding and imbuing inspiration in me, she has encouraged me to resist oppression and fight for justice. Alice is charming, sublime, and thoughtful with a copious amount of wisdom to share. She will always be one of the most influential people in my life. I hope to gain more knowledge and virtue from her. I am excited to ride on this road!

 *p. 163*

ALICE SHEBA CANICK

YEARS AS MENTOR: *1*

OCCUPATION: *Writer*

ALICE SAYS: Paldron is an inspiration to me, and I believe she will be a voice for her people. I look forward to our time together, sharing unlimited experiences, and watching her grow to be a powerful woman.

 *p. 162*

NAKISSI DOSSO

YEARS AS MENTEE: *1*

GRADE: *10*

HIGH SCHOOL: *The Young Women's Leadership School of East Harlem*

BORN: *NY, NY*

LIVES: *NY, NY*

PUBLICATIONS AND RECOGNITIONS: *Scholastic Art & Writing Award Honorable Mention in Poetry*

NAKISSI SAYS: I've always read other people's writing, but I never really thought about where they were coming from. Because Heidi's writing is so different from mine, even when we're starting from the same place, it helped me understand the process and personal perspective that goes into each piece.

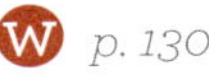
p. 130

HEIDI OVERBECK

YEARS AS MENTOR: *1*

OCCUPATION: *Account Director, Fenton Communications Firm; Chair, Media and Communications Network of NYC, Women's Information Network*

PUBLICATIONS AND RECOGNITIONS: *Hudson Review*

HEIDI SAYS: Each day with Nakissi is full of discovery. I am struck by how such different experiences can lead to the same place and point in time. Sharing the stories of our respective journeys has not only opened up new worlds of writing, but new worlds of thinking and feeling, too.

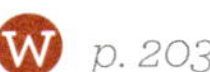
p. 203

ROBERTA NIN FELIZ

YEARS AS MENTEE: *1*

GRADE: *9*

HIGH SCHOOL: *Manhattan Center for Science and Mathematics*

BORN: *Curacao*

LIVES: *Bronx, NY*

PUBLICATIONS AND RECOGNITIONS: *Scholastic Art & Writing Award Honorable Mention in Poetry; YCTeen Magazine*

JALYLAH BURRELL

YEARS AS MENTOR: *4*

OCCUPATION: *PhD Student, Yale University*

PUBLICATIONS AND RECOGNITIONS: *Encore, The FADER, Portland Mercury, Vibe, Village Voice*

ROBERTA SAYS: Jalylah has been my coach when I needed to push myself and my muse when I needed inspiration. Working with her is a new world unto itself. It's a world where we can eat Clif bars or raw vegan pizza while chasing our dreams. She has shown me new parts of New York City and new sides of people I never knew existed.

 *p. 210*

JALYLAH SAYS: I hadn't thought about the Tao Te Ching for years until Roberta mentioned it in conversation. I subsequently searched for the highlighted copy my father sent me when I was in boarding school. She reminds me of myself, exceeding and enlivening the best of those memories. She works hard. Her work is attentive. Her work is honesty. Her work is a wonder. It's been a joy to wander with her.

 *p. 213*

TEAMARÉ GASTÓN

YEARS AS MENTEE: *2*

GRADE: *11*

HIGH SCHOOL: *Central Park East High School*

BORN: *NY, NY*

LIVES: *NY, NY*

PUBLICATIONS AND RECOGNITIONS: *Scholastic Art & Writing Award Silver Key in Poetry*

TEAMARÉ SAYS: My relationship with Katherine has grown a lot in the past year. She's taught me a lot about growing up and learning from the experiences we undergo.

W *p. 251*

KATHERINE NERO

YEARS AS MENTOR: *3*

OCCUPATION: *Writer; Film Producer*

PUBLICATIONS AND RECOGNITIONS: *For the Cause (feature film); 2001 Finalist, ABC/Disney Screenwriting Fellowship*

KATHERINE SAYS: Thanks to Teamaré, I have developed a greater awareness and appreciation of video games, webisodes, and other social media. Also, I admire Teamaré's ability and willingness to understand various viewpoints. As a result, she creates dynamic, multidimensional characters that build the foundation for compelling stories.

p. 282

NATHALIE GOMEZ

YEARS AS MENTEE: *3*

GRADE: *11*

HIGH SCHOOL: *Benjamin A. Cardozo High School*

BORN: *Rhode Island*

LIVES: *Queens, NY*

AMANDA BERLIN

YEARS AS MENTOR: *3*

OCCUPATION: *Writer; Life Coach*

PUBLICATIONS AND RECOGNITIONS: *Forbes.com, Renew, Teen Identity, Your Bella Life*

NATHALIE SAYS: I always felt like I was stuck in a hole that I had dug myself into, alone with no way out. But Amanda is always there to throw me a rope and help pull me up. I'm glad to have someone in my life who I can count on, and have been able to count on all this time.

 *p. 214*

AMANDA SAYS: Sometimes you venture into a new world by choice, other times you're forced down a path you had not researched. You're wearing sandals when all of a sudden the terrain demands Timberlands. When your life changes, sometimes the only way you can recognize yourself is by looking at the familiar faces of the people who walk beside you. I count Nathalie among my inner circle of skilled adventurers that walk beside me on this journey. As we both navigate challenging new territory, the mere fact that we choose to walk beside each other, for three years now, offers comfort, confidence and most importantly the assurance that neither of us are ever alone.

 *p. 294*

MENNEN GORDON

YEARS AS MENTEE: *2*

GRADE: *10*

HIGH SCHOOL: *Institute for Collaborative Education*

BORN: *NY, NY*

LIVES: *Bronx, NY*

PUBLICATIONS AND RECOGNITIONS: *Scholastic Art & Writing Award Honorable Mention in Poetry*

MENNEN SAYS: We did a lot of new things this year: there was a lot of editing, a lot of singing, and a lot of being shushed for being too loud. There was more rediscovering of Old Worlds than there was of New Worlds, from our constant change of venue to writing more in our favorite genres.

p. 287

JUDY ROLAND

YEARS AS MENTOR: *1*

OCCUPATION: *President, Roland Communications*

JUDY SAYS: Shared five-minute free-writes can yield anything from an original song by Mennen, which she sings soulfully and unselfconsciously in our café meeting place, to a sentimental family reflection by me. I feel privileged to be allowed into her world and to share mine with her. Oh, and we laugh a lot—a lot.

p. 100

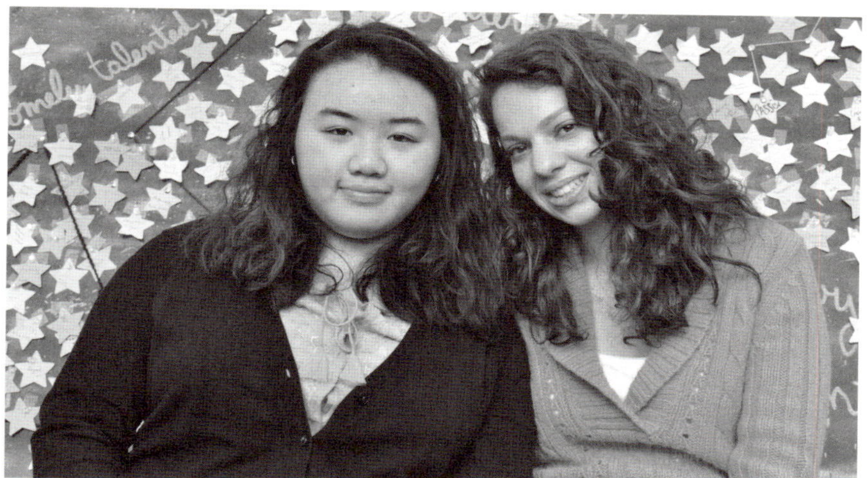

PRISCILLA GUO

YEARS AS MENTEE: *3*

GRADE: *11*

HIGH SCHOOL: *Hunter College High School*

BORN: *NY, NY*

LIVES: *Queens, NY*

PUBLICATIONS AND RECOGNITIONS: *Brooklyn Public Library Teen First Prize in Prose, GWN Poetry Ambassador, Poet-Linc Poetry Slam at Lincoln Center (3rd place), Scholastic Art & Writing Award Gold Keys in Poetry, Short Story; Silver Keys in Poetry, Painting*

ANNIE REUTER

YEARS AS MENTOR: *1*

OCCUPATION: *Music Journalist and Editor, CBS*

PUBLICATIONS AND RECOGNITIONS: *AOL, Billboard.com, Marie Claire, MTV, RollingStone.com, Venus Zine*

PRISCILLA SAYS: Living in New York, Annie and I are both lucky to be faced with fresh opportunities and original artistic ventures. During one of our first meetings, I took her into Koreatown to try some traditional Korean food, and she introduced me to her passion: music journalism. As she began to show me the true gems of country music, I accompanied her endeavors in first-person narratives. A mentee and mentor can explore new worlds together because we can give each other support along the way.

 *p. 152*

ANNIE SAYS: Having lived in New York for three years, it's hard to believe I have never visited Queens before. Since Priscilla lives there, one rainy Saturday we ventured to a crowded Barnes & Noble in Queens. As we waited to find seats, I found my first country review in *Billboard* magazine on the stands. It was a lifelong dream of mine to be published in print, and I was happy to share that moment with her, and to talk about our latest writing assignments. Priscilla reminds me of how I was at her age; she has an unyielding passion for writing that keeps me constantly motivated.

 *p. 84*

AMANDA HERBERT

YEARS AS MENTEE: *1*

GRADE: *12*

HIGH SCHOOL: *Democracy Prep Charter School*

BORN: *NY, NY*

LIVES: *NY, NY*

AMANDA SAYS: I learned to develop my writing in ways I couldn't have imagined over the last couple of months with Amy. I wrote a short story for the first time, and took lyrics from songs to create something new. Each process has made me a stronger writer and person. I am grateful for all that I have accomplished in these months we had together.

 *p. 220*

AMY S. CHOI

YEARS AS MENTOR: *1*

OCCUPATION: *Journalist*

PUBLICATIONS AND RECOGNITIONS: *BusinessWeek, The Philadelphia City Paper, Time Out New York, The Wall Street Journal, Women's Wear Daily*

AMY SAYS: Working with Amanda over the past year has renewed my sense of surprise when writing. She's reminded me that writing itself is a discovery, and each new endeavor (whether a poem or college essay) can open a new world unto itself. Also, we both work best under deadline!

 *p. 193*

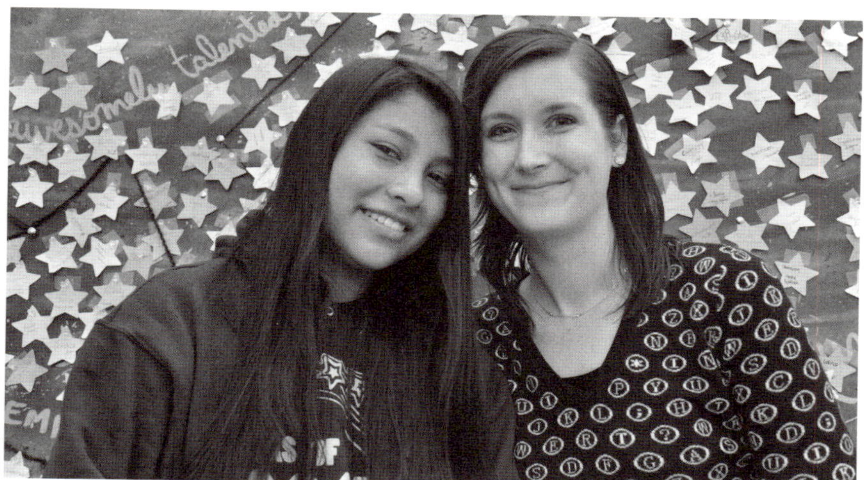

MONICA HERNANDEZ

YEARS AS MENTEE: *1*

GRADE: *12*

HIGH SCHOOL: *Manhattan Theatre Lab High School*

BORN: *Mexico*

LIVES: *Queens, NY*

MONICA SAYS: My relationship with Kirsten has been such a joyous adventure! The differences in our personalities have created such a dynamic between the two of us that boredom, the one single thing I truly fear, is never something I have to worry about when I am with her. Every new conversation becomes the grounds of a new world we create together, one based on our love for writing and our mutual love for one another.

 *p. 250*

KIRSTEN REACH

YEARS AS MENTOR: *1*

OCCUPATION: *Assistant Editor, Grand Central Publishing*

PUBLICATIONS AND RECOGNITIONS: *The Kenyon Review*

KIRSTEN SAYS: I've watched Monica deftly weave together the likes of Lewis Carroll, Vladimir Nabokov, heroes of Greek mythology, and *The Silence of the Lambs* in poems that are utterly her own. She's also one of the funniest, smartest women I've ever met. We've had a great year together, whether we're studying an ice sculpture of Belvedere Castle in Central Park or critiquing the dramatic adaption of *Frankenstein* in the Jekyll & Hyde Club in Times Square, or meeting as usual at Gregory's to read Elizabeth Bishop's poems (and our own) out loud to each other.

 *p. 277*

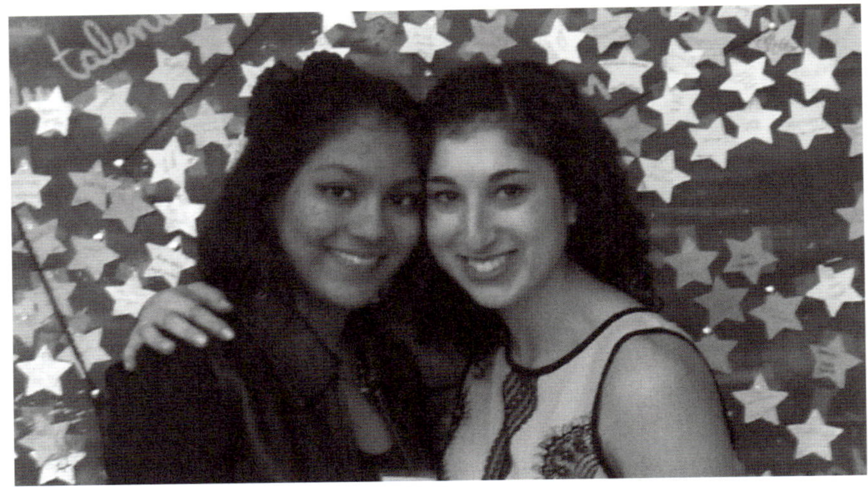

CHANDANIE DEVI HIRALAL

YEARS AS MENTEE: *1*

GRADE: *12*

HIGH SCHOOL: *High School 308 of Communication Arts and Technology*

BORN: *Guyana*

LIVES: *Queens, NY*

PUBLICATIONS AND RECOGNITIONS: *Scholastic Art & Writing Award Silver Keys in Poetry*

CHANDANIE SAYS: Three years ago, I published my first book *Black Roses and Other Poems and Short Stories*, and in recent months I've completed the manuscript for my first novel, *Moonrise in the Darkness*. I am nearly half-way into the sequel *Sunset in the Shadows*. Thanks to the opportunities presented to me by Girls Write Now, I won two silver keys in the Scholastic Arts & Writing Awards for two collections of my poetry, and was accepted to all the colleges and universities I applied to.

 *p. 170*

REBECCA HAVERSON
PROGRAM COORDINATOR

REBECCA SAYS: Armed with a self-published book of poems and a synopsis of her "in-the works" novel, Chandanie arrived to her first mentee interview full of her signature infectious energy. Her enthusiasm for writing, her fearlessness, and her belief in the power of a writing community are boundless. Chandanie is equal parts youthfulness and soul, and has shown maturity and grace in the face of the unexpected. Although her mentor was not able to continue with the program for the full year, Chandanie has truly been a mentee to all of us at Girls Write Now. As the sun sets on our monthly workshops, we can all count on Chandanie for a giant hug, a lot of laughter, and lasting inspiration.

IREEN HOSSAIN

YEARS AS MENTEE: *1*

GRADE: *12*

HIGH SCHOOL: *Young Women's Leadership School of Astoria*

BORN: *Bangladesh*

LIVES: *Queens, NY*

COLLEGE: *SUNY Plattsburgh*

IREEN SAYS: Speed dating: It's a nerve-wracking experience. How were we supposed to find a mentor in about five minutes? I was anxious to find my perfect match, and when we laid eyes on each other I knew she was the one. Nancy Hooper.

 *p. 95*

NANCY HOOPER

YEARS AS MENTOR: *3*

OCCUPATION: *Science writer*

PUBLICATIONS AND RECOGNITIONS: *Trade Secrets From a Three-Star Chef, Stopping Scoliosis: the Complete Guide to Diagnosis and Treatment; Discover, LIFE, People, The World Book Encyclopedia*

NANCY SAYS: Our eyes met across a crowded room at the Girls Write Now office. I heard her say, "I overthink everything." I thought, "That's the mentee for me!" My favorite mantra is: everything is NOT a big deal. It was my destiny to work with Ireen Hossain.

 *p. 277*

CHANDRA HUGHES

YEARS AS MENTEE: *3*

GRADE: *12*

HIGH SCHOOL: *Millennium High School*

BORN: *China*

LIVES: *NY, NY*

PUBLICATIONS AND RECOGNITIONS: *Scholastic Art & Writing Award Silver Key in Writing Portfolio*

COLLEGE: *Hampshire College*

CLAUDIA PARSONS

YEARS AS MENTOR: *3*

OCCUPATION: *Editor, Reuters*

CHANDRA SAYS: Claudia and I entered a new world together this year. Unlike other years, this year was less about creation and more about editing. We spent a good chunk of time editing the common application essay, followed by editing the Scholastic pieces, which led into the anthology piece. We also reviewed our own radio play, *Project Millennium*, and have entered the editing phase of that. As our last year together in Girls Write Now, I believe editing is our form of graduation.

 *p. 269*

CLAUDIA SAYS: This year has been all about college–how to get in, what it will be like, and what it was like for me back in the Stone Age. Chandra has always preferred writing about other worlds, so focusing on college essays and writing about herself was a new world for her. During one of our pair sessions, we wrote about the first day of college: she imagined what it might be like, I tried to remember. We met somewhere in the middle.

 *p. 292*

KIARA JOSEPH

YEARS AS MENTEE: *1*

GRADE: *10*

HIGH SCHOOL: *NYC iSchool*

BORN: *NY, NY*

LIVES: *Brooklyn, NY*

PUBLICATIONS AND RECOGNITIONS: *Scholastic Art & Writing Award Honorable Mention in Poetry*

KIARA SAYS: The first time I saw Rachel, her outfit screamed of awesomeness. From that moment I knew that I wanted her to be my mentor. Luckily they matched us, and she is the best mentor I could have imagined. We started off as journalists, and discovered the new world of poetry through sessions and workshops. I cannot wait until we are able to discover more new worlds later on. Rachel is truly a blessing.

 *p. 243*

RACHEL KRANTZ

YEARS AS MENTOR: *1*

OCCUPATION: *Homepage Editor, Newsweek and the Daily Beast*

PUBLICATIONS AND RECOGNITIONS: *Capital New York, The Huffington Post, Jezebel, Nerve, NPR, xoJane*

RACHEL SAYS: Kiara and I are both brand new at this whole mentee-mentor thing. That has meant this entire journey together has been a new world. Whether it's learning how to negotiate our busy schedules, or discovering a new love for poetry together, we continue to challenge each other in a way that feels increasingly honest and exciting. Kiara is a truly remarkable young woman, and I feel truly honored to be a part of her life. I can't wait to see how we both continue to grow as writers and friends.

 *p. 241*

KARLA KIM

YEARS AS MENTEE: *1*

GRADE: *11*

HIGH SCHOOL: *Hunter College High School*

BORN: *NY, NY*

LIVES: *Queens, NY*

SHERRY AMATENSTEIN

YEARS AS MENTOR: *1*

OCCUPATION: *Adjunct Professor at New York University and the New School for Social Research*

PUBLICATIONS AND RECOGNITIONS: *Q&A Dating Book, Love Lessons from Bad Breakups, The Complete Marriage Counselor; Family Circle, Marie Claire, New York Daily News, Redbook TV Guide, USA Weekend*

KARLA SAYS: I had never heard someone say, "Your story is beautiful." I had never considered my life to be very interesting, and preferred reading the memoirs of other Greater writers. But because of Sherry, I experienced the power of writing to help me discover new aspects of myself, and what I value. Within the short amount of time we had, we explored challenging subjects like racial bias and understanding our parents. Sherry showed me that good writing challenges you to see from different perspectives, and more importantly, that we should never let our limitations define our ability to write.

 *p. 124*

SHERRY SAYS: The first time I met Karla was on January 18th, 2013 at the Girls Write Now office. Waiting for her to arrive, I felt sad that we'd missed the first half of the year, but excited to get started.

I immediately sensed Karla's caring, sharing spirit, and soon became acquainted with the fire and steel lurking beneath. I am grateful to have this special person as a partner on our amazing Girls Write Now journey.

 *p. 126*

MAYA LASHLEY

YEARS AS MENTEE: *1*

GRADE: *12*

HIGH SCHOOL: *Bayside High School*

BORN: *NY, NY*

LIVES: *Queens, NY*

PUBLICATIONS AND RECOGNITIONS: *Urban Word Poetry Slam (2013 semi-finalist)*

COLLEGE: *Nassau Community College*

TRACY PEREZ

YEARS AS MENTOR: *1*

OCCUPATION: *Beauty Director, Parents Magazine and American Baby Magazine; Contributing Beauty Writer, TheNest.com*

PUBLICATIONS AND RECOGNITIONS: *InStyle, Prevention, Shape*

MAYA SAYS: Lost in the music, captivated by the sweet aroma of coffee, cinnamon chip scones, and success, Penn Station transforms into a writer's paradise. Sitting across from Tracy, it seems as if we are the only two people in the coffee shop, even though we are in the midst of various types of people. It's almost as if time freezes, and the people around us stand still, until our hour together is up.

 *p. 78*

TRACY SAYS: Maya and I share a passion for shoes and *Project Runway*. So one Saturday afternoon, we went to the Shoe Obsession exhibit at FIT. As we peered up from the Alaias, Louboutins, and Manolos, imagine our glee when we spotted Tim Gunn admiring the shoes too! We couldn't have timed it any better. I was so happy to have shared that moment with Maya. Funny how by walking just seven blocks from our usual meeting spot, a coffee shop in Penn Station, we ended up taking a once-in-a-lifetime trip.

 *p. 79*

RUMER LEGENDRE

YEARS AS MENTEE: *1*

GRADE: *10*

HIGH SCHOOL: *NYC iSchool*

BORN: *NY, NY*

LIVES: *NY, NY*

RUMER SAYS: As I think of all the meetings I've had with my mentor this year, it makes me smile. She made such an impact on my personal and writing life. She taught me to own my work and never apologize for my writing. Through working with Vivian, I've also discovered that there's so much more to me than being shy. I'm completely proud of all that I've accomplished. I'm also glad to have built a relationship with her that I will always remember.

 *p. 112*

VIVIAN CONAN

YEARS AS MENTOR: *1*

OCCUPATION: *Librarian; Writer*

PUBLICATIONS AND RECOGNITIONS: *New York Magazine, The New York Times; Creative Nonfiction Fellowship from the New York Foundation for the Arts, 2007*

VIVIAN SAYS: During these past six months, I have been continually amazed at Rumer's ability and willingness to write with emotional honesty. She's way ahead of where I was at sixteen. It took me until middle age to be brave enough to let people see my insides. I feel privileged to have been invited in.

 *p. 129*

JOANNE LIN

YEARS AS MENTEE: *3*

GRADE: *12*

HIGH SCHOOL: *Millennium High School*

BORN: *NY, NY*

LIVES: *NY, NY*

PUBLICATIONS AND RECOGNITIONS: *GWN Poetry Ambassador, Poet-Linc Poetry Slam at Lincoln Center, Poets Out Loud at Fordham University*

COLLEGE: *SUNY Albany*

JOANNE SAYS: Three years. Stepping into Girls Write Now, I had no idea what was in store for me. Opening my work for an adult mentor to read, opening up to a group of other girls who share the same passion, it was all new to me. Throughout these three years, an entirely new world has been created for me with the help of my mentor LaToya. To end my years as a mentee, I want to thank my mentor for all the laughs and wise words that we have shared. It is something I will remember for the rest of my life.

 *p. 82*

LATOYA JORDAN

YEARS AS MENTOR: *3*

OCCUPATION: *Assistant Director of Communications and Public Relations, New York Law School*

PUBLICATIONS AND RECOGNITIONS: *Mobius, The November 3rd Club, qaartsiluni, The Splinter Generation*

LATOYA SAYS: Although our road with Girls Write Now is coming to an end, I know that Joanne and I are entering a new world for our friendship, and hope that we'll continue to share our writing with each other. Joanne has kept me feeling young, inspired me, and has been a pleasure to hang out with for the past three years. The time flew by!

 *p. 81*

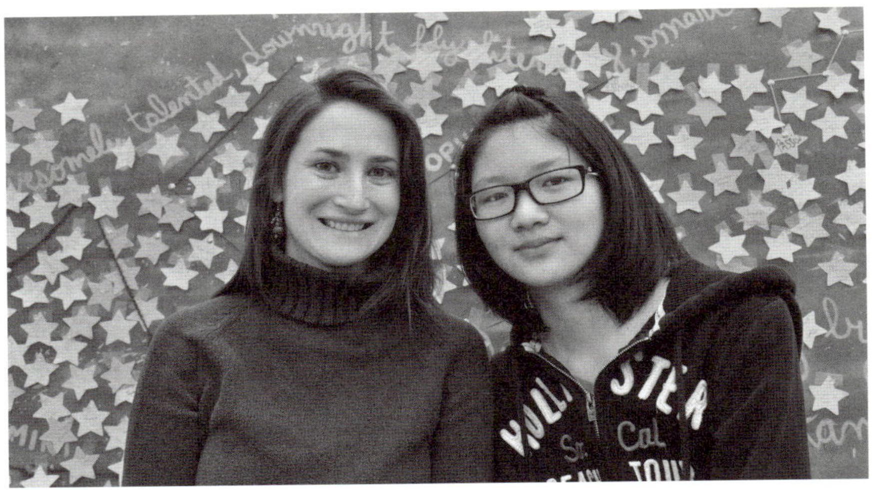

XIAO SHAN LIU

YEARS AS MENTEE: *1*

GRADE: *11*

HIGH SCHOOL: *International High School at Union Square*

BORN: *China*

LIVES: *Brooklyn, NY*

PUBLICATIONS AND RECOGNITIONS: *Scholarship to Barnard's Summer in the City Program*

ALYSSA VINE

YEARS AS MENTOR: *1*

OCCUPATION: *Associate Director of Media Relations, Barnard College*

XIAO SAYS: Joining Girls Write Now has given me a chance to improve my writing skills, but the best part is it has given me a chance to meet Alyssa. Alyssa and I were both new to the program, but it didn't take long for us to become friends. Alyssa is very gentle about the things going on around us. She always gives useful tips to help me improve my writing, and is tolerant of my English pronunciation. It is so fun with her, and it is my honor to have her as my mentor.

 *p. 284*

ALYSSA SAYS: Xiao Shan is full of enthusiasm, curiosity, and positive energy. I am constantly amazed at how hard she works, not only on her assignments, but in every area of her life. I am particularly impressed by her eagerness to use and improve her English. Writing in a second language is extremely challenging—we talk a lot about grammar and word choice. But this challenge is also closely linked with her creativity, and part of what shapes her voice as a writer. Xiao Shan finds ways of expressing herself that are truly original, translating Chinese words and phrases to convey her ideas in English. It is exciting to see her grow as a writer, and getting to know her this year has been a pleasure and a privilege.

  *p. 279*

RAYHANA MAAROUF

YEARS AS MENTEE: *1*

GRADE: *10*

HIGH SCHOOL: *Young Women's Leadership School of Astoria*

BORN: *NY, NY*

LIVES: *Queens, NY*

RAYHANA SAYS: My pair sessions with Anne are both work and fun. We move back and forth from the real world to the world of our imaginations. Before Girls Write Now, I used to write sentences like, "Chris went downstairs." Anne helped me see the difference between that and, "Chris crept down the steep staircase, clinging to the railing for dear life." Now I try harder to create word-images in my pieces. I have also discovered how much I enjoy memoir as a genre. Being a mentee has made me a better writer and a more self-confident person.

 *p. 83*

ANNE FEIGUS

YEARS AS MENTOR: *1*

OCCUPATION: *Former Litigator*

ANNE SAYS: From the moment that I first met Rayhana and she flashed her radiant smile, I had an intuitive feeling that our Girls Write Now experience would be a positive one. Still, I wondered whether we would be able to meet the program's expectations and our expectations of each other. An evolving relationship is akin to entering a new world because there is always the fear of the unknown and the fear of revealing oneself to another person. Happily, my world and my life have been enriched by Rayhana's presence.

 *p. 187*

BRIANNA MARIE MARINI

YEARS AS MENTEE: *2*

GRADE: *11*

HIGH SCHOOL: *The Young Women's Leadership School of Queens*

BORN: *NY, NY*

LIVES: *Queens, NY*

BRIANNA SAYS: My relationship with my mentor ended up teaching me how to travel by myself. Before this year, I wasn't allowed to take the train or go anywhere alone. Since we meet in the city, I needed to learn how to walk to our meeting place by myself. Travelling independently may seem like a small thing to most people, but to me it was a new and exciting experience.

 *p. 108*

KRISTEN DEMALINE

YEARS AS MENTOR: *3*

OCCUPATION: *Senior Editor, Today.com*

PUBLICATIONS AND RECOGNITIONS: *Akron Beacon Journal, Cleveland Plain Dealer, Eco Centric, Penny Ante*

KRISTEN SAYS: We've been discussing independence, and the responsibility that comes with that, a lot this year. Many of Brianna's circumstances echo my own at her age. I'm proud of how she's taking her own path. In my experience, it's not easy being different from your family or community, no matter how much you may also revel in that. I've been helping her figure out what she needs to know to explore the city (and the world) more. And some of that is reminding her how much she already knows!

 *p. 176*

KATHERINE MARTINEZ

YEARS AS MENTEE: *1*

GRADE: *11*

HIGH SCHOOL: *Aquinas High School*

BORN: *NY, NY*

LIVES: *Bronx, NY*

PUBLICATIONS AND RECOGNITIONS: *Scholastic Art & Writing Award Honorable Mention in Poetry*

KATHERINE SAYS: It was chaotic and cramped and too loud to be having a conversation with anyone the first time I met Amy. I honestly can't remember what we said, but what stayed with me was the very end of our conversation when we talked about how good some books smell. We spent the last few seconds smelling a book I was carrying around and basking in its scent. That's when I knew I had to have her as my mentor.

 *p. 159*

AMY FLYNTZ

YEARS AS MENTOR: *1*

OCCUPATION: *Copywriter; Manager of Online Customer Experience, Maxfield and Oberton Holdings, LLC*

AMY SAYS: I knew Katherine and I were a great fit when, during our first pair meeting, we spent three hours talking non-stop about writing, life, and everything in between. I didn't want our session to end! Poetry, fan fiction, and music inspires both of us. We even have the same music on our iPods! Not only is she one of my favorite people to spend time with; she's one of the most talented women I know. I feel so lucky that I get to hang out with her on a weekly basis!

 *p. 260*

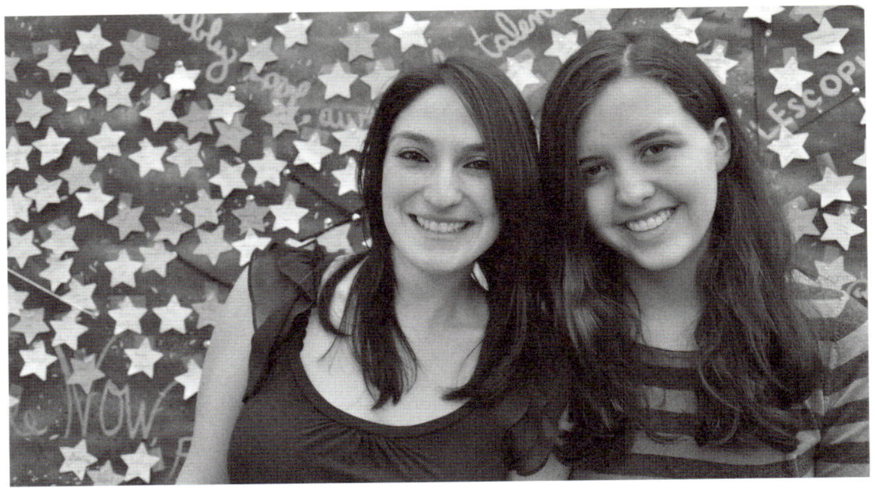

AMANDA DAY MCCULLOUGH

YEARS AS MENTEE: *2*

GRADE: *11*

HIGH SCHOOL: *Hunter College High School*

BORN: *NY, NY*

LIVES: *Queens, NY*

SAMANTHA CARLIN

YEARS AS MENTOR: *2*

OCCUPATION: *Executive Assistant, GOJO Industries*

PUBLICATIONS AND RECOGNITIONS: *Writer in Residence at the Norman Mailer's Writers Colony; Taglit-Birthright Alumni Essay Contest; Scholastic Art & Writing Award; Barnard College, Columbia University*

AMANDA SAYS: Samantha and I push each other to reveal our vulnerabilities. Together we've learned the vitality of being honest with ourselves and our readers. But being honest is harder than it seems, especially when we're trying something new with our writing. I lured Samantha into the world of memoir and urged her to try self-reflection. She identified places where I gloss over emotion and armed me with the tools to delve into those uncomfortable feelings. We're dedicated to helping each other break down self-imposed barriers, especially as we continue to explore new worlds.

 *p. 253*

SAMANTHA SAYS When Amanda returned from Nicaragua last summer, I knew she'd have wells of new material for our second year together. I've been privileged to work with her on many essays and memoirs about this journey. Amanda's reflections on the world and herself are courageous. Her bravery motivates me to "go there" in my own work, whether we're free-writing about images plucked from a dream dictionary, or tearing sentences apart in an epic editing session. And if I shy away, I can trust that Amanda will be first to call my bluff. In those moments, she's definitely mentoring me!

  *p. 255*

VALENE MEZMIN

YEARS AS MENTEE: *1*

GRADE: *10*

HIGH SCHOOL: *Medgar Evers College Preparatory School*

BORN: *St. Lucia*

LIVES: *Brooklyn, NY*

VALENE SAYS: During one meeting with Sara, I had an idea for a story but became stuck when I attempted to write it. I asked Sara for help, and with the utmost confidence in me, she told me just to write. One new thing Sara has taught me is that you don't need to think and plan and plot until your brain explodes. Most of the best stories happen once you take the first simple step of putting pen to paper.

 *p. 257*

SARA LIPPMAN

YEARS AS MENTOR: *1*

OCCUPATION: *Author; Sunday Salon reading series host*

PUBLICATIONS AND RECOGNITIONS: *Stripped: A Collection of Anonymous Flash Fiction; Big Muddy, GQ, Joyland, Mamas & Papas, Our Stories, PANK, Santa Fe Literary Review, Slice Magazine, Smokelong Quarterly, Women Arts Quarterly*

SARA SAYS: Valene is a writer with an affinity for mystery, a genre with which I have little experience. Plot is something I struggle with in my own work, so it was eye-opening to watch her cook up elaborate and fast-paced dramas. While I may never boldly tackle riveting twists like murder and amnesia in my own fiction in the way Valene does, she certainly has inspired me to raise the stakes in my own writing.

 *p. 114*

BUSHRA MIAH

YEARS AS MENTEE: *1*

GRADE: *10*

HIGH SCHOOL: *Vanguard High School*

BORN: *NY, NY*

LIVES: *NY, NY*

PUBLICATIONS AND RECOGNITIONS: *Scholastic Art & Writing Award Honorable Mention in Short Story*

GILLIAN REAGAN

YEARS AS MENTOR: *2*

OCCUPATION: *Public Editor, Director of Marketing at Capital New York*

PUBLICATIONS AND RECOGNITIONS: *Bloomberg Businessweek, The New York Times*

BUSHRA SAYS: I can only begin by saying that working with Gillian is such a blessing, and I still won't be able to truly emphasize how amazing she is or how she's affected me. She's inspired me in numerous ways and brings out unprecedented optimism, something I didn't think was ever possible. I'm forever grateful to her for indirectly opening the doors to my changed perspective about writing, personal creativity, oblique philosophy, and much more. Most importantly, the experience of discovery and learning I have had while working with her has been divine and miraculous.

 *p. 86*

GILLIAN SAYS: When I first met Bushra, she introduced herself with a lot of "I don't," "I'm not," and "I can't." She claimed she's not creative, can't be imaginative, and isn't personable. Over the next few months, it would become clear to both of us that Bushra was completely wrong about herself. She is incredibly talented, innovative, sweet, and friendly. Writing and working with Bushra helped me realize how I create my own boundaries in my creative work. We both learned how to trust and open ourselves up through communication, kindness, and imagination.

 *p. 188*

AVA NADEL

YEARS AS MENTEE: *2*

GRADE: *12*

HIGH SCHOOL: *Millennium High School*

BORN: *NY, NY*

LIVES: *Brooklyn, NY*

PUBLICATIONS AND RECOGNITIONS: *Performance Award Scholarship*

COLLEGE: *Guilford College*

JESSI HEMPEL

YEARS AS MENTOR: *2*

OCCUPATION: *Senior Writer, Fortune Magazine*

PUBLICATIONS AND RECOGNITIONS: *BusinessWeek, FORTUNE, TIMEAsia*

AVA SAYS: Every weekly meeting with Jessi involves picking a slip of paper out of the back of Jessi's notebook. We take the next ten minutes to respond to the prompt. One prompt was to write about meeting a celebrity and eventually finding a dead body in the trunk of their car. In the end, I wrote a short but humorous scene about a young girl running into Hugh Jackman and finding an unconscious Oprah Winfrey in the trunk of his car. When I finished reading, Jessi sat there chuckling. Was the door of a new world open? Most definitely.

 *p. 283*

JESSI SAYS: Oprah Winfrey? How did Ava get there? That's the question I wondered—the question I always wonder—when Ava reads her response from our opening exercise. We always start with the same phrase or assignment. We write by ourselves for ten minutes, following the odd twists of our imaginations. And then we share, only to discover that the same phrases have taken us into different worlds. When we come together, share our work, and help each other edit, we create something new. We see things differently.

 *p. 217*

AMANDA NERVAIS

YEARS AS MENTEE: *2*

GRADE: *11*

HIGH SCHOOL: *Academy for Young Writers*

BORN: *Brooklyn, NY*

LIVES: *Brooklyn, NY*

AMANDA SAYS: My relationship with Kate has become more open this year. I feel much closer to her than I did last year, and she's always the first one I reach out to by email when I'm frustrated with whatever is going on at the moment in my life. She's always pushing me to take what I'm feeling and get it down on paper, even when I don't feel like it. Next thing you know, a new story is born.

W *p. 227*

KATE JACOBS

YEARS AS MENTOR: *3*

OCCUPATION: *Editor, Roaring Brook Press*

KATE SAYS: Mandy is one of the toughest people I know. She has a determination and resiliency to hold on to beauty and hope whenever life gets difficult. One of my favorite things is opening my email after Mandy's had a tough week and finding a poem or essay unpacking what she's experiencing. There is always a metaphor or turn of phrase in her writing that I take with me into my day, and it helps me make sense of my own experience.

p. 226

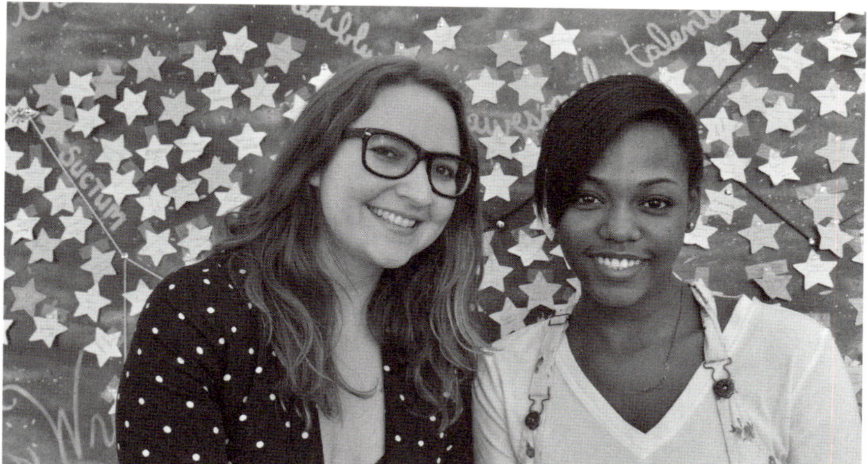

BRE'ANN NEWSOME

YEARS AS MENTEE: *2*

GRADE: *10*

HIGH SCHOOL: *The Urban Assembly Bronx Studio for Writers and Artists*

BORN: *NY, NY*

LIVES: *Bronx, NY*

PUBLICATIONS AND RECOGNITIONS: *Scholastic Art & Writing Award Silver Key in Poetry; GWN Poetry Ambassador, Poet-Linc Poetry Slam at Lincoln Center, Poets Out Loud at Fordham University*

CHRISTINA BROSMAN

YEARS AS MENTOR: *3*

OCCUPATION: *Talent Department, ID Entertainment PR Firm*

PUBLICATIONS AND RECOGNITIONS: *...And Then She DIES at the End!*

BRE'ANN SAYS: During my second year with Girls Write Now, my mentor Christina and I have remained partners in crime. Something is improved upon with every workshop and outing we have, whether it's confidence, chemistry, or a new piece. I'm fortunate to have a mentor I trust to help develop my work and remind me of how far I've come.

 *p. 239*

CHRISTINA SAYS: It's been so amazing to bear witness to all of Bre's work as a Poetry Ambassador this year. Seeing a sophomore in high school possess so much talent, drive, and self-assurance is incredibly impressive. Sometimes, in the best way, I feel like I'm just along for the ride. I'm thrilled to see her continued progress from one meeting, piece, and performance to the next. And I'm looking forward to exploring the great new worlds our third year together will surely bring.

 *p. 238*

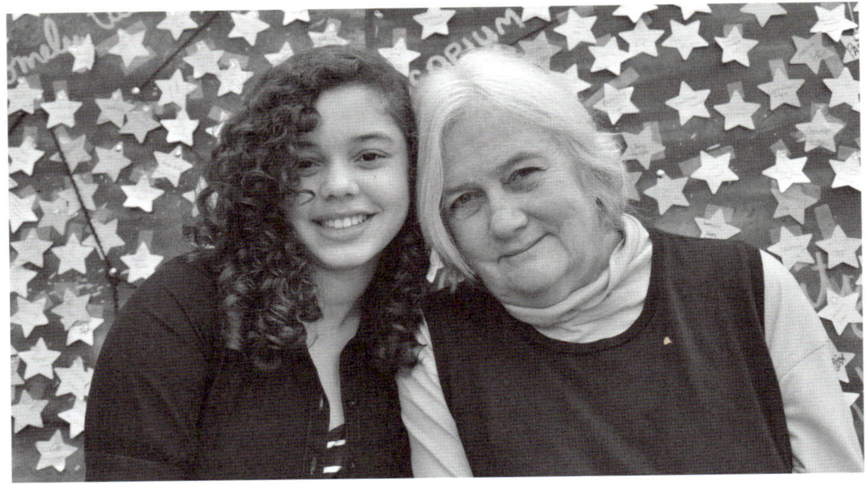

KATHERINE ORTIZ

YEARS AS MENTEE: *1*

GRADE: *9*

HIGH SCHOOL: *Metropolitan Expeditionary Learning School*

BORN: *Dominican Republic*

LIVES: *Queens, NY*

KATHERINE SAYS: My relationship with my mentor has provided me with the insight to view my writing with a different perspective. I no longer dwell on fiction and I now incorporate my own personal experiences into my writing to make it seem more realistic. Together we've explored new genres. We saw our writing in different forms and explored the unexplored within our pieces.

 *p. 248*

MARY PAT KANE

YEARS AS MENTOR: *1*

OCCUPATION: *Writer; Teaching Artist*

PUBLICATIONS AND RECOGNITIONS: *The Brooklyn Herald, The Christian Science Monitor, The Philadelphia Daily News*

MARY PAT SAYS: My relationship with Katherine has opened me up to new music genres! (I research the groups she talks about.) And she is so conversant and easy with computer programs that she has inspired me to do more. Our weekly meetings produce fresh from-the-now writings that I cherish.

 *p. 190*

EMELY PAULINO

YEARS AS MENTEE: *4*

GRADE: *12*

HIGH SCHOOL: *Young Women's Leadership School of Astoria*

BORN: *NY, NY*

LIVES: *Queens, NY*

PUBLICATIONS AND RECOGNITIONS: *2012 Urban Heroes Award*

COLLEGE: *Bard College*

JESS PASTORE

YEARS AS MENTOR: *4*

OCCUPATION: *Fundraiser, ACLU*

EMELY SAYS: I don't know how to fully express how grateful I am to have a mentor. Jess helps me make sense of the craziness in my life, but most importantly, she inspires me to write. When I am being hard on myself she reminds me that good writing takes time. After more than five drafts of my college essay and reading piece, I found that my writing improved substantially. The *New Worlds* theme truly fit my experience with Jess this year, as she helped me make my way through the college process and explore new topics in my poems as well.

 *p. 259*

JESS SAYS: As we began our final year together, I knew we'd be treading new ground. I expected it to be tough, and I knew I'd need to be there every step of the way as she entered this new phase. What I didn't expect is how transformative the year would be for me as well. As she looked ahead to college, Emely inspired me to take a deeper look at my own journey to where I am today. I've found inspiration, strength, and friendship that is at the heart of a great writing partnership—one that I hope will continue long after the last reading.

 *p. 153*

KIRSTIE PLASENCIA

YEARS AS MENTEE: *1*

GRADE: *11*

HIGH SCHOOL: *Urban Assembly for Media Studies*

BORN: *NY, NY*

LIVES: *NY, NY*

 *p. 218*

CHERISE WOLAS

YEARS AS MENTOR: *1*

OCCUPATION: *Full-time Writer; Co-President, Ovie Entertainment*

 *p. 268*

KIRSTIE & CHERISE SAY: A hot chocolate, a decaf skim latte, the beat of Colombian instruments

Caja drumming, tiple and estrellia thrumming

Others: heads in books, fingers on laptops, ears cauliflowered by phones

Not us, we who are focused on the magic of the short story, the purity of language, enchanting syntax.

Flying ether drafts, lines spun, words plucked

The birth of themes, characters bursting through shells, orchestrating their wobbly next steps

"There is a lot of food in this story!"

The essential art of editing, whittling story bones

Progression notes, forward movement

"At this pace, you could have several short stories by the end of the year."

Talking about writers who make our hearts jump, TV shows of momentary obsession, movies recently seen

"Let's apply to the digital workshops."

"Yes, we'll be futuristic!"

Week after week, word-by-word, until new worlds are constructed, built by us together.

EMILY RAMIREZ

YEARS AS MENTEE: *1*

GRADE: *12*

HIGH SCHOOL: *Brooklyn Technical High School*

BORN: *NY, NY*

LIVES: *Brooklyn, NY*

PUBLICATIONS AND RECOGNITIONS: *Scholastic Art & Writing Award Gold Key in Personal Essay/Memoir*

EMILY SAYS: Being paired with Jennifer as a mentor has truly been amazing. I have learned so much from her. She has inspired me as a writer and encouraged me to continue by writing about things that I care about. And she encouraged me to create my own blog. I always thought that I'd have to be published to be a writer, but Jenn convinced me that I already was.

 *p. 184*

JENNIFER CODY EPSTEIN

YEARS AS MENTOR: *1*

OCCUPATION: *Novelist; Adjunct Professor, Columbia University*

PUBLICATIONS AND RECOGNITIONS: *The Painter from Shanghai, The Gods of Heavenly Punishment; The Asian Wall Street Journal, Mademoiselle, Parenting, The Wall Street Journal*

JENNIFER SAYS: Working with Emily has opened my eyes to how people with the same goals and values can be different. Our backgrounds are so vastly different, and yet we share very similar passions for writing, literature, and social change. We find endless things to talk about with one another. Knowing her has made me realize how hard some have to work for the things that came to others more or less automatically–and reminded me how valuable those things are, regardless of your background.

 *p. 182*

TEMA REGIST

YEARS AS MENTEE: *2*

GRADE: *11*

HIGH SCHOOL: *Midwood High School*

BORN: *NY, NY*

LIVES: *Brooklyn, NY*

PUBLICATIONS AND RECOGNITIONS: *Scholastic Art & Writing Award Silver Key in Poetry; GWN Poetry Ambassador, Poet-Linc Poetry Slam at Lincoln Center, Poets Out Loud at Fordham University*

JOANN DELUNA

YEARS AS MENTOR: *1*

OCCUPATION: *Journalist*

PUBLICATIONS AND RECOGNITIONS: *Bodega Monthly Reading Series; New York Minute, Poet-Linc: Poetry Slam Anthology*

TEMA SAYS: My relationship with my mentor has opened me up to many new experiences, lessons, and discoveries. We have gone to poetry slams at Lincoln Center. We have tried many different poetic styles. When we visited Fordham University for the poetry translation workshop, it was amazing to see how popular poetry is, and how it is a universal language. My mentor and I had many amazing experiences.

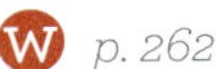
p. 262

JOANN SAYS: "What do you want to do in our sessions?" I asked Tema. "I write a lot of love poems so I want to write other types of poems," she said. Damn—I tend to write a lot of love poems, too. How am I going to help her? "Well, we'll learn to write non-love poems together," I said. Then she offered to read me one of her love poems from her phone. Wow, I thought to myself. This girl is so young, but she's experienced so much.

p. 263

SARA REKA

YEARS AS MENTEE: *1*

GRADE: *11*

HIGH SCHOOL: *NYC iSchool*

BORN: *Albania*

LIVES: *NY, NY*

SARA SAYS: Kathleen has broadened my horizons, developing both my writing skills and my taste in bakeries. I knew we'd instantly get along; she was funny from the get-go and we understood each other perfectly. She always knew what I was trying to say, even when it wasn't clear to me. This pairing is great, I thought, when Kathleen told me of her tales in Kosovo. Being that I'm Albanian, we found that we had a lot to talk about. We always have a lot to talk about. I've also found that Kathleen is more than a mentor, she's my friend.

 *p. 137*

KATHLEEN KRAFT

YEARS AS MENTOR: *1*

OCCUPATION: *Creative Movement Teacher, Stevens Cooperative School*

PUBLICATIONS AND RECOGNITIONS: *Anderbo, Drash: Northwest Mosaic, Foundling Review, Gargoyle, The Madison Review, Pirene's Fountain, REAL: Regarding Arts and Letters*

KATHLEEN SAYS: Getting to know Sara has been a new world for me. Our conversations about what it means to be a New Yorker, Eastern Europe, and all matters of poetry have been so gratifying. It has also been fun to walk around the city with her and explore museums, seeing the world through her eyes. Sara's passionate temper really comes through in her writing, and working with her has reinvigorated that element in my own work. Last but not least, Sara is receptive to feedback, and is an excellent reviser!

 *p. 140*

KIARA KERINA-RENDINA

YEARS AS MENTEE: *1*

GRADE: *10*

HIGH SCHOOL: *Frank Sinatra School of the Arts*

BORN: *NY, NY*

LIVES: *NY, NY*

KIARA SAYS: Whether we are joking about our regression into childhood, telling stories of the hilarious variety, or eating croissants, everything I do with Rory is a learning experience. This year we focused on memoir, and through this we explored new worlds, discovering things about both ourselves and other writers and people. We have exchanged so much of our knowledge about history and experiences that I feel like I might explode from all the information that I've learned and discovered, but I would do so in an eruption similar to that of a phoenix being reborn.

 p. 135

RORY SATRAN

YEARS AS MENTOR: *1*

OCCUPATION: *Content Director and Editor, Opening Ceremony*

PUBLICATIONS AND RECOGNITIONS: *About Face: Women Write About What They See When They See When They Look in the Mirror; Opening Ceremony, The Washington Post*

RORY SAYS: Our twin iPhones face each other on the tiny table at Café Angelique, the Bleecker Street spot where we meet every Sunday. Kiara pulls hers out to look at my notes on her anthology piece, to show me a recent self-portrait from art class, to pull up photos of a mutant tree she saw in the Dominican Republic. I admire a new cupcake sticker on her phone, then grab mine to show her a photo of an incredible sticker-art piece in Lena Dunham's bedroom. Technology is omnipresent. New worlds are at our fingertips.

 p. 190

NAJAYA ROYAL

YEARS AS MENTEE: *2*

GRADE: *10*

HIGH SCHOOL: *Benjamin Banneker Academy*

BORN: *NY, NY*

LIVES: *NY, NY*

PUBLICATIONS AND RECOGNITIONS: *Radical Teacher Journal; GWN Poetry Ambassador, Poet-Linc Poetry Slam at Lincoln Center, Poets Out Loud at Fordham University*

ANUJA MADAR

YEARS AS MENTOR: *3*

OCCUPATION: *Editor, Frommers*

PUBLICATIONS AND RECOGNITIONS: *Marriot International*

NAJAYA SAYS: My mentor has opened my eyes to different ways of editing my work, and convinced me to step out of my comfort zone. We are still exploring the new world of growing up and making smart decisions. It's a world you can learn from and get hurt by (or both), but it's the most valuable of them all and our journey has only just begun. Wish us luck!

 *p. 290*

ANUJA SAYS: This year has been a learning experience for me; who knew high school was so intense? I am constantly shocked by what kids today have to deal with in school, and I am consistently impressed by how Najaya handles it all. She rises above whatever challenges are put in front of her, and has made some tough decisions that would be hard for someone twice her age. Together we are exploring a world where decisions are not always easy, and for every few steps forward there may be a step back, too. I'm confident that we'll be able to navigate it easily, especially since we're doing it together.

 *p. 291*

ANGELICA ROZZA

YEARS AS MENTEE: *1*

GRADE: *11*

HIGH SCHOOL: *Long Island City High School*

BORN: *NY, NY*

LIVES: *Brooklyn, NY*

PUBLICATIONS AND RECOGNITIONS: *Scholastic Art & Writing Award Silver Key in Short Story; Finalist for The Polozzo Strozzi High School Renaissance Award*

JOANNA LAUFER

YEARS AS MENTOR: *1*

OCCUPATION: *Writer; Editor; Writing Coach*

PUBLICATIONS AND RECOGNITIONS: *Inspired: The Breath of God, Child Magazine, Dance Spirit, Dance Teacher, The Antioch Review, Greensboro Review, StoryQuarterly*

ANGELICA SAYS: I consider myself extremely lucky to have Joanna as my mentor. Whether we are at one of our pair meetings, pair outings, or just on a phone call, I always feel like I'm growing as a writer. When I try new genres in my writing, Joanna always supports me with an unlimited amount of confidence boosts and expert advice. We not only understand each other as writers, but also as friends, which makes it so much easier to pitch ideas and utilize constructive criticism. We also have this in common: we both love the workshops' free brownies.

 *p. 120*

JOANNA SAYS: This year I learned to be more prolific from working with Angelica. Wednesday afternoons at Juan Valdez Café, after emailing editing suggestions throughout the week, I sometimes feel that I am sitting across the table from a colleague. I marvel at her fearlessness, passion, and ability to write and revise so quickly and so well. She has inspired me to abandon my tendency to edit as I write. We have a strong personal connection, similar tastes in writing and art, and a mutual love for Dylan's Candy Bar.

 *p. 119*

ASHLEY SANDINO

YEARS AS MENTEE: *1*

GRADE: *12*

HIGH SCHOOL: *School For Excellence*

BORN: *NY, NY*

LIVES: *Bronx, NY*

PUBLICATIONS AND RECOGNITIONS: *Manhattanville Presidential Scholarship*

COLLEGE: *Manhattanville College*

ASHLEY SAYS: "Oh, no, I'm so embarrassed." It was my initial thought the very first time she read my writing, putting myself down by believing I'm just an amateur, forgetting this is something I've done since I learned to spell my name.

But since that first time, I haven't felt scared around her anymore.

By having these memories I created with her, I realize the goal was not to be writing all of the time, but to actually get out and experience the world. Having the experience of feeling scared and a little embarrassed, courageous and accomplished, has given me so much to write about.

And she has been there every step of the way.

 *p. 264*

LYNN LURIE

YEARS AS MENTOR: *1*

OCCUPATION: *Author*

PUBLICATIONS AND RECOGNITIONS: *Quick Kills, Corner of the Dead; Juniper Prize for Fiction*

LYNN SAYS: Starbucks. Friday at 5:30PM. Lexington and 78th. Computer opened, words on the screen. You stare straight ahead asking me to read, waiting for me to comment. I know you from what you write. I have questions about the story, the point of view. You want me to direct. The weight of your expectation, how difficult it is to cancel out the surrounding noise, but you are waiting.

 *p. 264*

ILANA SCHILLER-WEISS

YEARS AS MENTEE: *3*

GRADE: *11*

HIGH SCHOOL: *School of the Future*

BORN: *China*

LIVES: *NY, NY*

PUBLICATIONS AND RECOGNITIONS: *Scholastic Art & Writing Award Silver Key in Personal Essay/Memoir*

INGRID SKJONG

YEARS AS MENTOR: *4*

OCCUPATION: *Digital Editor, Departures Magazine*

PUBLICATIONS AND RECOGNITIONS: *Departures*

ILANA SAYS: When I first met Ingrid, I had no idea how to pronounce her surname. I still don't know, but it shows you how you can come to know someone very well without even being able to pronounce her name. We talked about a wide range of topics throughout our pair meetings. It was great getting to know her, and to trust her wise feedback and judgment. Every time I told her a story about something in my life, Ingrid encouraged me to write it down. Thanks to her, little by little, I've begun to use writing to help make sense of the world.

p. 89

INGRID SAYS: I learned something critical about Ilana after our first few meetings: she has a penchant for burying the lede. Case in point: one day, after a half hour of chatting about how our day went, the weather, and what we planned to have for dinner, she paused, looked me in the eye, and said, "Oh, and I'm going to China for spring break!" Clearly that is news of the up-front variety, and when I said as much she just smiled. Her tendency is delightful and I always find myself wondering what new and monumental announcement she's going to make me wait for next.

p. 88

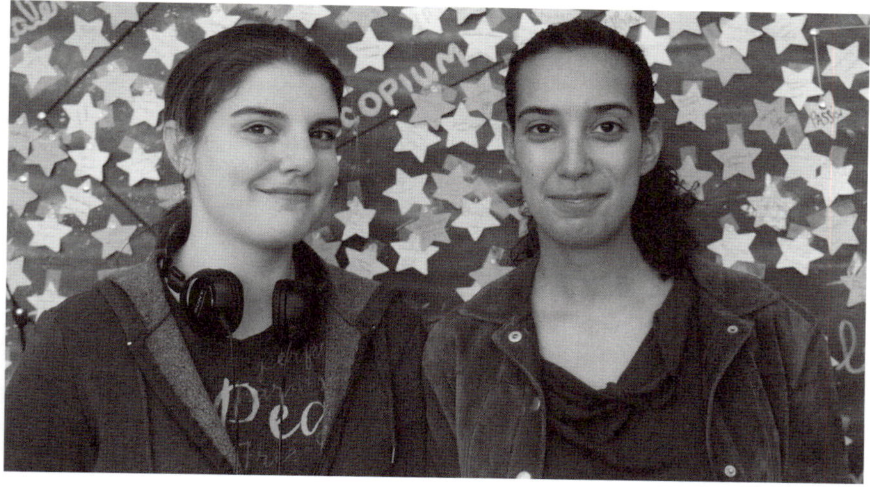

ARIANA SPATOLA

YEARS AS MENTEE: *1*

GRADE: *11*

HIGH SCHOOL: *Susan E. Wagner High School*

BORN: *NY, NY*

LIVES: *Staten Island, NY*

ARIANA SAYS: The amazing dynamic duo of Luciana and myself began with the mere mention of cats. With only a little bit of conversation the first day we met, I simply knew we'd be one awesome pair and we are. I'm forever thankful I've met Luciana. I can recall every pair session with a smile on my face. She's a kindred spirit who never fails to motivate and lend her ear to me. With her, I've grown as a writer and a person.

 *p. 158*

LUCIANA LOPEZ

YEARS AS MENTOR: *1*

OCCUPATION: *Journalist, Reuters*

PUBLICATIONS AND RECOGNITIONS: *Reuters*

LUCIANA SAYS: Ariana and I would have fun pair sessions anywhere, but living in New York provides us a bonus–the significant cultural institutions of the city. Together we've gone to plays, museums, Central Park, exploring the city and its various narratives. Every time we stumble onto something new, I feel again how lucky we are to be where we are, doing what we are.

 *p. 199*

SADE SWIFT

YEARS AS MENTEE: *2*

GRADE: *12*

HIGH SCHOOL: *Beacon High School*

BORN: *NY, NY*

LIVES: *NY, NY*

PUBLICATIONS AND RECOGNITIONS: *WNYC Schoolbook; Lang Dean's Scholarship*

COLLEGE: *Eugene Lang College*

SADE SAYS: In a nutshell, Linda is a narrative genius. She has a way with words that makes you want to hear more. Linda has helped me and pushed me to explore other genres, and I think I have done the same for her. We decided to "show, not tell" this year and we have kept each other to that. Linda has taught me to appreciate and take pride in my work, while remaining open-minded to changing it.

 *p. 195*

LINDA CORMAN

YEARS AS MENTOR: *3*

OCCUPATION: *Journalist; Teacher*

LINDA SAYS: Sade has led me to push genres. Our early exercises focused on writing poetry; I came up with some hash between poetry and narrative. Now I love to write with the intense attention that poetry demands, and I'm more inclined to read poetry. Sade has also helped me realize that I need to seek out readers for my writing. I've gradually shared more of my work, and I'm gaining the courage and determination to get more feedback from her and others.

 *p. 194*

LAWRENCIA TERRIS

YEARS AS MENTEE: *1*

GRADE: *11*

HIGH SCHOOL: *Arts and Media Prep High School*

BORN: *St. Lucia*

LIVES: *Brooklyn, NY*

LAWRENCIA SAYS: Working with Juliet has opened many new worlds for me. The most recent one was journalism. We tried interviewing an employee at a coffee shop, which didn't turn out so well, and led to me to the other new world: being shot down. It was a good lesson because I learned that as a writer, my ideas will sometimes not work out the way I want them to. The only way to get over it is to move on to other ideas.

 *p. 206*

JULIET WERNER

YEARS AS MENTOR: *1*

OCCUPATION: *Associate Producer, The Daily Show*

PUBLICATIONS AND RECOGNITIONS:
The Onion,
The Queens Tribune

JULIET SAYS: My relationship with Lawrencia has opened the new world of being a mentor. Do I feel like I've lived up to such lofty title? Not necessarily. I know I introduced her to a new kind of cream cheese, and she now thinks she's "addicted to lox." But beyond that, have I made a difference? I think the difference is that Lawrencia and I are now friends, whereas before we were not. And our friendship, because it's fueled by two brains that love observation, could potentially expose others to new ways of seeing things.

 *p. 225*

TESSA LEE-THOMAS

YEARS AS MENTEE: *1*

GRADE: *12*

HIGH SCHOOL: *Urban Assembly Institute of Math and Science for Young Women*

BORN: *NY, NY*

LIVES: *Brooklyn, NY*

PUBLICATIONS AND RECOGNITIONS: *Girls Inc. Award*

COLLEGE: *City College*

KATHLEEN SCHEINER

YEARS AS MENTOR: *2*

OCCUPATION: *Writer*

PUBLICATIONS AND RECOGNITIONS: *The Arts Cure, Dance International, L'Ecran Fantastique, Publishers Weekly, Toxic*

TESSA SAYS: Meeting Kathleen at Girls Write Now has opened me up to new experiences. I had never shared my love for writing and horror with one person at the same time. Our differences are what connect us. We both come from two different worlds, but at the end of the day, we are able to merge and create this one new world for ourselves. In this world there are zombies and horror, there are colored pens and paper, there are words and drama, but there is also love and respect. In this dynamic world, two come together to create a world that we have bonded together.

 *p. 207*

KATHLEEN SAYS: Tessa and I rode the subway and decided to do some writing together. The prompt we blindly picked was: sitting on the subway going under the East River, and all of a sudden it stops. That's the world Tessa and I have shared this year—one of synchronicity. In the sun-lit cafeteria of the Brooklyn Museum, we trade horror movie recommendations, and then get down to the business of writing about zombies and paper-cuts and snow and deserted streets. We write and share our darkest fears, and by making up stories about this, we become more powerful together as women writers.

  *p. 209*

IRIS TORRES

YEARS AS MENTEE: *2*

GRADE: *11*

HIGH SCHOOL: *The Young Women's Leadership School*

BORN: *NY, NY*

LIVES: *NY, NY*

PUBLICATIONS AND RECOGNITIONS:
Scholarship to Syracuse University's Summer College Program

IRIS SAYS: Working with Heather has offered me such great opportunities. Not only does she broaden my mind, but she also takes me on a journey without ever stepping out of New York City. From Brooklyn to Bombay to Asia to South Africa, Heather and I have explored a lot this year. Not only do we go on these wonderful adventures, but we also remember to have some fun every now and again!

 *p. 160*

HEATHER KRISTIN

YEARS AS MENTOR: *6*

OCCUPATION: *Writer*

PUBLICATIONS AND RECOGNITIONS:
Glamour, Live and Let Love, New York Press, Slate, Smith, St. Petersburg Times, West Side Spirit

HEATHER SAYS: Iris has taken me on a journey to new worlds with her writing. In her poetry she explored the people of Palestine, in her fiction she's explored the Far East, and in her digital writing she's taken me to Africa. I've traveled the world with Iris without ever having to jump on a train, plane, or automobile.

 *p. 166*

MOIE UESUGI

YEARS AS MENTEE: *1*

GRADE: *10*

HIGH SCHOOL: *Bard High School Early College Queens*

BORN: *NY, NY*

LIVES: *Queens, NY*

PUBLICATIONS AND RECOGNITIONS: *Scholastic Art & Writing Award Honorable Mention in Short Story*

MOIE SAYS: I'll try to keep this as light as I can, because clumsy everyday life is the world Savannah has helped lead me back into. Amid Mayan prophecies, weird coffee shop music, and many blackened drafts about a girl and a grave, the theme was: keep it light. Maybe that's why she still lets me off the hook when I show up for everything approximately eight minutes late, and we never seem to finish within an hour. To say it simply: our theme this year was whipped cream—the homemade kind that creates patterns both in my hot chocolate and in my writing.

 *p. 185*

SAVANNAH ASHOUR

YEARS AS MENTOR: *1*

OCCUPATION: *Editor, Workman Publishing*

SAVANNAH SAYS: Working with a writer outside my everyday professional context has given me the luxury of being able to focus on craft, to linger on thorny questions or interesting ideas, without being so goal-oriented. Moie loves to untangle linguistic or structural challenges, so her enthusiasm for digging in makes our side-trips all the more rewarding.

 *p. 234*

CARMIN WONG

YEARS AS MENTEE: *1*

GRADE: *11*

HIGH SCHOOL: *Boys and Girls High School*

BORN: *Guyana*

LIVES: *Queens, NY*

CARMIN SAYS: My mentor has helped me discover more about myself as a writer. I learned that a piece of writing does not have to create itself in one day, but can start out as a single note or list, and evolve over time into something beautiful. I have also opened up to trying new genres.

My mentor and I have explored each other's writing styles and have realized that a big part of why we write is to have self-expression and power, something that is not common for females in the worlds we come from.

 *p. 188*

HADIA SHEERAZI

YEARS AS MENTOR: *1*

OCCUPATION: *Master's student, St. John's University*

PUBLICATIONS AND RECOGNITIONS: *The Vanguard; named to Who's Who Among Students in American Colleges and Universities*

HADIA SAYS: Having had wonderful writing mentors, starting with my father, I was always amazed by their patience and dedication. Being on the other side of that relationship has allowed me to pass on the wisdom that was handed down to me.

From trying crepes for the first time, to tiptoeing outside our comfort zones and experimenting with "shape poetry," we've visited all kinds of worlds–those familiar to one of us, and others that were entirely new territories. But most importantly, we've had fun every step of the way on this journey.

 *p. 146*

LULJETA ZENKA

YEARS AS MENTEE: *1*

GRADE: *9*

HIGH SCHOOL: *Susan E. Wagner High School*

BORN: *NY, NY*

LIVES: *Staten Island, NY*

LULJETA SAYS: At our meetings, Lizz always has some tale to share of what happened on the bus, while I have more insane stories to tell. In between the storytelling we learn about each other. We may seem like opposites, but we get along well and have a lot in common.

 *p. 127*

LIZZ CARROLL

YEARS AS MENTOR: *1*

OCCUPATION: *Communications Manager, Digital Media, CFY*

PUBLICATIONS AND RECOGNITIONS: *Latina Magazine, SCRATCH Magazine*

LIZZ SAYS: I scrunched my eyes and peeked at the screen. Damn, only 30 minutes left! I took a deep breath and squinted... I can do this, right? I've been editing for over ten years for God's sake! "Oh, and by the way, I forgot to tell you..." I lift my face to look at Luljeta. "Yeah... uh... it's 700 words over the word count." My shoulders fall. I shake my head and break out into a disbelieving smile. "You know I'm gonna kill you, right?" We burst out into laughter.

 *p. 293*

RACHEL ZHAO

YEARS AS MENTEE: *1*

GRADE: *10*

HIGH SCHOOL: *Millennium High School*

BORN: *NY, NY*

LIVES: *Brooklyn, NY*

RACHEL SAYS: One of the first things I noticed about Nina is her love for mint tea. When I learned how to write a proper newspaper article, balancing detail with information and compressing events into words, I thought about how writers had to learn these techniques throughout history as they ventured to all corners of the world during peace and war. Luckily, I didn't have to do it alone as Nina was there with me, dissecting each part of an article, with the smell of mint tea grounding me as I scribbled down the current state of our world.

 *p. 147*

NINA AGRAWAL

YEARS AS MENTOR: *1*

OCCUPATION: *Policy and Communications Coordinator, Collaborative for Building After-School Systems*

PUBLICATIONS AND RECOGNITIONS: *America's Quarterly, Feet in Two Worlds (Website and Podcast)*

NINA SAYS: Being Rachel's mentor has reopened the world of being a teenager in high school, while also compelling me to explore new writing genres and techniques. Prior to working with Rachel, I had written mostly nonfiction in the form of journalism. I hadn't focused on the techniques of fiction or poetry, but because Rachel excelled in these genres and wanted to learn more about them, I explored them with her.

 *p. 280*

evolution

EXPLORE THE ART OF POSSIBILITY

She was ready to go somewhere extravagant, have a luminous time, explore the art of possibility, and relish the joys of life.

Bushra Miah, p.86

My mentee Sara Reka talks to me about going home to her native Albania, how the place "remains inside of her," and that she knows "how to navigate" when she gets there. I imagine her on streets I've never seen, making her way to a relative's home, feeling like both an insider and an outsider as she has described. As I listen, I think about how we all have places we navigate throughout our lives, and that it's these places that turn us onto the road of who we are and who we become.

In the following stories and poems, the narrators navigate their homelands, schools, cities, and jobs, but mostly their changing, growing selves. They explore their memories and their changing beliefs about their place in the world, as well as their abilities and dreams. They describe the "second chance" of turning eighteen, the memory of losing kindergarten ice cream money, a secret garden in New York City where the narrator experiences herself as part of an ancient Persian tapestry, and so many other profoundly transformative experiences.

Sara remarks how moved she is by the vulnerability and the courage expressed by these girls and women. I was also moved: it is a privilege to read their stories.

KATHLEEN KRAFT
2013 MENTOR AND
ANTHOLOGY COMMITTEE MEMBER

TRAIN TO EIGHTEEN
MAYA LASHLEY

 *Perez, p. 79*

 *p. 43*

I've got a one-way ticket
to eighteen, burning
a hole in my back pocket.
I'm speechless as
my words hold my
emotions hostage.

It seems like just yesterday
I was a pile of clay
young and afraid
yearning to be
molded into a
fearless woman.

Sleepless nights
and tear-soaked notebooks
full of broken dreams
consumed the old world
my soul used to inhabit.

As God's grace would have it
I received a second chance
to make my old world new again.
To change
and rearrange
my goals,
and my future
to become the woman
I've always wanted
to be, the woman
who was always
hidden inside of me

As I travel into the
brave, new world
ahead of me
I say farewell to
the sadness of
the past. I'm on
my way, so look out
world, here I come!

Standing here on
life's subway platform

waiting for the train
to eighteen,
a breeze of the future
flies through my hair
filling my head with
endless possibilities.
I won't be seventeen
for very long,
because soon I will be
catching the train
to eighteen.

EIGHTEEN FROM THE OTHER SIDE

TRACY PEREZ

 *Lashley, p. 78*

 *p. 43*

If I could tell my eighteen-year-old self
what life would be like now
I'd say get ready for a ride
filled with unforgettable people
dreams fulfilled
and a heart broken
but not beyond repair.
I call New York City home
that much I figured.
But I hope I never stop exploring
never stop taking a leap of faith
Into what can't be planned or explained.
If I could tell my eighteen-year-old self
about the journey I've taken thus far
I'd say I haven't regretted one minute.
I found myself in an unexpected place
but it's exactly where I need to be.

THE DOLLAR
CORRINE CIVIL

My friends really enjoy my retelling of this experience. In writing this, I realized that maybe I should carry some of my five-year-old self into the new worlds I encounter from now on.

 *Henig, p. 223*
 *p. 22*

I was sitting at the round, pink table of the school cafeteria with a few friends, and we were all casually chatting over our (as usual) uneaten school lunches when the topic of childhood came up. Wasn't it funny how we all thought as kindergarteners that the value of the dollar was way more than it actually was? Back then, I thought a dollar could buy someone a feast of all my favorite foods. That's why I was so devastated the time I lost my dollar at school and couldn't buy an ice cream bar.

Back in kindergarten, I never felt I fit in. So when my mother handed me a dollar bill that morning, it was remarkable that I could finally buy a treat at lunchtime like the rest of the kids. I folded the bill into four, slipping it carefully into one of my little Tommy Hilfiger school shoes. It seemed like a great day. I had on my favorite shoes, the plaid uniform skirt that I could finally wear after a long, cold winter of slacks, and the money that would allow me to enjoy one of my favorite treats. Not even M, the evil girl who had colored on my clean, white homework folder, could take me from the bliss I felt.

This all took a turn when lunchtime finally came around.

I discarded my tray and poured my milk into the smelly trash can that was specifically designated for milk. Slipping back into my seat so I could grab my dollar from my shoe, I stuck my pinkie finger into it just where I had left it that morning. The money was not there.

I checked my other shoe, though I was 99.99% sure of where I had placed my money. I placed my hands on each of my hips, attempting to check my pockets. But I had no pockets! I was wearing my skirt that day, so there was nowhere I could have placed the dollar bill by mistake. Slouching over, I gave up on the desperate search. I was angry, let down, and overall devastated. It was gone, it wasn't coming back, and there was no way I would be eating ice cream along with the other kids that day. I wasn't close enough to any of the other girls to ask one of them to lend me a dollar until the next day. I tried to think of which classroom my older sister might have been in to see if she could lend me some money, but I quickly abandoned that plan; I couldn't remember if she was in the fifth or sixth grade, and I realized she probably didn't have a dollar either. My planned leap that day to social recognition amongst the PS 96 kindergarteners was NOT a success.

I walked out of the cafeteria, unable to avert my eyes from the students licking their cold treats in delight. I didn't cry, but disappointment overcame me as I got into the girls' line to head back to Ms. Messer's classroom. I trudged unhappily

into the hallway, and being surrounded by my chattering and happy peers added to my chagrin. It was not the great day I had imagined.

Now, at the pink table during the sophomore lunch period, I shared this horrible experience with a few of my many amazing friends, Tazrin, Amira, Amber, and Naomi, who all burst into a laughter that somehow grew more intense when Lauren looked at me directly and told me to "man up." But my laughter turned into real tears as I cried as if I were back in kindergarten, reliving that terrible day all over again. They found it hilarious that I was emotional as I shared a bad experience of my childhood, and in my opinion it was; I was laughing as much as I was crying. However, my mind could not stop analyzing how much I had changed since kindergarten.

My preference for ice cream has never faltered, but my bad luck with friendships disappeared about a decade ago. Today, I have several friends who would be at my side during lunch, each offering me a dollar so I could have FIVE ice cream bars. If my sister went to my school, I'd hunt her down until I found her and ask her for the dollar I know she would give me. I know now that I do not have to be alone, and that if I want something, I'm going to have to go for it.

GO

LATOYA JORDAN

M *Lin, p. 82*

P *p. 45*

Not a single soul
was out in the dark city.
The girl skipped along
the deserted yellow lines
of the two-way street,
her path dimly illuminated
by moonlight.
The city's only sounds:
her boots hitting the asphalt,
her humming to still a
racing mind. Her hands shook
faster than the beating of her
heart but her legs kept moving,
they did not understand fear,
only go.

A DARK CITY
JOANNE LIN

 *Jordan, p. 81*

 *p. 45*

The city was dark, and it seemed as if not a single soul was out. The moon was alone that night. For the first time in a number of years, New York City was quiet. There were no televisions on, no laptops surfing the Internet. There were no cars roaming around, no heels slamming on the sidewalk. No buses picking up passengers.

It was the second night without power and my family was huddled in my parents' small bedroom. We had several candles lit and a flashlight pointed at us for light. My dog, Yuki, lay between my mother and me, her tiny body pressed against my leg as she slept. My brother sat on a small stool and my dad rested on the computer chair. We were using the small amount of light to play poker.

We were staring down at our cards, and my brother's eyes were frustrated as he scanned his hand and my dad slapped down an ace. It was one of the rare moments we had time together. We used to have a tradition, huddled around the same cards on the same table. But between growing up and life's naturally changing, the tradition slowly faded out of our lives.

The last time we had a poker game was six years ago; I was in fifth grade and scared of middle school. I thought I was taking the biggest step in my life, leaving my best friends and entering a new world. Now, I am graduating high school and starting my first year of college soon. It certainly feels like the biggest step of my life once again. Life changes quickly, yet there will always be a constant in my life: my family. That night, while the city was cold and dark, we were warm with bright smiles.

THE SKY'S THE LIMIT

RAYHANA MAAROUF

My experience at Aviation High School has inspired my anthology piece. I drew upon my childhood fascination with airplanes and explored how that passion has affected choices about my future and the new worlds that await me after graduation.

 *Feigus, p. 187*

 *p. 47*

Airplanes have captivated me from a very young age. My friends loved playing with Barbie and Ken dolls, but nothing delighted me more as a kid than taking daily walks with my father past Aviation High School in the neighborhood where my family lived—Sunnyside, Queens. At the time, I was unaware that the students who studied there learned everything there was to know about airplanes. But I did understand how excited I felt when I gazed at the five huge aircraft that sat on the ground behind the school. The planes were painted a vivid golden color that sparkled brightly in the sun. To add to the excitement, my father would point to planes passing overhead on their way into or out of New York City. Now I realize that those were not just special moments that I shared with my father; they were moments that foreshadowed my future.

I will never forget my first plane ride. I was five years old, and my family, who are Muslim, were traveling to Morocco. I remember a pretty brunette in a uniform coming over to my seat and asking me how I was enjoying the flight. I responded with a toothy grin that earned me a big smile and a chuckle. The stewardess reached into a cart and brought out a pencil case that she placed on my tray table. The pencil case had a black background. On the background was a sky-blue jet plane surrounded by an ivory moon and twinkling stars. The jet was smiling broadly and had a speech bubble next to it that said, "Bon Vol," which means "Good Flight" in French. That pencil case sits in a place of honor on my desk to this day.

Needless to say, I had no doubt which high school I wanted to attend. But I had to apply to Aviation because it is a competitive high school, and many more kids apply to it than get in. My heart was thumping wildly when the letter arrived in the mail, and my hands were shaking as I tore it open. I shouted, "I made it!" as tears of joy slid down my cheeks. Many people told me that I wouldn't be able to handle the work because it was a "man's job." I ignored their warnings and accepted the challenge enthusiastically. I spent the whole summer researching the school and friending anyone on Facebook who went there. I studied the different types of aircraft and memorized the parts of a Boeing 747. Until then, airplanes had been my passion. Now they were my obsession.

My first day of school was exhilarating. I picked out my favorite abaya, which to me is a symbol of self-respect. I wanted to make a self-confident impression on my teachers and my peers. Little did I know that a big surprise awaited me on that first day. Everywhere I looked, as I walked through the halls, I saw posses of guys. It turned out that only 16% of the students in my class were female. But I have never let that gender imbalance intimidate me.

On my very first shop project, I proved that I was as capable as any guy. Aviation has an extremely rigorous science and math program as well as shop classes in which students are required to construct actual parts of an aircraft. For that shop project, each student, working independently, had four months in which to build a component of an aircraft wing known as an aileron. By coming to school early on weekdays and going in on Saturdays over the course of more than three months, I was able to complete that project two weeks before it was due. Not only did I earn an A from my instructor, but many of the guys in the class asked me for help finishing their ailerons. With that early success, I completely shattered the myth that the work at Aviation was "too hard for girls." Since then, my motto has been, "The Sky's the Limit."

TAKING THE SPOTLIGHT

ANNIE REUTER

Guo, p. 152

p. 35

I've always been the quiet one. Never wanting to be the center of attention, most family dinners during my childhood consisted of my sister ruling the conversation.

Don't get me wrong; I didn't mind. In fact, I was grateful. The less I had to say, the better.

Naturally, I became a writer.

My notebook was my source of comfort. As long as it was in my hand I felt I could say whatever I wanted.

As a kid I idolized Katie Couric. Every morning Dad and I would watch The Today Show over breakfast and I aspired to be her—something I forgot about until very recently.

This past January, while sitting in a meeting discussing the upcoming Academy of Country Music Awards, the topic of who would host our weekly Country Rewind show arose. A long-lost dream deep inside of me floated to the surface.

"Annie, do you know any country journalists in New York?" my boss asked.

I knew a few, but none would go on camera.

As names were called out this nagging voice inside of me just wouldn't shut up.

"You should do it. Speak up! You know everything there is to know about country music."

Then my conscience got the best of me.

"Annie, if they thought you could do it they would have suggested you."

This had to be true. So, I dismissed that constant nagging to volunteer myself. But it just wouldn't stop! So, at the end of the meeting with just my boss in the room I spoke up.

"John, if you can't find anyone, I'll do it. I'm not comfortable on camera but I can practice."

"Annie, I don't want to make you do anything you're uncomfortable with," he said.

"I know," I said, and added, "I'll sleep on it and come to a decision in the morning."

A month later, I was gearing up for my very first live shoot. Despite the three dress rehearsals, I just couldn't shake those nerves! As soon as I walked past the newsroom and saw cameras set up, a big knot in my stomach formed and I wanted to throw up.

"Why did I decide to do this?" I asked myself. But it was too late to back out now.

I wrote the very first script I had to recite on air and had interviewed three of the artists I was discussing in the first episode, so you'd think it'd be easy. The first take I had to redo because I wasn't loud enough and they said I needed to smile more.

"This is silly, but can we add smiley faces into the script? Maybe that will remind me."

It worked! By the second try I was certain I could do better.

I took a deep breath and pretended I was talking to my friends about country music and that seemed to do it.

THE CHANGE
BUSHRA MIAH

The main character, Aomame, not only physically discovers a new world when traveling from her native Japanese land to the European continent, but also explores new aspects of her own thoughts and emotions.

 *Reagan, p. 188*

 *p. 52*

Upstairs, Aomame rushed between the closet and her duffle bag, doing last-minute packing. Even as she hurried, every article of clothing was neat and tightly folded. She packed her personal bag, a duffle bag containing only necessary clothing and sanitary supplies for three days, and her business bag. While carrying everything at once, it seemed as though the weight of the bags would overwhelm her thin frame and she would tip over, falling face-forward. But she remained balanced, not showing the tiniest bit of discomfort, taking every step with calculated precision.

Although this was her first time traveling out of the country, she didn't seem nervous at all. Instead, she left the house just as she would for a regular day of work: she grabbed her keys from the coffee table, tucked her wallet into the side of her personal bag, turned off all the lights, and used the flat of her right hand to gently touch the largest photograph of her late parents, one of many photographs which hung in a maze-like pattern near the door.

On the way to Haneda International Airport, sitting in the passenger seat of the cab, she made some mental notes. *Dress suit, check; pencil skirt for the meeting, yes; comb, got it; toothbrush, in the front zipper; deodorant, mmhmm...*

After checking in her bags, obtaining her boarding pass, and going through the metal detectors, she stood near the gate where her flight was scheduled to take off, fiddling with her smartphone. Despite eyeing a Starbucks and simultaneously hearing her stomach grumbling in call for food, she remained still, as if any movement would break the glass surrounding her.

After waiting for a couple of minutes, she looked at her silver Fossil watch. The longer hand was in between the five and six, while the shorter hand was exactly on the one, which meant it was now 5:05 a.m. It was five minutes past the time scheduled for her flight. Wait... did she miss something? Perhaps an announcement? She double blinked, making sure this wasn't blurry vision. She stared at her watch for a couple of seconds, making sure it still worked. She looked to make sure the sign read "Gate 19." Then, she looked up at the screen containing the arrival and departure information, making sure that beside the Japanese Airlines logo and flight JA1915, it read "NOW DEPARTING." Confused, she looked down at her black heels, then looked right back at the screen. It now read "FLIGHT CANCELLED." Bewildered and unable to think clearly, she looked at the desk below the screen and saw a mixture of eight Japanese Airlines

employees and flight attendants rummaging through papers, speaking in hushed voices, with looks of both concern and disapproval on their faces. There wouldn't be any flights going to the US for the next week.

Two of them came onto the airport loudspeakers and delivered the uninvited news. Within seconds, she found herself slumping down in a dirty wooden chair, weak and dehydrated. With the words "FLIGHT CANCELLED," her life shattered onto the cold airport floor, like broken pieces of irreplaceable glass.

This wasn't any short trip. It was a "make it or break it" opportunity to work for the number one American graphic designing company in Salt Lake City, Utah. To Aomame, it wasn't just a job or simply a career, but the rest of her future. She had spent so much time and effort making herself eligible for the position... and now, all of that was wasted.

"No way... no way! This cannot be happening right now," she mumbled to herself. Before she was even able to accomplish the first step of her dream, it vanished right before her own two eyes.

Shock and disappointment formed tears in her eyes. Refusing to sob, she acted stoic. The screen of her phone opened to a text message she received from a friend: "Good luck with everything. After the meeting, have some fun; go shopping; enjoy yourself! Call me when you land!"

Aomame observed her surroundings, her eyes and ears absorbing all they possibly could, like a sponge. When hearing a woman bawling, she turned around and saw a husband and wife, cuddled together. The husband had his hand on his wife's back, trying to console her, while she shed tears and repeated: "My father. My father... heart attack... died."

Quickly, Aomame turned back around, closed her eyes, and made a small prayer. She wasn't the only one caught in a dilemma. And even if so, this was merely the reality of life. Looking back at her phone again, she reread the text message. So what if her flight was cancelled? With every calamity, there was always an opportunity.

Focusing on wanting what she couldn't have was causing her to fail in appreciating what was right in front of her. She was ready to go somewhere extravagant, have a luminous time, explore the art of possibility, and relish the joys of life. With that, she stood, walked up to a desk, and booked the next flight to London, England.

MOVE IT ALONG
INGRID SKJONG

 *Schiller-Weiss, p. 89*

 *p. 66*

My mentee, Ilana, recently wrote about her desire to enter the working world—and the unexpected turn her first interview took. A first job, like so many things in a sixteen-year-old's life, is a gateway to entirely new worlds and experiences. Watching her go through that gateway and more is exciting and reminds me of how much change a teen can experience in the last few years of high school. Change, of course, doesn't stop there, a point I remembered last year after a particularly hefty number of shake-ups.

In the space of twelve months, beginning in January 2012, I left a job I had been in for seven years to freelance; moved into a new apartment with my then-fiancé across town from the neighborhood I had lived in for seven years; unexpectedly took a new full-time job a few months later; and planned a wedding, marrying said fiancé twenty-six days shy of the first anniversary of our engagement.

It was... a lot. But it was also thrilling, offering fresh perspectives nearly every day, from navigating the layout of my Upper West Side 'hood to navigating the transition into married life. In a funny way, New York became new to me again even after living there for nine years.

Now fully settled, I've fallen into routines that add a bit more structure to 2013 in comparison to how 2012 unfolded. (It's nice to, say, use my Kindle Fire to read a book versus using it for wedding invitation design research.) But that doesn't stop me from anticipating the next change, whatever that might be—and really looking forward to it.

CAROLINE BERGER, MENTOR 2005-2007

I didn't understand that one could be a writer until college. In high school, I only knew that I coveted well-crafted sentences like hard candies, that novels were my confidants, and notebooks my life rafts. I scribbled my way into the life I wanted.

YOU'RE (NOT QUITE) HIRED

ILANA SCHILLER-WEISS

This is an account of what went wrong on my first job interview. I was excited to embark on a new journey into the working world, but little did I know, it would turn into a completely different kind of adventure.

 *Skjong, p. 88*

 *p. 66*

It seemed almost too good to be true. The internship coordinator from my school had set me up with a job interview at a school-supply company. The pay? Nine dollars an hour, which seemed like a dream wage. I was incredibly excited at the idea of making money but was even more thrilled by the thought of having my first job. I looked forward to the responsibility, and to telling people that I was a working woman.

The night before the interview, I laid out my clothes—a striped dress shirt, black corduroy pants and a velvet-like blue blazer—and combed the Internet to find more about the company. Oddly, there didn't seem to be a scrap of detail about the job anywhere, but I ignored that tidbit and thought that maybe its website was down. I could barely contain my excitement and had some difficulty getting to sleep.

The next day seemed to drag before I was finally released from the fiery gates of school and hopped onto the uptown 6 train. I got to the site of the interview twenty minutes early and waited outside near the building for my mom. (If all went well and I got the job, she wanted to be there for this significant turning point in my life.) I entered the dark brick building and saw two doormen. I walked up and handed them my ID card, told them the name of the man I was supposed to see, and signed in. As I was about to step into the elevator to press the button, one of the doormen said, "Be careful."

"Sorry?" I said.

"Watch out!" he exclaimed. "He scams."

The doors closed before I had time to answer. Jesus, there must be some serious rivalry there, I thought. I didn't take his warning to heart, but I did keep it in the back of my mind.

When I got to my floor, the interviewer introduced himself as the leader of the company and proceeded as if he had already hired me, telling me what to do. His instructions had nothing to do with how my internship coordinator had described the job: data entry and working part-time around the office. The job the man went on about seemed to entail selling odd stickers with stay-in-school slogans—a far cry from what I thought it would be.

The whole thing felt weird.

Midway through the interview, the receptionist called me out—my mom had an emergency and I needed to go. I didn't think a family member had died in the last fifteen minutes so I figured it had something to do with what the doormen had warned me about earlier. As I left, I was surprised that I didn't feel embarrassed. Instead, I felt relief that I could get out of there, due mainly to sheer nervousness.

I departed and the interviewer looked stunned. He stood at the door of the elevator and it was suddenly clear to me that he didn't buy the excuse of a family emergency. He knew exactly what was going on.

As my mom and I walked away briskly, she revealed that she had learned the interviewer had been arrested and was wanted in several states. He was a con artist, tricking high school kids into scamming other people and never paying his hires. I felt shaken, but mostly deflated—like a tire that ran over a sharp, rusty nail. I had dreamed that by the end of the day I'd be gainfully employed. Alas, that wasn't the case.

Some people are trustworthy, but how do you know who they are? There is a life lesson in here somewhere, but I haven't yet figured out exactly what it is. I suppose I should have trusted my gut and left the interview on my own initiative when I felt that the job was not right. But I didn't want to seem rude or hurt his feelings; that nice-girl thing is too ingrained in me. Next time I am in a situation like this, which I hope is never, I promise myself that I will be the one who rescues me.

CROSSING THE BRIDGE

MEG CASSIDY

M *Camara, p. 92*
P *p. 15*

The drive into Brooklyn that September afternoon
Felt like a second trip through the birth canal
Slow, painful, sticky
After hours of rain
The storm clouds following her
Through the mountains of PA
Rush-hour mugginess set in
The old Toyota's windows rolled all the way down
(Its AC had given out long ago)
But there was hardly a breeze
Let alone
A hint of autumn in the air

Heartbreak on her mind
And in her tape deck

The skyline seeming impossibly far away
Even at the mouth of the tunnel
And Brooklyn
Where she was moving
But had yet to step foot in
Even further out of range
Beyond that

After crawling along Canal Street
A jarring stretch for a Midwestern driver
(Windows hurriedly rolled up
triple-checking doors were locked)
She found herself atop
That massively beautiful bridge
She'd only seen in picture books

For the first time ever
She didn't mind being stopped in traffic
And as soon as she turned onto Joralemon
A street that was simultaneously
As slender and grand as any she'd seen
It felt like a load had been lifted from her
aching shoulders
And she was home.

INSPIRATION FROM MY MOTHER

FANTA CAMARA

This piece came about when I was applying to college. The college application process was not easy, but because of an awesome mentor and my mother's inspiration, I made it through.

 Cassidy, p. 90

 p. 15

I am from Guinea, a small country located in West Africa. In Guinea, elders believe that marriage is more important than education. They believe that education can only be important at certain points in one's life. They also believe that marriage is a symbol of dignity and an honor to the family. While in school at the age of sixteen, my mother was a very smart girl. Her teachers never complained about her academic performance. But her parents took her out of school to get her married to my father. Although marriage was the last thing on my mother's mind, she was never given the chance to choose between her education and marriage. She married my father, whose family promised that she would continue her education.

After getting married to my father, she did not go to school again due to some financial problems in the family. Instead, my mother started to do business at the market place in her neighborhood. At that time she was not happy. After six years of marriage, she realized that only education could help her get where she wanted to be, so she went back to school and became a nurse. Going back to school did not only change her life, but it changed her children's lives as well. Watching my mother struggle, I realized that education is what will help me get to the top of the mountain. I believe in education and I will do all I can to make sure I get my degree.

Does history repeat itself or do people allow it to repeat? I know that my mother suffered a lot, but I will not let the same thing happen to me. My mother is the person who had the biggest influence on me. My mother is my history, my present and future. The only history that I will allow to repeat is the one that bettered my mother's life, which was getting an education. Even though everything in her life gave her the right to give up on her dreams, she never did. She fought for her children and herself. Thinking about her reminds me of the many responsibilities I have in my life.

One year ago I received a call from my grandmother. It was very strange because the communication between my grandmother and me decreased a lot when I came to the United States. She wanted me to marry someone she had chosen for me. I thought about what happened to my mother being married at such a young age. My mother's struggles and living in the United States made me stronger and helped me realize that the decision is mine. No one can force me to get married. I am pursuing my education because I am the leader of my life. I chose to go to college and make my mother proud of me. I choose to be educated.

LOVE FROM LONDON

MADELYNE ZOLLO

After reading Brenda's work about London, I thought it would be interesting to explore the events that led up to her protagonist's moving abroad. My piece is a prologue to hers.

 *Bota, p. 94*

 *p. 12*

It was a postcard that first planted the idea
in my mind—

Sent to me accidentally, with the name of
someone else scrawled across the front.

On it a collage of little pictures—

Of rivers and palaces and churches and
storefronts.

I imagined the clicking of heels on
cobblestone streets, the tolling of the
bells—

The smell of fresh-cut flowers wafting in
the salty chilled air.

The streets would be filled with people
bustling around, much like here—

But with fine smile lines carved into their
flushed faces, not scowls.

What if I were there too, an espresso
warming my hands as I browsed the
markets—

Or sitting on a rod iron bench, watching
red double-decker buses roll by.

What if I switched lives with the person
who sent this postcard?

Would I too be writing home saying I'm
never coming back?

Would I too be signing my letters with *Love
from London*—

Tharsa?

THE "NORMAL" LIFE

BRENDA BOTA

Not only is London a place I'd like to see for myself one day, I'm drawn to everything about it, from its culture to its lifestyle. I used this poem to explore what it'd be like to live there, while also playing around with the idea of anonymity and starting afresh.

Zollo, p. 93
p. 12

My name is Tharsa Jackson.
(In New York, my family knew me as Katherine Slimore).
Now it is acceptable to keep my hair natural.
(In high school, I was always teased for having such puffy hair.)
Here, my accent is rare and up-to-date
(Where back home, I was corrected when I said "wa-ta" to water.)

Every corner of this town marks an event—
Statues depicting historic heroes, battles won
Or state-of-the-art exhibits and beautiful gardens.
(While every corner of my old town marked nothing special—
Another street not clean, papers everywhere;
Cars parked in illegal spaces, windshields covered in dust)
I could drink tea before bed without a fuss
("Katherine!" Mom would call. "It's 8:30 p.m., why the tea!?")
The streets are quiet too

(Unlike the screaming of strangers, the honking of cars, construction being done since the sun rose...)

I went to my first ball.
(I remember Zara used to call about going to apartment parties.)
The dress I wore was a soldier-like uniform, but military chic was the fashion—
Navy blue, long lace sleeves, buttons running down the front, flowing bottom
(versus my old, skintight, leg baring, bright-colored party dresses).

Harrods is across from my flat and every time I go for a walk I see new things—

Piccadilly Circus, Westminster Abbey,
the London Eye
(Rather than yet another apartment
building, grocery store, line of buses).

Two months passed,
Then six...
It's still a journey—
A whole new beginning.

London.

ON THE RIGHT TRACK

IREEN HOSSAIN

 *Hooper, p. 277*

 *p. 39*

We all have that one thing we hate but
love.

The one thing that no matter how hard we
try to settle feelings for,
it ultimately wins and pulls us back.

The scent of urine,
the littered train tracks,
mutated rats,
a Spanish woman selling churros,
the languages of the world spoken in
tongues per minute,
the aspiring rapper,
attractive men dressed in their classy
business suits,
families with Target bags,
a woman reading *Fifty Shades of Grey*.

I see everything in the subway.

It's super filthy—but it's cool—a very
important part of my day.

Yes, I'm in a dysfunctional relationship
with the NYC subway.

When I'm riding the train, I feel like I'm

in the audience of a
way-way-way-off Broadway show.
I hear opera singers singing their hearts out!
Funky dancers that look like fish out of water!

All of this for the price of $2.25!

I should have gotten used to the subway, having been raised

in NYC for seventeen years, but honestly, where's the fun in that?

The subway takes me to the places I need to go:

To The Young Women's Leadership School of Astoria,
where confused young daydreamers—like me—
become lifelong learners.

It took me to my first internship in Dumbo, Brooklyn
where I gained "real world experience"
of working from nine to five in an office
where I could hear my coworker's
deep breathing five cubicles away!

The subway takes me to Girls Write Now,
where professional women writers
eat bagels spread with grape jelly,
polish writing skills,
and listen to rants about math teachers who hate kids.

To Coney Island, where summer nights are spent with my family.
We go to all areas of the park except for the beach,
because it's not necessary for Muslims to get a tan.

The subway takes me to Times Square to shop with friends,

where the tourists are so slow,
I could run to Russia and be back in time
for lunch.

FLASHBACK: When I was younger, my
dad and I would visit our
friends and we would take the subway.

Since my dad is a taxi driver,
he preferred to take the subway so that he
could sit back and relax.

I would hold onto his big rough hands,
standing on the platform and waiting for
the train.

My eyes would widen with excitement
from the blue and white spark caused by
the train running on the tracks.

Train rides will take me to the places I'll be
heading to one day.

Each stop the train makes is a stop closer
to my crazy hopes...

of becoming an international movie star,

wearing Prada,

meeting handsome men,

and collecting TWENTY CATS to live with
me in my oceanfront mansion,

as well as taking me to my realistic dream
of becoming a registered nurse.

Watching a homeless man stumbling onto
the train is a reminder for me to become a
woman with a future.

I want to learn from my professors,
debate with fellow students
and be the conductor of my life.

I want to read Japanese...eat Albanian food
...dance to Egyptian music—

and experience all that the world has to offer.

That homeless man?? He's also a reminder to me that for every person, there's a path...

I can't wait to get started on mine.

A POEM FOR MY NEIGHBORHOOD: ON THE PROSPECT OF MOVING FROM ARTHUR AVENUE

ALLISON ADAIR ALBERTS

 *Aviles, p. 179*

 *p. 7*

I.

Four bakeries. Two flower shops. One shop for potted plants.

Five pastry shops, distinguishable by expertise: cheesecake, biscotti, cannoli.

Two Green Carts.

One spice market. One produce market.

Two fishmongers, three butchers: one of each I call my own.

Three mysterious social clubs, one closed by the health department last fall.

Two cigar lounges, populated by old men in white shirts and their dominos.

Two wine shops, one vastly better than the other.

One pasta shop, whose line snakes around the block on Sunday mornings

and before important feasting occasions: Easter, Thanksgiving, Christmas.

One glorious cheese shop.

Three delis. Half a dozen bodegas: the

one up the block hosts dance parties on Saturday nights.Two beauty shops. Three barbers.

Four different languages spoken on the sidewalk at any given time.

Two churches. One convent.

II.

I wake and move with the bells of the church.

When there was no pope, there were no bells.

Disoriented, I could no longer divide my hours into quadrants

and resorted to setting my alarm for the first time in six years.

III.

When I leave you, I will have sifted my hands
through your raw materials
Molded my story from the shards of your sidewalk,
from your bounty,
from your Saturdays, bustling with tourists,
from your quiet weekdays.
In the cheese shop I heard a woman ask,
"Who really lives here, anymore?
My family moved years ago."
But I do. I live here. When I leave you,
I will have made and broken bread here.
I will have married my one true love.
Read hundreds of books.
Written thousands of words looking out over your corridor.
Walked down your sidewalks in joy and in sorrow,
through sun and snow and Sandy.
I will have taken part in your feasts

and celebrated your saints.
When I leave you, you will not miss me.
But you have etched yourself
as a central character in my
künstlerroman,
the story of my place in this city.

MY SECRET GARDEN
JUDY ROLAND

 *Gordon, p. 287*

 *p. 34*

Has there ever been a place that was so special to you that you selfishly wanted to keep it to all to yourself, while at the same time you were bursting to share it with others so they could experience it, too? That's the way I feel about the Conservatory Garden in Central Park.

It's a part of Central Park but apart from it. Unlike Frederick Law Olmsted's people's park, this later addition looks far more like something that was lifted intact from an aristocratic European country estate and plunked down on the park side of Fifth Avenue and 105th Street. I suspect Mr. Olmsted may have found it ostentatious.

To me, the Garden is magical. It's one of the few places I know where I feel perfectly in tune with nature, life, and its continuum. I can sit on a bench along one of its two allées of crab apple trees and instantly be transported to Paris.

I recall once being spellbound by a white dove—most likely a refugee from one of the many wedding photo sessions in the Garden—sitting on a lilac tree branch just before dusk on a late spring day. I couldn't help feeling that both the dove and I were part of some ancient Persian tapestry, the visual equivalent of an Omar Khayyám poem.

On another occasion, just after saying a final goodbye to my mother-in-law at nearby Mount Sinai Hospital, my husband, my father-in-law, and I wandered over to the southern end of the Garden for relief and peaceful contemplation. As we sat there, a lovely monarch butterfly hovered over us, then lit on the nearby branch of a magnolia tree in full bloom, where it remained for some time. Is it mere fantasy or wishful thinking to believe it could have been the spirit of my mother-in-law that had just been released?

Anything is possible in my secret garden.

relationships

YOU LEFT A SKETCH OF YOURSELF

instead of the body
the next morning
you left a sketch of yourself
on your side of the bed

Christina Butan, p. 102

A moment of transformation in a relationship can be tied to physical change—a prerequisite for becoming a vampire is one unearthly bite—but it can also arrive in more subtle moments between two people. A certain slant of smile from a friend can change the implication of an evening together; a man returning from war might fail to say the right words when he opens the front door of his family's home. Each story and poem in this chapter has a certain twist that threatens to change a relationship forever, a fulcrum of fear and excitement that leaves you with a delicious sense of possibility or a sour feeling of disappointment.

Monica, my mentee, introduced me to the world of "shipping" this year. Short for relation*ship*, for those unfamiliar with the term, it's a world of online forums in which emotionally invested fans imagine their favorite characters getting together (no matter how unlikely those pairings might seem). The pairings tend to be romantic, though that's not always the case.

Heather Graham's story *(p. 107)*, which brings together Ziva and Tony from the television show *NCIS*, is a direct example of fan fiction like this. But if you study the other stories carefully, you'll find yourself rooting for Frida Kahlo to return to Diego, for two sisters to forgive one another, or for one friend to finally break free from another.

Savor the chemistry between these characters as you turn the page.

KIRSTEN REACH
2013 MENTOR AND
ANTHOLOGY COMMITTEE MEMBER

VIVA LA FRIDA

CHRISTINA BUTAN

Frida Kahlo may be gone from our world, but she's an everlasting presence in mine. A woman filled with passion and determination, and strongly rooted in feminism; a woman I am inspired by.

 *DiLuna, p. 103*

 *p. 13*

last night
you painted your way
into my bed with your
gray suit and short hair
that i gripped every time
your red mouth formed into
the letter o and serenaded me
with mexican lullabies
i traced the scars on your
thin feet and got visions of you
walking on the waters of hell
letting el diablo diego rivera poison your
colorful palm lines with the drunken
kisses placed on his fingertips by
putas that weren't you
i always wondered how you
sprouted flowers from your hair
so you showed me your green thumb
and whispered
te quiero mas de lo que puedo expresar...
while planting love in my belly button
in hopes that one day i bear a child
and preserve the umbilical cord
instead of the body
the next morning
you left a sketch of yourself
on your side of the bed
nestled in a long skirt
sealed with your lips and coated
in gold dust
every time i touch it i hear
the bus crashing
your bones breaking and your heart
thumping wildly within mine
viva la frida
viva la frida

FINDING FRIDA

AMY DILUNA

After Christina wrote her poem, we popped into the MoMA to see the Frida Kahlo painting they had on display. I had never gone to a museum just to find one painting, making all of the other work background noise while we were in search of a treasure.

 *Butan, p. 102*

 *p. 13*

We almost missed the painting entirely. We were wandering, room to room, distracted by the Magrittes and the Rothkos and some stuff splashed on the wall.

We paused at paintings of stripes, paintings of nothing, paintings of men at work. Finding Frida took another lap around the floor, and a glance at a wall we hadn't seen when we'd rushed through before, fixated on a particularly funky Picasso in the distance.

But we found her, all thick eyebrows, holding a monkey. We found Diego Rivera's painting first. Diego jumped out at us in a way Frida hadn't. I read a piece by an artist in the Paris Review about their differences in scale. He was a mural painter, after all—his work was bigger, louder, made you step back to take it all in. Her square masterpieces whispered; his shouted.

When we found it, we were triumphant. It was nestled in an opulent frame. Later, we stood in a room that housed one work: on an enormous screen, a video of an elephant played on an infinite loop.

Back at home, I re-read Christina's poem, a twelve-point ode to a woman who was broken, by a bus crash and the drama of a remarkable life.

"last night you painted your way into my bed"

Each tiny stanza was a miracle.

"every time i touch it i hear
the bus crashing
your bones breaking and your heart
thumping wildly within mine"

It doesn't take a mural to make the world stand back.

THE END

RACHEL CANDELARIA

When writing this piece, I focused on the way that change can be unpleasant. The girl in this story will outlive the boy by a few centuries.

M *Caster, p.114*
P *p. 16*

It seems like it takes a day rather than a decade for their world to collapse.

The changes are gradual, subtle things: a schedule that no longer fits together flawlessly, shorter conversations online, and, when they do meet face-to-face, an unspoken tension that weaves silence between them. Both develop new nervous ticks to cope: Lucene brushes herself off continuously, as if the unnerving stress between them is simply a palpable grime, while Tornun adjusts his goggles endlessly, as if just an imperfect angle is blocking him from seeing satisfaction.

Their dates continue like this, filled to the brim with tangled words and underlying emotions. Lucene is frantic, scheduling one outing with him after another, then upping her workload with the jewelry design studio until she's a jittering, thrumming mess of a girl, hair slowly losing its luster and paint flaking off her once-maintained nails. They kiss and cuddle and talk to each other still, but all they notice are the flaws that they'd trained themselves to ignore, but are slowly but surely getting harder to deny: he begins to get uneasy under her inquisitive, hyper stare, while his height and lankiness make her feel small and vulnerable in the worst way possible.

Gradually, they begin to fall apart in very separate ways, trying to retain a thin sheet of normalcy even as everything is disrupted.

Lucene feels a part of her drowning, choking on something she refuses to acknowledge, and so she uses her designs as a life-raft, plunging deeper into her work—further and further, until she dreams of hot molten metals and the hard edges of countless precious gems. He doesn't love you, her cold heart screams, and she mainlines work even more, eyes cloudy and unfocused from watching the moon become the sun and back again.

Tornun feels it too, but he welcomes their disintegration with open arms, grateful not to have to take the first move in ending their relationship. It's not that he doesn't care for her—God, no—but even as she glows like one of the gems she works over, eyes sharp, witty with her quick tongue, he can feel himself decaying slowly, tissues falling apart and not coming back together. He's dragging out their time together, he knows that, but he isn't dead enough to want to leave her just yet, even though she's so close to falling apart at the seams already and more time with him will just hurt more later on. But he's unable to let go—he's like her own personal parasite, draining her until she's nothing but an empty pretty husk, bits of dust and fluff where a heart used to reside. If he leaves her now, right this

instant, she'll be able to shake off his memory like a bad feeling. But every time he starts to set up the perfect moment to break it off, her face breaks through his resolve like a yank on tissue paper and he's back to square one. He tries to convince time to speed up, to ferry him away as painlessly as possible for them both, leaving him no opportunity to hang around any longer and make it even worse.

THE GREAT DAISY BUCHANAN

ANDREINA AVALOS

This story was inspired by The Great Gatsby *by F. Scott Fitzgerald. The story is told by the "beautiful fool" Daisy Buchanan, in which she unravels different surprises during a matter of seconds that will change her life.*

 *Graham, p. 107*

 *p. 6*

James, I love you. Don't leave me... And then I woke up with cold sweat running down my body. I held in my tears. I couldn't cry out loud because Tom was sleeping next to me. I slowly got out of the bed, went outside, and walked toward the green light on the dock, staring at the night sky. I spotted an extravagant, wild party across the river. So far, yet so close.

"Why are you out here?"

I turned around.

"Nothing, Tom. Just admiring the night sky."

"Let's go inside."

"No, please, I just want some fresh air."

He smiled and took my face between his hands. Then I felt a huge slap on my face. I wasn't shocked, but I released the tears I was holding back.

"I said let's go inside!"

He pulled me into the mansion. I felt all five fingers grasping my skin hard. I tried pulling back but it was useless.

"Let me go! Tom, please stop, you're hurting me!"

I tried pulling back but his grip got stronger every time. As we got into the bedroom, he threw me onto the bed. I saw the room from a different angle. I felt so impotent. He made my skin crawl.

I asked myself why I married him but the answer was obvious. I'm a W.A.S.P. and a beautiful fool. Every second I felt more anger stirring in my veins. When he finished I stood up and quietly said, "Tom, I want to divorce you."

Again he smiled and then chuckled.

"I said I want a divorce. I'm tired of you! I'm leaving now."

"Really?" He laughed loudly.

"You make me sick. You think I'm a fool but you have no idea that I know about your affair with Myrtle Wilson. Now if you'll excuse me, I'm leaving now."

I rushed to gather my belongings into my wooden trunk. I quickly closed my eyes when Tom started to hit me once again, but he stopped mid-air.

"Four years ago, I knew about your romance with Gats. I wanted you in my arms, so I moved heaven and earth to get him away from you. I paid for his draft into World War I, hoping he would die there."

I exploded, slapping him, cursing at him and hitting him with all my might. I ran to the Ford and drove to my cousin Nick's house on West Egg. I drove so fast that I didn't see the woman crossing near his house until I hit her. I was so scared to even look. I parked the car in front of the house and ran to ring the doorbell.

"Nick! Open the door!"

"Daisy! Why is your face bruised? And what is this ruckus?"

"I just ran over a women! I'm so scared. I don't know what to do."

"What! The police will send you to prison."

"Nick, please help me. We grew up together."

"Come, go to bed. I'll take care of it. We will act like we do not know anything if the police ask us."

In the morning, Nick and I went to the crime scene. Tons of policemen were surrounding the area. My Ford was nowhere to be found.

I saw Jordan Baker. She saw me and came over. "Daisy! The policeman said that the victim was a woman named Myrtle Wilson. What a horrible way to die. I wonder what she was doing out here at night."

I was paralyzed with surprise. I could barely speak. I was about to collapse when Nick took a grip on my arm. Then Jordan said, "Oh, here comes my boyfriend. I want you to meet him."

I was in such shock that I didn't see the man approaching. I looked up. It was James Gats. Another shock. My heart couldn't handle all this.

"Gats?" I said. His eyes sparkled and he smiled at me. I must be dreaming.

ZIVA AND TONY: BENDING RULE #12

HEATHER GRAHAM

Andreina suggested we write fan fiction, so I wrote about NCIS*, a world of crime-solving inside the military that I love to get lost in. As one of many fans who want Ziva David and Tony DiNozzo to declare their love, I wrote a piece that puts them there.*

 *Avalos, p. 105*

 *p. 6*

Ziva was just lying there, staring at the ceiling. She kept replaying how it all went down. She had been sure she was going die at the hands of a terrorist in that dark hole somewhere in Somalia. She knew her father—Mossad director Eli David—wouldn't send anyone to find her. It was Gibbs, McGee, and Tony who came for her.

She was so grateful. Seeing Tony's face, beaten but still smiling, and sweet McGee... Gibbs saved them all with a clean shot to the captor's heart. But she was also still angry. She felt as though she were caught between worlds. She was really a Mossad officer on loan to NCIS. But her father had betrayed her. She felt Tony had, too. It was Tony's visit to Ziva's apartment that started the entire situation in motion. Tony shot Michael Rifkin in her living room. Yes, Michael killed an ICE agent and a handler for an LA-based terrorist cell, but Michael was a friend, once her lover. Ziva thought that Tony went to her appointment to question her loyalty to NCIS and she was angry.

She couldn't sleep, but Ziva preferred lying in bed, in the dark, watching the faint lights of Washington, D.C through her gauzy curtains. There was a low, soft knock on the door. She almost didn't hear it. It came again, a series of slow raps that had just a hint of sadness. She knew who it was. She left her gun on the side table and went to let him in. When she opened the door Tony was resting his left arm above his head on the doorframe.

"Officer David," he said, "I've come to do a post-debrief debrief."

"Tony, what do you want?"

"Oh, just to see what's new. Maybe have a pillow fight."

"I do not want to talk to you."

"Ziva, I know you're angry..."

"I do not want to talk about it again." She walked into the apartment.

Tony followed her. "Ziva," he said firmly. He grabbed her arm but she twisted out of his grip. "You questioned my integrity. If you do not trust me, then I do not trust you," she said.

"I do trust you. C'mon. Let's not end up like those girls in Beaches who have a fight and then stop talking until one of them finds out she's dying. It's a real tearjerker."

Ziva sighed and collapsed onto her lush leather couch.

Tony sat next to her and wrapped his arms around her. She started to move away, but she didn't want to fight anymore. Ziva succumbed to her exhaustion and slumped into his torso, resting her head just below his chin. "You are my best friend, Tony."

"I know," he said, kissing her lightly on the top of her head. "And you are mine."

"I know." She looked up and softly kissed his cheek. They sank down into the couch without losing their embrace.

"I love you, Ziva David," he said. "Sometimes I think we should break rule number 12."

"I think we already have, Tony."

MOVING ON
BRIANNA MARIE MARINI

 *Demaline, p. 176*

 *p. 48*

Standing in front of the door to my French classroom on Monday morning was more than nerve-wracking. I'd compare it to that moment when Harry's talking to his family in the Forbidden Forest before he goes to Voldemort to sacrifice himself in *The Deathly Hallows*, but I'm not that dramatic. Usually.

Today's the day I get to go back out into the real world after hiding for two days.

Our friendship had just disappeared, shoved under some large object that I couldn't move on my own, left there to rot.

To be honest, it'd been long overdue.

Friendships are rarely ever equal. There's usually someone who gives more than they should (me), and then there's the person that takes more than they should (her).

For five years, I'd bitten my tongue over a lot of things. I'm not the type of person to hop straight into a confrontation, so for peace's sake, I'd stayed quiet.

Now, I'm kind of the opposite. I stand up for myself a little more than I have to and never let things slide. I'm in a period of learning, settling, and readjusting—figuring myself out is a part of that period.

When she called at three in the morning, crying over her latest breakup, I'd be the one to comfort and soothe her so she could go back to bed. When she whined about her mother and their constant arguing, I'd be the one to agree with everything she said even if I didn't agree. I'd be the one to walk her through the English homework that she could do if she tried a little harder, leaving mine for later because she needed me.

When I called her in the middle of the afternoon just to talk, she'd never pick up the phone. "Sorry, I was busy," she'd say, and that'd be the only explanation I got every time. When I complained about the family drama in my house or the Spanish project I had to help my brother with, despite my not knowing a word of the language, she'd cut me off to talk about her problems. When I asked her for help with math homework, which she knew off the top of her head, she'd say she didn't do it, and leave me alone to struggle with geometric shapes and the confusing equations that accompanied them.

I had no idea what happened. I had no idea why I was suddenly being avoided at all costs, why all my efforts to fix things were completely ignored.

Then came the trash-talking, the belittling, and the rumor-spreading. In girl-world this is completely common; however, I wasn't exactly part of girl-world. I thought all of that was beneath me, and beneath her—though I was proved wrong about that in the end.

When two people spend five years making a place in the world their own, there are always memories left behind. Our initials carved into a bathroom stall door with the end of a metal ruler in the tenth grade, the place we'd go to skip geometry on the third floor in the ninth grade - they seemed little back then, but now they seem so large that they're almost suffocating.

I take one, two, three deep breaths. The brass doorknob turns underneath my hand and the wooden door opens.

"Bonjour, Madame," I say a little breathlessly. The class is working on a worksheet, but they all look up when I come in. Madame hands me the worksheet and I walk over to my desk.

Completing the worksheet takes little effort on my part, even with her eyes burning a hole into the back of my neck. She's developed a habit of staring now, as if waiting for me to show a bit of sadness or anger that she would immediately say I'd shown because I was without her. Her stare hasn't left me since I walked into the room and a part of me wants to snap.

It won't be long until I get to go to college and into a new world, one where the broken friendships and drama of high school are long behind me. All I have to do now is wait.

EPISODE 9: THE TRUTH HURTS
JENNIFER BEAN

Fantasy as a genre invites people to imagine new worlds. This episode is part of a book-length fantasy series called My Life, *which looks at the intersection of love, fear, friendship, high school, and vampires.*

 *Pottroff, p. 191*

 *p. 10*

At school, people swarmed the halls in all different directions and voices blurred in conversation. A fluorescent light shone on Bart as he walked up to Michelle.

"Hey, Michelle, is there something wrong with Sam? She's been acting really weird," Bart said.

"Well, there is something, but I promised Sam that I won't say anything about Lucas."

"Lucas?"

"Shit!"

"What about Lucas?" She was looking at the ground trying to avoid the question.

"Michelle, what about Lucas?"

She sighed. "Lucas kissed Sam."

"What! That son of a bitch is dead!"

"Wait, there's more. Sam kissed him back."

His eyes filled with hurt. "What? How could she do that?"

"But it isn't her fault."

"How is this not her fault?"

"Well, Lucas is a vampire."

He laughed. "You're joking, right?"

"It's true. He does not have a reflection."

"I'm sorry; I have to get to class."

She turned back to her locker and said to herself: "I know I'm going to regret this, but I have to tell Sam." She walked slowly up to Sam, dragging her feet because, as a best friend, she knew exactly how Sam was going to feel.

"Sam, I have to talk to you."

"Yeah, what's up?"

"Well, I sort of told Bart about Lucas."

Her eyes grew wider. "You did what?"

Michelle's voice, full of guilt, pleaded, "I'm sorry; it just sort of slipped out."

"What exactly did you tell him?"

"I told him that you guys kissed..."

"And..."

"I also told him that Lucas was a...vampire."

"Great, now Bart's gonna think that I'm fucking crazy."

***

After school, Sam went to Michelle's house to hide from Bart even though she knew that he would find her anyway. As usual, she felt more comfortable being around Michelle than by herself. Then the girls heard a knock at the door; Michelle opened it and found Bart.

"Hello, Bart."

"Is Sam here?"

"No, she is not here."

"Look, I know she's here. Can I please talk to her?"

She turned to Sam, who nodded her head. Michelle let him in, and Bart and Sam had a very awkward moment.

"Can we talk?"

"Yeah, sure." The couple sat on the couch, and Michelle left them alone.

"Michelle told me what happened."

"I know you must hate me."

"No, I don't."

"Oh, do you think I'm crazy?"

"No, but I saw it."

"Saw what?"

"He didn't cast a reflection."

Sam sighed. "I knew this would happen."

"But I found some information on them though."

"All right, let's see it."

"Well, a vampire prince must find a pure human girl for his queen."

"But he should be able to sense that I'm not a virgin anymore."

"It also says that vampires have the power of seduction, so that's why you kissed him."

***

So the plan was to make sure that someone was with Sam at all times; however, late the next afternoon all her friends were busy and she was left alone. Sam was walking down the hall when she felt a large pain on her head. She collapsed on the cold floor. She woke up and was in the old abandoned room in a beautiful long dress. Lucas appeared in the room and said how beautiful she looked. As he came closer to her, he started kissing her even though she did not have the strength to push him away. Then, suddenly, she felt a sharp pain in her neck and became dizzy.

SWITCHING BEDS

RUMER LEGENDRE

 *Conan, p. 129*

 *p. 44*

When my sister limped through the doorway of the room we shared, it was clear there was no way she could climb the ladder to her top bunk bed. My parents delivered the news: we would have to switch. Since I'm seven years younger, I'd always slept on the bottom—until the day Erin tore her ACL during a soccer game.

Ascending to the top bunk, the first thing I noticed was how close I was to our old, white, wobbly ceiling fan. Anger built up in me as I looked down to see my parents helping Erin get comfortable on the only thing I could lay claim to. Our room was supposed to be shared equally, but it had never been equal. Erin's clothes always found their way to my side of the closet, and her books were always on my shelves. The worst was the door, where big block letters nailed into the wood spelled ERIN. Until I was born, this was her room, and no matter how much I protested, my dad refused to remove her name. That night, I wasn't in the mood to talk, so I faked a yawn and, despite my anger, fell asleep.

For the next few days, before she went to work, my mom woke Erin, helped her out of bed and into the living room, made her a hot breakfast, and ensured that she was comfortable on the sofa. The major change came when my mom said I'd have to take over. I felt as if it were the end of the world, but there was no way I could object. I knew my mom could get fired if she kept arriving to work late.

My mom's routine became mine. I woke an hour and a half before school, rushed down the ladder, and assisted Erin in getting out of bed. I did everything my mom did, but I wasn't loving it. My idea of breakfast was milk and cold cereal. Feeling like a servant, I made sure Erin was comfortable on the couch by propping pillows under her leg and adjusting the cushions. I even had to find a television channel she wanted to watch. Before I grabbed my school bag, I went back into our room, passing the ERIN sign, so I could get her crutches and put them near her. For weeks, each day my resentment grew.

One morning when I woke, I was surprised to see Erin's head right next to my mattress. She was standing, hunched over on her crutches. I was still in a sleep daze; it wasn't until I climbed down the ladder, fully conscious, that I realized my sister had gotten out of bed without help from me. Shocked that she had taken such a bold step and done something on her own, I opened the door to let her walk through to the living room. It was the first sign that she was getting back her independence. And a sign of hope for me.

The next morning, Erin dug out a bright yellow blouse from the top dresser drawer without my assistance. From then on, each day she did little things, like brushing her hair, doing exercises at night, changing outfits, finding her own station on TV, and getting onto the couch by herself. I never admitted it to her or my parents, but with each new sign of her recovery, my smile grew.

A few weeks after I first saw Erin standing by herself, I had just come out of school and was talking with my friends in the dismissal yard. In the midst of all the conversations, I heard: "Hey, Rumer, isn't that your sister?"

Turning, I spotted Erin across the yard, standing with a cane. As I walked over to her, I thought it was so unreal that she had walked ten blocks to my middle school. Although she'd been making steady progress, she'd never walked outside by herself. "I decided to venture out on my own," she said when I reached her. A big part of me was glad that of all the places Erin could have chosen, either around the corner or a block from our house, she had decided to walk specifically to my school. For the first time since her accident, I was proud of my sister.

From then on, everything was back to normal except the bed. I didn't ask for the bottom bunk because I knew Erin was making big steps to recovery. And although the bed was upsetting, I wasn't resenting her as much because she wasn't depending on me anymore.

That all happened five years ago, when I was eleven. Just this year, I had to write an essay on someone I admire, and my sister came to mind. She got through a really difficult thing, despite my not-so-gracious help. I did eventually get my bed back, and I'm sure it was one of the best days for me, but I can't even remember it. What stands out for me about that time is Erin's strength.

ONCE
SARA LIPPMANN

 *Mezmin, p. 257*

 *p. 51*

once
we shared pears
 in coney island
rode the carousel
 at whim
we read books
 once we wrote a story together
you said
 "we could have been — "
in another life
 in this life
hold on
 around and down
my braided neck
 sprayed a fool's gold
chips in your grip
 we spin threads
in a steel wheel
 stop
here is candy
 eat fast
lick your fingers
 toss out the cone
once it dissolves

MALLO CUPS
WENDY CASTER

 *Candelaria, p. 104*

 *p. 16*

Sarah practically skipped into the rehearsal room. After months of unemployment, she had finally gotten a gig as second violin on a musical. But when she saw who she'd be sitting next to, day after day, she froze. "Seriously?" she thought. "*Seriously?*"

There, in the first chair, was her ex, Allison. Allison, who had left her for a flute player.

Allison looked up and saw Sarah. Shock flitted across her face, and she looked away.

Sarah dragged herself to her seat, grunting hello to Allison. Allison grunted back.

"Since she left me," Sarah thought, "it's up to her to break the ice." But by week's end, the ice had thickened into an Arctic shelf. Finally, after a Tuesday night performance, Allison told Sarah, "We need to talk."

"Okay," Sarah thought. "Better late than never."

After the other musicians had left, Allison said, "You keep going sharp on 'Bring Me Love.'"

Sarah sputtered. "I do not—how could you!"

Allison said, "You've always—"

Sarah yelled, "I've always?! What about—"

She shut up abruptly. This was a work conversation and she needed to behave professionally.

Allison said, "You're sharp on 'Bring Me Love.' That's all." She strode to the door. Without quite turning around, she said, "You know the breakup wasn't all my fault."

That night, Sarah took down the tacky tumbler she and Allison had bought in Hawaii. She poured Scotch up to the knees of the dancing girl on the glass, and then to the top of her grass skirt. "What the hell," she thought, and filled the glass to the dancing girl's neck.

Pacing her small apartment, drinking and remembering every negative thing Allison had ever done, Sarah worked herself into a frenzy of anger. Around midnight, she was thoroughly sick to her stomach, then fell asleep on the cool tile of the bathroom floor. When she woke, cramped and uncomfortable, defenses destroyed, she felt the truth creep into her brain.

She and Allison should have split long before Allison met the flute player. They weren't ever a great match, really, though they had had their moments. Sarah flashed on them laughing at movies about musicians, cooking lavish meals, savoring obscure brands of chocolate. She remembered how they loved announcing to each other, about events and items big and small, "Now that is a good thing."

The next day, on the way to work, Sarah thought about talking with Allison, but realized there was nothing left to say. Not far from the theater, she ducked into a candy store. She surveyed the different brands of chocolates. And then she saw them: Mallo Cups! Perfect.

In the orchestra pit, Allison was twisted in her chair chatting with a viola player, so Sarah slipped the Mallo Cups onto the music stand, then took her seat. And suddenly she was so nervous that her mouth went dry.

Allison turned forward and saw the distinctive yellow package. Sarah could barely hear her whispered "Wow." Allison picked up the Mallo Cups and traced the illustration with her finger. She made eye contact with Sarah for the first time since they'd started working together and said, "Now that is a good thing." They smiled at each other for a moment, then picked up their violins.

THE LAMB THAT ATE THE LION

MAXINE ARMSTRONG

Even though mutants don't exist, we do have outcasts in society who are voiceless. This is the beginning of a story about teenagers who set out into the Midwest to find the main character's mother.

 Pylväinen, p. 118
 p. 5

Lions had a tendency of roaring so loud that they began to think they were the only ones who could, when really, everyone had a roar—only the voiceless could hear it. The lions here had guns for teeth and flags that danced in the winds for claws. They sat in their houses fat on the meat they called Justice and laughed at the likes of us. The food chain was simple, a dollar bill got you a ladder, and bruised hands from working got you an anchor. We don't count our blessings; blessings were something you didn't count when you were born and the doctor said: "It's mutant" before: "It's a boy." They hunted us before they hunted animals, and in church we clutched our Bibles, praying, "Protect me from those demons, those demons who are different and therefore deadly." In the land where money is power and power a privilege, weakness was the plague you inherited when even money couldn't change what you were. You can say this land is brave and free, but to get there, the lions had to chain down those who could fly—after that, they threw out the key.

***

The smell of burnt blunts and rusted steel is better than breakfast in Tully; that much I've known since I was a kid. The streets around here are always barren—only wooden planks and parts of torn warehouse gates are your company if you're alone. And here, you barely are. After we walk about three blocks from my house, Boone begins to talk.

"So what's up with you?"

I glance at him, brows raised, a look on my face that is almost no look at all. "Nothing. Why does something have to be up?" Boone doesn't answer when I look at him.

We stop at the light, even though no trucks invade the streets and not even a gust of dry wind creaks against the crumbling buildings. Boone brings his fingers through his bright blonde hair and places his hands inside the pockets of his worn-out jeans. When our eyes meet he grins. "I was just asking you how your morning was, if that's okay with you," Boone says through a toothy grin. There are days when Boone could say nothing and I know what he's thinking. I let out a breath as we turn the corner toward Jack and Husky's place.

“Fine.” I look east toward a closed sugar factory, the remains of a painted pink panther dancing on the aged brick. Tully is nothing but steel and brick. When I look back Boone isn’t by my side—I turn and he’s got his arms crossed against the chest of his light grey pullover, hazel eyes on mine, the kind of look on his face that says too much for a conversation. I don’t bother to speak, my mouth still open as if it doesn’t know what my head knows.

“Zippy...” Boone says, his black eyebrows raising bright blonde hair, slowly turning to a diluted grey that almost matches his pullover. Sometimes I wish I had what Boone had: you could never really guess how I felt, you could just look at me and know. When I look up to the sky I hear my name again but it doesn’t register that it’s me he’s talking about, that my name left his mouth. “Did you have another—”

“I’m fine.”

I walk at a pace that’s made for the two of us, the kind of pace we’ve had since we were kids. Slow, yet too fast for anyone else. I hear his footsteps behind me and when I look behind my monstrous shadow I see his, his head tilted my way. “Hey bird boy, will you slow down.” I turn sharply to him grinning from ear to ear like a fool.

“What did you call me?” I say, and Boone smugly points to my back, fingers brushing against a feather.

“Seems to fit the part.” I shrug lightly and look at his hair.

“At least I’m not a pack of crayons. Crayola should pay you for the publicity it’s getting.”

Ever since we were kids we’d known when enough was enough, the difference between pushing someone’s buttons and stabbing them in the chest. We both try not to smile at each other. I look down at my feet to stop myself. Before I can get my head up Boone says, “It will only get worse if you don’t tel—”

He stops and looks between us.

I sigh.

“You haven’t told him yet have you?” Boone says, shooting me a look. I begin to walk, glancing at the buildings I’ve known since birth but have left and dreamt of a hundred times. “You’ll have to be more specific.”

Boone catches up like he always does. “Your father. Shit, anybody. One of us. Andy, Jack, Ryder, one of your uncles. Mac—”

“Mac?!” I scream and Boone doesn’t look terrified like the others. Boone stands where he is.

“Yeah, your brother Mac, remember him?”

“Fuck off.”

THE FIRST MIGRATION

HANNA PYLVÄINEN

Early on in our sessions, Maxine and I talked often about her interest in literary fantasy or science fiction. During one session, we each assigned the other a topic to write about, to practice our skills of making an unbelievable moment believable. This is the result of that exercise.

 *Armstrong, p. 116*

 *p. 5*

I was late to class the day he came in, so I was only annoyed that I had missed the fuss, but then I was disappointed because he didn't look anything different. I remember even then wondering how everyone knew, but I suppose like all rumors it came from the lady at Pat's Grocery Store. Isn't that strange, though, that I can remember the name of the store, but my sister is always saying I try to offer her lunch when we've just eaten lunch. But my doctor says I ought to write things down to help my memory, one memory a day, but my hands hurt so my helper is writing things down. (I have just apologized to her for not remembering her name, but she's very kind.)

The first week wasn't so bad—he sat next to us and got the answers about as wrong or as right as the rest of us. Some kids took him into the bathroom and locked him in there with a greased pig and said they wouldn't let him out until he had killed it and smoked it for all of us to eat, because they knew he could. It sounds like bullying, but I suppose people just wanted to see him at work, the way you want to touch a pregnant woman's belly to feel the kick—you know there's something in there, but the sight of it isn't enough. I suppose that was the problem, then, before the Second Migration—they didn't look like anything special.

I don't know how long it was before we began to ignore him. It wasn't a small thing, the ignoring—I mean that we put a silence on him. We were so solidified in our responses that some of the teachers gave in, and did not call on him. At least no one beat him up, although I think he might have preferred it. Once a gir—not even a popular girl, with bad teeth the way no one had anymore—told him to tie her shoe. When he leaned down, she kicked his face, but even then he didn't flare. But if I remember, no one laughed. Or maybe that's how I want to remember it, that we were nicer than we were.

I know I haven't given any details of much interest yet, especially to what was on the news later. I suppose that's the nature of celebrity—you cling to whatever connections you have, no matter how faint. But even my grandchildren now, when I tell them that he sat next to me in history class (an irony I only recognize now), and that his parents had moved them to the Upper Peninsula so no one would find out—well, even they listen. The fact is, I was the only one who saw him before he killed those people, I mean, really saw him. The fact is that he was a very nice kisser.

AFTER HOURS

JOANNA LAUFER

Angelica and I selected two lines from a story she wrote and used them as the last two lines of new stories.

 *Rozza, p. 120*

 *p. 64*

The pond behind the cider mill froze enough to look frozen, but he keeps checking to see if it is. Each day he looks at the small waves that have frozen in wrinkles, the patches of gray that keep changing.

The air is settling into winter now. It will be mild, then it will freeze up, then both. Almost a month has passed since the morning he first told the lie that he had saved a boy from drowning.

I like the lie. It's noble. It brings more customers to the orchard to hear his story—a solution after business had slowed down. Walking toward the orchard store, I call out to him. Only certain sounds carry in air that quiet. In that kind of quiet, you can hear trucks cough, the swoosh-roar of snowplows, shovels scraping against ice. And quiet things, like boot steps, carry. Things that are supposed to, like words, don't always. Words sometimes sound like birdcalls or like the cries that come and go in open air.

His wife has pulled away, ever since business has been bad. I like that, too. But she listens and draws closer when he talks about the boy.

There is an absence in his life—not of reasonable things, but of reasonable things working out. Owning the orchard is reasonable, but he can't count on it anymore. Marrying his wife was reasonable, but the marriage has grown cold. These unexpected losses, someone drowning in his pond—though one has happened and the other has not—mean, to him, that something reasonable that isn't working out is worse than something unreasonable that could.

He confides in me. He says his voice seems to come from somewhere else when he hears himself lying about the boy. One day it just started, before he even knew why. But it took that voice to maybe save a life.

I wait for him in the store after hours. It is gray outside, light enough this night to look like day. He pushes the door open and is overcome with a heavy silence. This is the kind of silence that carries the weight of some hidden truth.

HOMECOMING
ANGELICA ROZZA

 *Laufer, p. 119*

 *p. 64*

Clouds hang low above the miles of rolling green hills that stretch far beyond my porch. I can't help staring up at the flawless shade of blue that paints the heavens as I light my third cigarette. It's amazing to me how the simplicity of the sky can hover above so much sin and still manage to remain so pure. A warm summer breeze tickles my face, causing ashes to trickle onto the crumbled note I clutch in my hands. The note—now stained by a bad habit—reads nothing more than: I'll be home by August 15th. I miss you dearly. It is not signed, but the handwriting is unmistakably Marvin's. I have received so many letters in the past three years claiming that Marvin will be home before Christmas, before I give birth to Dianna, before Louis learns his first words... before I stop loving him. For years, I yearned and waited for him to march up our stone path beneath the willows and embrace me with all the love lost time can store. But he never returned from fighting overseas. With false hope and two children who were deprived of a figure to match the word "daddy," I knew I had to move on.

I hear Steven in the backyard playing catch with the children. Their laughter turns my mind briefly away from the fact that today is August 15th. I bury my face in my hands. All those meaningless letters I replied to now weigh in as miserable missed opportunities to tell him that our relationship is over. I imagine Marvin sitting in a train car, fidgeting with our wedding photo. For all he knows, he's returning to the woman in the white dress with bright green eyes who married him shortly before he was drafted. But he's only returning to what he has missed, the children blossoming to another man who sleeps on his side of the bed. And although I hoped from the bottom of my heart that I could postpone his return, the breeze carries the thick stench of his cologne.

After a fourth cigarette, I retire to my bedroom to powder my face. The mirror tells the most awful truths. I retrieve a checkered dress from the closet and pull it over my bloated body. I resemble nothing of the woman Marvin married. I am now a woman aged by war. And although the skirt's zipper won't slide all the way up my hip, I am relieved. Maybe Marvin won't want the new me.

Dianna and Louis are fast asleep on the sofa and Steven is reclined on the love seat reading the newspaper. The room is covered in the love of a new family. I stand before them, staring at them through the eyes of someone lost between present and past. Steven peers up from his newspaper and nods in reassurance that I can handle the situation accordingly. Sick to my stomach, I nod back and drag a stool from the kitchen to the window in the den and sit in silence for what seems like hours.

Every second or so I peer at my children. Not Steven's children, but Marvin's. After an hour of waiting by the window, and three years of waiting altogether, a small, black car finally pulls up in front of our pathway. I stand up so quickly the stool tips over, alerting everyone in the room to gaze out the window. My children stare in awe at the masculine gentleman waving the cab away. Almost running with a smile on his unchanged face, Marvin, in his uniform with a duffle bag slung across his shoulder, makes his way up the pathway underneath the willows and approaches the front door. I hold my breath like I don't deserve to breathe and collapse to my knees. He pushes the door open and is overcome with a heavy silence. The kind of silence that carries the weight of some hidden truth.

IDAMARIS PEREZ, MENTEE 2010-2012

Before Girls Write Now, writing and I were separate entities. Writing was just writing and I was just me. I treated writing as just a simple venue for getting out nagging feelings, thoughts, and observations. Our relationship was emotionally distant, but the passionate and creative workshops of Girls Write Now bonded us into one. They challenged me to step out of my comfort zone and write my words above and beyond. I discovered that writing is part of my identity.

EMMA STRAUB, MENTOR 2009-2011

At fifteen, I was a poet. I wrote poems non-stop every day, love letters to the world. Looking back, I think there was something magical going on in my brain, a chemical reaction that I couldn't control. Pure, mad, joy. There is nothing better in the world.

history

I COME FROM A BACKGROUND

> *My background is filled with colors, sounds, loud jewelry, and music. I grew up watching my aunts and cousins wearing colorfully magical hijabs; some that sparkle and some that shine. I also come from a background of strong women. Women who would never agree to be "oppressed."*
>
> *Nishat Anjum, p. 144*

History. Roots. Legacy. However we think of it, our past is a wellspring of emotion and memory. A source of power and sometimes of pain. It's where we come from, and can give us clues to where we're going. And perhaps most importantly, our history is where our story begins.

Whether our respective roots are close enough to touch or fading from memory, rich with joy or rooted in tears, they're irrevocably woven into our identities.

Our histories teach us about where we came from, and may light the way to where we could be going. They illuminate the people around us, and enlighten us to what we hold inside ourselves.

And whether we prefer to embrace our past or run from what we think it means, our histories are a rich source of introspection, self-discovery, and inspired storytelling.

In the end, whether our histories shape us or shame us, make us laugh or provoke questions, they're a springboard for every story we wish to tell. And for that, we are grateful.

JILLIAN GALLAGHER
2013 MENTOR AND
ANTHOLOGY COMMITTEE MEMBER

ERASING RACE

KARLA KIM

I wanted to explore race, something that's integral to my identity. I challenged myself to think about perceptions of ethnicity, and how these perceptions have shaped me. During this process, I faced my fear of understanding and evaluating the importance of my insecurities.

 *Amatenstein, p. 126*

 *p. 42*

Micro-aggression. I wish I had known that word sooner.

A classmate I'll call Susan turned to me as we walked through the school hallway and said, "Isn't Phoebe really pretty for an Asian?"

I silently seethed, feeling as if someone had peeled away my skin and jabbed at what defined me. It was much later that I learned that what I had just experienced had a name. Micro-aggression: brief and commonplace, often unintentional, verbal indignities that convey racial bias. I should've known I wasn't being oversensitive.

My school prides itself on being race-blind. You won't hear overt slurs like, "Ching chong ling long!" or "Go back to where you came from!" ricocheting around the corridors of our brick, prison-like building.

We were expected to be mature and open-minded. Anyone who acted otherwise was not a true member of our "enlightened" community. Like my peers, I wanted to be completely unaware of race. I swore skin color would not be a factor in how I viewed others because I wanted to be accepted by being the most accepting person on earth.

But it wasn't long before I realized race-blindness was impossible in a school with a population of forty-five percent Asian and fifty percent Caucasian students. No one shunned anyone for being different, but I began to notice the large pockets of Asians sitting a room's length away from non-Asians. Sometimes, our 'race-unaware' school seemed split in two.

Slowly, my ears became increasingly attuned to phrases like, "It's okay, I only 'Asian failed.'" I was ashamed; the corners of my lips curled downward when I overheard, five minutes before class, "Don't worry man, just ask an Asian kid for the math homework."

I wanted to believe that such comments actually proved that our school was race-blind. Maybe we could imply racial bias because we couldn't possibly mean it. But it was difficult to filter any statements—joke or not—related to my skin through the sieve of race unconsciousness.

Determined not to become the target of micro-aggressive comments, the implications of my ethnicity set up by both society and myself, I steered clear of those pockets of Asians and desperately tried not to align myself with my color. Maybe I wouldn't feel so uncomfortable and race-conscious.

I began to label for myself what was acceptable and what was not, eliminating the little mannerisms and habits that screamed out, "I'm an Asian!"

It was like finally stepping into the light and seeing all the muddied spots on your body, the grime stuck in your nails and the dust in your hair. All you want to do after that is wash it all away before more people notice that you're not normal.

Monitoring my every action to check and evaluate, "Is that too Asian for me to say?" I'd have a ten-second panic attack when I saw someone reaching toward my iPod, afraid they would ignore my Norah Jones playlist and fixate on my collection of Korean pop music.

Yet I refused to tolerate the same hiding from others.

I rolled my eyes when my Asian friend Cady proudly called herself a Twinkie—yellow on the outside and white on the inside. "I'm practically white," she exclaimed with a smirk. I wanted to demand of her, "Why are you white-washing yourself to lose your culture?" Instead, I smiled in agreement.

How could I attack her when I was no different? Like Cady, I longed to easily step outside the boundaries of our race. She and I were doing whatever it took not to be the typical Asian and escape the negative, unspoken labels: over-achieving, politically quiet, stoic, artless, uncreative, calculating, and timid.

I thought erasing any signs of my race would offer me a chance to truly be Karla, just myself.

Seeing my hypocrisy, it became untenable to continue to allow hidden generalizations and my personal bias to define how I view my identity. Though I am the girl who enjoys singing in front of an audience, reading Shakespeare, and avidly watching Downton Abbey, I am also the Korean who's been taught not to stare directly into the eyes of an adult, can reel off the names of the most authentic Korean restaurants in Flushing, and who loves to hear the traditional Korean tales of rabbits and their face-washing routines.

I am more than my race, but still part of my race. Although I am miles away from being completely comfortable in my own skin, I know I can sit with whomever I want—be it large pockets of Asians or my non-Asian friends. I can pursue whatever I desire and speak only when I want to, without being wary that I seem too immersed in a culture that molds me.

I won't go back to race-blindness; no one should erase race. I'm both Korean and American, and it's okay that I'm still trying to work out how to reconcile the two.

MY INNER BIGOT

SHERRY AMATENSTEIN

My piece was inspired by a spirited discussion Karla and I had about race and belonging. Her brave recounting of her struggle with her feelings about heritage made me decide it was past time to reveal my own prejudice.

 *Kim, p. 124*

 *p. 42*

I prided myself on being a person who wasn't prejudiced.

A child of holocaust survivors I'd seen the effects of hate and ignorance up close and personal. Not just the unimaginable horrors of what my family endured at Auschwitz and Dachau, but the quieter indignities.

Such as my mother's longtime neighbor, Rita DeMartino, tossing off during a coffee klatch at Chez Amatenstein, "Bernice, I don't know any other way to describe this guy who stiffed me but he was a cheap kike."

My mother, petite but vocally mighty, instantly lobbed back, "I guess the only way I should describe my feelings about you right now is ignorant wop." Rita apologized and the coffee klatches continued, though more sporadically.

So after enrolling at Wurzweiler School of Social Work in Washington Heights seven years ago, I assumed the required course called Cultural Diversity would be a cakewalk. The class was designed to help future therapists get in touch with their inner bigot.

Our first assignment was keeping a "bias" journal. I was clueless about what to write, being perched on my holier-than-thou pedestal. It took two days to tumble from the heights of hubris.

I'd known Wurzweiler was part of Yeshiva University, yet I hadn't expected to see so many Orthodox Jews on campus. Being devoutly reform myself, their side locks and black hats made me uneasy.

Unease upgraded to disdain when a fellow student I'll call Chaim pushed ahead toward the swinging door into the classroom, ignoring both my "Hi" and that I was juggling a load of textbooks. His jostling spelled doom to my unsteady grip. The books went "thwack" as they hit the floor.

Up bubbled a long-buried memory of a sunny Sunday over a lox and bagel feast, staying quiet when my companion, also reform, said of our Orthodox brethren, "They act better than us but they're a disgrace!"

Unleashed, my journal filled with ire at Orthodox classmates who espoused dismissive views toward gays, women, and non-religious Jews. I wrote, "God forbid non-Jews think people like Chaim 'represent' all Jews. As I seem to think Chaim represents all Orthodox Jews."

True, Orthodox Jewry helps keep some wonderful traditions of our religion alive. I looked down at Orthodoxy for what I viewed as rigidity, Puritanism, and the quality highlighted by the swinging-door-episode rudeness.

My entire life I've fought against being roped in. I dislike being told how to act, feel, and dress. Live and let live. Still, I'm the product of my background. My parents carried to their graves distrust of those were different.

In class, Chaim seemed unaware he'd annoyed me. I was too chicken to speak up. By telling Chaim what he did "wrong" I'd have allowed a seemingly decent person to see sides of himself he might work to change. Squelching my resentment allowed my prejudice to build.

The more I accept my imperfections, the more I can allow others to be imperfect. Acceptance can lead to tolerance, then respect, and ultimately to a bridge connecting humanity.

MY BEGINNINGS

LULJETA ZENKA

 *Carroll, p. 293*

 *p. 74*

When I was born, my mother was only twenty-one and my father was thirty-three.

I, being the firstborn of my parents, was regarded as the prized possession of the family, even though my mother has always told me that my father had been looking forward to a boy. As immigrants, my parents had little knowledge of what it was like to raise a child in the US, but I would like to think they did a good job.

As of 2013, my immediate family consists of my parents, my two brothers, my two sisters, and my grandmother.

Eight people. Imagine eight people living in an apartment with three bedrooms and one bathroom in the middle of Ridgewood, Queens until 2010. With all the craziness that came with those living conditions, my parents were the rock. They kept going for my siblings and me because they wanted to give us the life that they never had.

Sometimes it sucked that I didn't get all the toys I wanted, or that I didn't have my own room, but I didn't care because I had my family and that's all that mattered. My parents made that perfectly clear over the years.

Everyone in my family knows that my mother is a force to be reckoned with. She has the power to not only scare all my cousins, but also seem like an angel in front of my friends.

With me, my mother is almost two different people.

She can be that friend who makes jokes about everything and shares the latest gossip. She can be easygoing and she gives me snacks late at night. It's just one of her thoughtful gestures.

However, she can also be strict. She chastises me for my improper behavior and, like every other daughter and mother, we argue. We argue over my chores, my attitude, my grades...over almost everything! I know it's because she's worried for me and because mother knows best and all that stuff, but my stubborn head won't let me realize that until the end.

Being a teen is hard, but being a teen who's a first-generation American is even harder. Old and new clash all the time and there's nothing to do about it. I'm thankful that my mother is there to help me. Yeah, she doesn't understand some stuff sometimes, but she knows me best. She knows the person I am and she helps me decide what to do.

My father, on the other hand, is the king of the castle—or so he likes to believe. To me, he's that weird type of funny that you can't live without.

I think the funniest thing he ever did was when he named our two parakeets Lady Gaga and Persian Prince.

My dad and I are alike in so many ways. Our sense of humor is quirky and a bit snarky, we both have loud voices, we both love joking around with my mom (we're always torturing her), and we're both stubborn.

I won't say that we're perfect because that's not true. My dad and I have communication problems sometimes, too. Our stubborn attitudes clash and we can get mad, but we don't stay mad because there's no point. There's no lingering anger in my family. Just love with a hint of trouble.

I'll admit my father was never able to provide us with the best of anything. My parents' combined salary got us through each month, sometimes with nothing left to spare. While other children had iPods and all the video games they could ever want, we just had a computer, a TV, and our imaginations.

He makes up for it by telling stories to us about where he came from and where he has been. Even when he's too tired, he'll playfully chase after his youngest children and still makes time to talk to us big kids of the family. He does the best he can.

In no way am I ashamed of my parents' professions or background. Why would I be? In fact, I use what they tell me to push myself forward because that's what I am supposed to do.

I am so grateful that I have two loving parents who, while we may not get along sometimes, are there to support me.

They were the ones who taught me to do simple math and they were the ones who

taught me to read English even though their accents prevented them from saying the words correctly.

I may complain when they ask me to babysit or clean, but, in all truth, I would do anything for them.

They were the ones who pushed me to join Girls Write Now, the ones who take me to the meetings, and the ones who push me in the right direction.

They may not know what I'm talking about when I talk to them about writing and the Girls Write Now program, but I don't care. They're there and they're listening and they're supporting me.

And that's enough.

LUNCH

VIVIAN CONAN

It's World War II. I'm three years old. The men are in Europe. The women go to work. In Brooklyn, my Greek-Jewish immigrant grandmother takes care of the children. I'm used to my father's strictness, so this is a new world for me.

 *LeGendre, p. 112*

 *p. 44*

I loved Nona's house. Aunt Sophia knit me a white angora sweater, combed my hair, and told me how pretty I was. Aunt Rae gave me a doll with a lace dress. Aunt Diana bought me a colored metal fish that came with a magnet, then showed me how to go fishing in a pail of water. And I was with my cousins all day, playing in the backyard, or climbing up the mountain of fabric scraps in the basement near the sewing machines, then sliding down.

Most of all, I loved the way Nona fed us lunch. After she gave Marvin his bottle and settled him in his playpen, she drew Jerry's highchair up to the table. George and I sat in regular chairs. White kerchief tied tightly over the coiled gray braid at the nape of her neck, small gold earrings swaying gently from her pierced ears, and lips sucked in over toothless gums, Nona carried a delicious-smelling pot from the stove to the table. Except for that pot, one of several she had put over low flames in the morning before she went down to the basement to sew, the table was bare. Nona dipped in a spoon and loaded it with a flavorful mush of potatoes, meat, tomatoes, and string beans. Holding her hand under it to catch any spills, she brought it toward my face. I opened my mouth and she slipped it in. While I chewed, she refilled the spoon and ferried it to Jerry's mouth. Next was George's. By the time she came to me again, I had swallowed and was ready for another bite. If any food dripped down our chins, Nona scraped it upward with the spoon and guided it into our mouths. All the while, she told us stories.

"De farmer, he work hard to plant ta vegetables. He put water and take out alla ta weeds."

My turn for the spoon.

"He no see de horse what come in de night to eat ta vegetables."

Jerry's turn.

"And he tink to himself, why alla ta vegetables dey disappear lak dat? What's happen?"

George's turn.

"And he say, I gawn find out who take ta vegetables."

The farmer hid in the field with his gun. There was a loud BAMMMM! Nona always timed it perfectly. Just as the horse was running away, spinach dangling from his mouth, the pot was empty. After she released Jerry from his chair and we got up to play, Nona walked to the sink, swaying from side to side on her bowed legs, and washed the pot and spoon. Then she paused at the stove to lift the lids from the supper pots and give their contents a stir before she went back down to the basement.

WEST PHILADELPHIA

NAKISSI DOSSO

To open yourself up to a new world, you have to start with what you know already, and that requires reflecting on your past. My summers in Philadelphia with my uncle shaped who I am today and who I hope to be tomorrow.

M Overbeck, p. 203

p. 30

Besides being the place where the popular '90s television show The Fresh Prince of Bel-Air was based, West Philadelphia is actually quite the hangout. Coming from New York City, it's very quiet and a change of atmosphere. Somehow the air is much fresher, and there are fewer crowds. In the summertime, the parks are filled with people, and the underground studios come alive. The rap and music scene is beyond interesting, and listening to up-and coming-rappers who give out demos and mix-tapes is more fun than anything.

Since everyone lives right across the street from each other in houses ranging from colors of green and sky blue to the typical white house on the corner, it seems you

always have someone to invite to a summer BBQ. And don't forget about the local homeless man who gets his change by standing on the corner reciting Chris Rock and Steve Harvey comedy lines, always sure to let you hear some of Bernie Mac's harsh but hilarious jokes about children and childbirth—that is, for an extra dollar!

The slang in West Philadelphia goes right along with the tang of the taste in the popular Philly cheesesteak sandwich we all know and love. It's never a disappointment to head out to West Philly.

Especially when your childhood lives there.

...

Blood is thicker than water, you're told,
and no one ever really knows the
Meaning
until you are subject to the grieving,
to the loss of your humble beginnings.
My childhood couldn't be without my
summers with my uncle.
Losing everyday contact with him sent me
to a world of uncertainties.
As cliché as it sounds it's the only constant
in my story.

He held a small part of my heart and when
he left to go back home he took it with him.
Being stuck in the limbo of not seeing him,
not hearing his jokes, not hearing his laugh
Living without actually living,
Always reminiscing about the fun you used
to have because he is now oceans away.

A family of immigrants is a family of strength,
a family of endurance, a family of emotion.
Not being granted guaranteed access
to a place because you've come from
somewhere else.
Therefore living in doubt, and isolation.
Being split like you've never been split before.
Being "sent back" because you were not
born with a country's social security number
when you only left for the prospect of
having a better life.
You are told to follow your dreams, but
what if you're stopped by a country's border?

MORRAL
SHANNON DANIELS

This piece was written in response to my first trip to Louisiana. It was a very different world, in which I explored New Orleans and visited the Atakapa-Ishak tribe of the Mississippi.

 *Jacoby, p. 134*

 *p. 27*

I've known rivers:
I've known the Hudson,
who has hugged this urban playground of an island
from Whitehall to 220th, swallowed every bottle of soda
and half-eaten hot dog without hesitation, balls
its chubby fists and curses morning commuters
with sidewalks slick with tears.

I've known the Mississippi,
who claims to have a muddy bosom that
turns all golden in the sunset,
but now I wonder if that glitter is just
dispersed oil.

Rosina collects the scales of fish
I cannot pronounce,
wears a braid trailing down her back
like her crescent of a Southern accent.
Her tribe members feel with their nets
for writhing treasures—sometimes three-eyed
or blind—in this poisoned womb.

My soul has grown deep like Rosina's.

I've known the French Quarter,
pastries with names that hang off
my tongue like tutus over purple colonial balconies.
O beautiful for spacious skies and
horse-drawn carriages, every remnant of bird or squirrel
scraped clean from storefronts.
Shimmering masks to
erase frowns. Freedom from want and suffering and
flooding.

Yet I've known the empty lots of the Ninth Ward just as well –

Eight years, but the houses have still not
been rebuilt from the hurricane that
never gave back what it took, the graffiti
from what remains
still wet on my fleshy palm.
The bungalow with the black netting over
the porch
to mourn the nine-year-old who met the
bullet on the other
end of the door.

I've known too many dreams deferred—
college, marble-lined stoops,
a world without gangs or empty pockets or
suffering—
and the disparities that erode them.

I've learned that poetry is not a bandage,
that my words will not bring together
fragmented marshes or build stronger
levees
or save struggling families from the next
disaster.
But I will forever know Rosina's words—
when she told me that even though
the Mississippi is reclaiming its land
day by day, swallowing species and
communities whole,
the sweet plant, *morral*, can still grow out
of this wetland,
polluted and damaged as it is.
The children love the taste, she tells me,
and it's the first time
I mirror her beautiful, crooked smile.

I've known rivers:
I live in an ancient, dusky limbo between
the green-gray grandmother of the South
and the child of the North that I've
returned to.
New York City skylines don't conjure the
same ache
in my chest, Louisiana is at the crest
of torrents of torment. How badly I wish I

could mend
this internal war,
this eternal war.
This house of myself, this an, split
irreparably,
roof ends curled toward overcast skies
the same white as the liquid absolution
beneath me
breaking surface, open water,
slippery, inky mud.
My soul has grown deep
like the rivers.

STOP LOOKING AT ME, JESUS!

WHITNEY JACOBY

Shannon and I have often discussed the way religion has impacted our lives. These discussions inspired me to write about the first time I experienced religion, which was a brand new world to me, as I was raised as an atheist.

M S. Daniels, p. 132
P p. 27

During the entire trip from JFK to LAX, I received warnings from my mother, punctuated with snide comments from my father. For five hours straight, nothing but, "Your Aunt Nora is very religious—more so than me and Grandma," followed by, "Crazy is what she is." My mother was raised in the Philippines, so by default she was Catholic and, growing up, went to church every weekend. She doesn't go to church anymore, but I've always thought of her as religious, especially compared to my atheist father. As far as my twelve-year-old self was concerned, believing in God meant you were religious.

The first thing I noticed when stepping into my aunt and uncle's house in Pasadena was the Jesus shrine decorating the entryway. This isn't so bad, I thought to myself... until I actually entered the house. Every room was decorated with a three-foot-tall Jesus nailed to the cross. As someone who was raised without a single religious artifact in my house, this was quite a

shocking sight. Why did a mutilated Jesus need to watch me while I got dressed? While I made breakfast? And most shockingly, while I peed? Is this what it meant to be religious: constantly uneasy and scared?

My discomfort was just beginning. That first night my aunt prepared dinner and when we sat down to eat, she casually suggested I say grace. Now, I had never eaten at a table where grace was recited, let alone said grace, so I had no idea what to say or do. I sat frozen at the table as I imagined what one of the Jesuses would do to me if I refused. Luckily, my father saved me by storming away from the table, screaming about how inappropriately Nora was behaving. The room filled with silence and even though I didn't understand why my dad was so upset, I knew something horrible had just happened. Secretly, I was grateful for my father's outburst, because as the tears rose in my throat and panic filled my chest, my aunt said grace. Once Nora was finished, we started eating and my father returned to the table without a word. As though nothing happened, we commenced the usual chit-chat that occurs between family members who have not seen each other in years. We never again mentioned that moment, which will forever be one of the most uncomfortable I've ever experienced and instilled in my mind the association of religion with fear.

FOUR EYES
KIARA KERINA-RENDINA

In this piece I explore a world of family history and memoir, where I run backward and forward in time between my father's and my own experiences.

 *Satran, p. 190*

 *p. 62*

I have my father's eyes, eyes that are the color of an oak tree. Eyes that are pulled down by invisible strings on the outermost corners. Eyes that gravity pulls down like a hunched back. Eyes that have seen so much, but understand so little. Eyes that share love and experiences that will last forever through our memories.

His eyes stayed awake on school nights, burning from fatigue, whispering one last page as their lids brushed together. His eyes watched pages fade to darkness as psychedelic plots floated in the space between the cornea and the optic nerve. My eyes stay alert from five to ten, skimming lines of documents and watching television in a tempest of letters and images. My eyes rest at night, drooping low from overuse like withering orchids.

His eyes skimmed parents' bookshelves for mature novels, famished for something of substance. His eyes found themselves devouring The Godfather and The Drifters as a small herbivore would devour a plant. My eyes spin through Barnes and Noble in a frenzy, searching for the final book of a seemingly endless Song of Ice and Fire series. My eyes swim through sheets of paper in a lake filled with unraveling subplots and dying characters.

His eyes watched blood seep out of two holes where a glass bottle had sliced a leg swimming in a quarry. His eyes watched as fish nibbled at these fissures that didn't seem so bad until they needed eight stitches to be sewn back together again. My eyes watched a small thumb stick itself too close to the door when it slammed and promptly turned the color of the fingernail to that of a plum. My eyes felt tears well up and overflow quickly like a bathtub faucet that has been left alone and forgotten.

His eyes watched as term papers about the legalization of anything less than conservative were stamped into a crisp, blank sheet. His eyes watched those term papers receive grades from an angry teacher, as fruitless as an apple tree in a desert. My eyes strain over a computer screen that blinks white and black in a pattern of vowels and consonants, shooting pages out of an eager printer. My eyes watch anxiously as a classmate hands them back, grades as satisfying and filling as a warm cup of tea being sipped in a soft place.

His eyes watched pizza dough thrown by his father fly higher than they could see, feeling a head tilting backwards to watch. His eyes watched that pizza come down as gracefully as a ballerina from a bluebird lift. My eyes watch an older version of the same patriarch as he instructs hands to fill ravioli with a mixture of cheese and spices with the same, perfect amount each time. My eyes watch as small bits of filling ooze out when the ravioli is flipped over and squeezed to be sealed and readied for mealtime.

Our eyes saw the bleached pillars of Pompeii rise high, fighting other tourists for an inch of shade. Our eyes saw each other stagger up a mountain, sweaty and silent as we pretended that our feet weren't hurting. Our eyes stayed up until early hours, watching old movies and new releases and everything in between. Our eyes see each other.

MY FAIR CITY
SARA REKA

This poem came about through memories of my birthplace, Albania, and my experiences in New York City. Additionally, it was written as a tribute to Adem Reka, my deceased grandfather who was honored with the title of Hero of Socialist Labor.

 *Kraft, p. 140*
 *p. 61*

I wake in the lonesome planet of New York,
where mornings stir only the restless souls.
Outside my window I see the spine of the city
that lay beneath our feet,
supporting unyielding buildings as they grow
like Jack's beanstalks.
I long for the face of my fair city now that I know its framework,
its streets and boulevards, modern traffic lights and signs.

I remember the Grand Canyon as a marvel encased in gold,
with jutting boulders and cliffs, tangles of rock tinted amber,
like eager brown eyes.
Hawaii, too, was a miracle of the world.
I would listen to life buzzing loudly in every level of brush
in Honolulu's rainforests, along its winding paths.
But I remain unsatisfied, still searching
for a landscape worthy of my fair city's face.

I find myself sitting on Pier 40's wooden benches,
eyes glued on New York's skyline.
I always favor the last few benches,
where my faint graffiti stains still remain.
I used to claim everything, from walls to trucks
to entrances and exits.
This is my bench, my pier, my Hudson, my city.
My thoughts are clearest by the murky-scented waters.

New York's many facades are exotic displays of man's hard work.

I find possibility on these silver streets.
A homeless man grins at the coins in his hand,
grins at the jogger rushing past,
and my lips stretch into a smile instinctively;
the appreciation he feels for the simpler things boldly exposed,
the hope that many long to feel.

The contrast between this country and my motherland, Albania,
overwhelms my differing selves
but they have found common ground in New York City.
We left Nana behind in Albania,
along with my cousins, aunts and uncles,
and I abandon them every two summers,
all over again, when my plane departs.

The first nights of my stay were the most restless.
I remember the echoes of meows in the night
as the neighborhood cats fought and loved
and the white dove's songs at sunrise.
Sleep was nearly impossible to come by.
The same boy crossed my part of town every afternoon,
carrying milk and wearing dusty clothes of little worth.

I wondered if he knew my last name
and wondered if he knew of my grandfather
or of his great death.
Hero of socialist labor is his title.
Dad would point out the particular crane that took his father's life,
and I was left speechless every time.
He still has the medal of appreciation locked away
in our jewelry drawers in New York.

Grandfather's blood status, unlike mine,
never was challenged.
Parading the streets of dear old Durres
with foreign makeup and clothes,
I watch women disapprovingly take in my
image,
inhale my aroma, and snicker at my speech.
I know better than to expect a grand
welcome.

I walked the daring line of Albanian-
American,
and the citizens of Durres listened to my
descending footsteps
all the way back to New York.
The morning sun now rises and peeks
through my window,
and my evasive mindset finally commits:
More than being Albanian, more than
being American,
New Yorker pumps through my blood.
In the mirror, I finally glimpse the face of
my fair city.

POOJA MAKHIJANI, MENTOR 2004-2009

I discovered the power of writing as a teenager through a very personal journey in the world of books. Writing for me, then and now, has not been about making sense of things, but in discovering deeper meanings. Writing confronts reality with a singular memory—one's own—and by extension the realities of a whole society.

RECALLING KOSOVO

KATHLEEN KRAFT

This piece was inspired by meeting Sara and talking with her about Albania and Kosovo, where I worked several years ago. It brought back so many memories of that challenging time, and I was finally able to write about it. (This piece will also appear in REAL: Regarding Arts & Letters *in the Winter of 2013.)*

 *Reka, p. 137*

 *p. 61*

Here to do meaningful work, but too tired
from all that happened in the last year,
the dynamic duo of lay-off and legal
separation.
Disoriented in Pristina, a capital anything
but pristine—
communist tower blocks, watery streets,
espresso cups
that dot every table like stubborn mushrooms,
and the unpredictable darkness, whims of
a faraway grid.

Three days in: click of the front door—my
friend back
suddenly from work—relieved until she
says *Turn on the TV.*
We watch: smoke and plane, smoke and
plane—downtown
billowing from so many mysterious angles.
I want to be there, in my desperate city
among transit workers and delis
that sell flowers in every Easter color.

Voices from home say, *Stay, It's bad here,*
Maybe it's safer there, We're OK.
So I start the job. I write. I write for work.
I walk among ruins—people's homes.
I go to a Serb enclave: SERB ENCLAVE—
the words a stubborn riddle. *Clave, cleave*—
to adhere and to split.

A startling poverty in the dimness—
Roma children wander toward me in rags.
One smiles dark and bright, the others
are gray.
Generators drone the hours of sorting and
reporting,
thrumming my broken sleep.
I'm given a cell phone, my first ever. I stare
at it,
flip it over in my hand, take comfort in its
small smoothness.

We buy things with Deutchsmarks, one of
three roaming currencies.

Change is never exact, and the coins are heavy.
I write an article about a successful moment in sheep farm rehabilitation and briefly feel happy.

I laugh sometimes with old and new friends, sometimes drink beer.
I watch myself watching.

The ajvar from Macedonia is fresh and delicious,
a pretty, vibrant red in a place of little color.
Some of us go skiing over patchy terrain, loud music tears
through the ragged mountain. I grow quieter, book my ticket home,
say goodbye to my friend, and land in an empty JFK
just before new year.

BECAUSE OF THEM

KATHRYN O'DELL

This piece is based on the stories I've heard about my ancestors over the years. I filled in and fictionalized any information I didn't have.

 *Barnes, p. 271*

 *p. 8*

I am because they were. I am because they explored new worlds.

1838. Somewhere in Tennessee. Great-Great-Great-Grandmother O'Dell.

After weeks of walking from the Deep South to the South, Fountain Ella's father said they would escape *Nu na da ul tsun yi, The Place Where They Cried, The Trail of Tears*. They never walked to Cleveland, Tennessee. They never stayed in the concentration camps there. They were never rounded up in Red Clay. They never forcibly walked to Oklahoma.

1881. Skurup, Sweden. Grandpa Monson's uncle.

Bengt Truedsson Monson sits tied to a kitchen chair with rags, what used to be a tablecloth or curtain. The woman who took him in removes the goiter on his neck with a few painful, but skillful, incisions. At the first sign of the goiter, Bengt's father had decided his son was worthless for anything but manual labor, so Bengt worked on his father's farm with the Russian peasants who came across the Baltic Sea—until he ran away. Now the woman's family gives goiterless Bengt a place to stay and a little money, which he saves in a sock. Saves it to escape again. He'll find an older brother who lives in Mankato, Minnesota, Blue Earth Country. *Blue Earth Country* his brother wrote in a letter, a letter he carried with him in a burlap sack to the kind woman's home, a letter he will carry with him to America.

1913. Šibenik, Yugoslavia. Great-Grandmother (Trovone) Clarence.

Amelia Clarence squats, scrawny thighs shaking over a Kilner jar. Her knobby knees make the ends of a V. Her pee, coming out of the V's vertex, is the color of saffron when you rub it between your fingers and the red bleeds yellow. The glass jar is warm, its contents foamy at the top. She giggles, and then pours it over the balcony on the boy who wants to marry her younger sister. A month later, she is shipped to Canada to marry a family friend from Split.

1939. Mankato, Minnesota. Grandma (Guiessinger) Monson.

Richarda wipes her clean hands on her clean apron, and then she takes a piece of strawberry-rhubarb pie to the lanky man in the threadbare suit, who had only ordered coffee. Three weeks later, she is in Frederic Monson's Plymouth Sedan, heading east toward Michigan. The blue sky never looked so big.

1941. Flint, Michigan. My Grandpa O'Dell.

JB and his cousin JR came from Tennessee to work at GM. One night after their shift, they get drunker than skunks on scotch and beer and head down to the local recruiting office to join the war. They stagger in, swaying and swinging. They're sent to a hotel to "sleep it off, boys" and told to come back in the morning. JR gets enlisted, but JB doesn't. Flat feet. He starts hanging out at local dances on Friday nights without his drinking partner. Sits in a chair, drinking beer with his shirtsleeve rolled up, showing off his indigo Cherokee-chief tattoo, watching Jean Clarence dance.

CONVERGENCE

JULIE SALAMON

Working with Nishat for the past several months has taken me back to the beginning, before I'd racked up thirty-five years as a professional writer. As the title suggests, this piece is about the convergence between her experience and mine.

 *Anjum, p. 144*

 *p. 4*

For the past few days I've been thinking about the Holocaust and Nishat's hijab. My mother and my mentee. Past and present.

The convergence of our New Worlds struck me after a phone conversation I'd had with my mother about her upcoming talk to a high school class in the Bronx. The teenage students are all recent immigrants to the United States, mainly from West Africa and the Dominican Republic, and have been studying the Holocaust. My mother is a ninety-year-old survivor of Auschwitz.

"I thought I would start by telling them how lucky they are to be living here," my mother began. "How this is the greatest country in the world."

I felt annoyed, as though I was a teenager again. "No!" I objected. "A lot of these kids are having a tough time adjusting to New York. They didn't necessarily choose to come here; they don't want platitudes."

"Okay," my mother said calmly. "What do they want?"

"They want to know what happened to you," I said. "Just tell your story the way you have so many times before."

She said, "That's good," and changed subjects. We both understood that my brief flash of irritation was habitual, a daughter's practiced resistance. Neither of us was really worried about her talk. My mother has led a remarkable life and talks about it with the flair of a born storyteller. I might have forgotten our phone call altogether if it hadn't taken place just before the Girls Write Now reading at the Scholastic Auditorium.

That night I sat in the audience filled with pride and worry as Nishat, my mentee, took the stage. She was wearing a hijab as always and (as always) had fastened her brightly colored headscarf with an insouciant bow. I was nervous for her but confident. I'd read many drafts of "The Understanding" and knew how good it was. I'd heard Nishat practice reading it until I mouthed the words along with her. Still, I felt a jolt when she reached the climax, describing a moment that passed between her and her father after a tense evening.

"I sat down on my steps, preparing myself for a long lecture about educational advantages provided here in America," she said. "Instead what I received were his memories of what happened to him and his family during the Bangladeshi Independence War, stories I had never heard before."

This time her story carried an echo of the conversation I'd had with my mother—and the lifetime of similar conversations we have shared. Nishat reminded me how much I appreciate my mother's willingness to talk about painful matters, to reach across the vast gulf between her experience and mine.

I took many photos of Nishat at the reading. They are positioned on my iPhone camera roll next to pictures of my mother at our family's Passover seder. There they are, hijabi and Holocaust survivor, divided and joined by history and culture, decades apart in age, connected through stories that confound expectations.

THE HIJABI
NISHAT ANJUM

The Hijabi is a glimpse into my inner world. It shows the way I think and the background that created me. This piece is also a peek into how many Muslim women think.*

 *Salamon, p. 143*
 *p. 4*

At eight years old, I went to a funeral. Looking back now, that funeral may have been the beginning of my prolonged evolution. That funeral was the first time I had seen a corpse; it was also the first time I saw so many people wear white. In Islam, white is the color of death. I don't remember who had died, just being stuck in a house full of weeping strangers.

I was ecstatic going home; in the car my mom put a gift from my aunt in my lap. The scarf was onyx-colored and silky in my hands. With streetlights blurring by, it seemed silver in places, and in my drowsy condition, I made out the words Calvin Klein. This hijab was one of many, as I later found out, but at 8 I believed that it was my own special scarf.

From then on, I wore that hijab almost every week to Sunday school. Eventually I wore it to certain family dinners and parties. I noticed two things. One, it was easier to get ready without having to do my hair. And two, it was easier for me to speak to people. I wasn't my usual socially awkward self. Putting that scarf on was like putting on a mask of sorts—at least at first.

It wasn't until the summer of 2010 that I gave serious thought to wearing the hijab. For the past two years I had been going to a summer camp for teenage hijabis, Muslim women who choose to cover their hair. The best part of this camp (or not, depending on your perspective) was that it took place entirely in the city. We had BBQs, beach trips, and games, as well as lectures from prominent Islamic figures. During my second year at this camp I reached a realization.

One of the lecturers was an African-American man who had converted to Islam as a teenager. They say that respect is earned, not given. If there was any better way to earn a person's respect, then he would have beaten it. If I hadn't been born into a Muslim family I don't believe I would've converted to Islam until I was older. To make such a life-changing decision at such a young age is staggering to contemplate. I listened to this man's tale of how he was abused and ridiculed for becoming a Muslim and saw how easy my own life had been. In that moment I decided to take the jump and wear the hijab. When I walked up to my friends on that first day of high school none of them batted an eyelash or looked taken aback at my new wardrobe choice, as I had feared. They simply said hello and demanded to know why I hadn't been in contact with any of them.

My background is filled with colors, sounds, loud jewelry, and music. I grew up watching my aunts and cousins wearing colorfully magical hijabs; some that sparkle and some that shine. I also come from a background of strong women. Women who would never agree to be "oppressed."

In my mother's time, not many women from Bangladesh wore the hijab. My mother herself chose to wear the hijab eight years ago, after she had recovered somewhat from lupus, an incurable autoimmune disease. I wouldn't say that religion is the most dominating factor in my life; it is, however, a major aspect. A lot of Middle Eastern cultures have been mixed in with Islam itself. Wherever Islam has spread, it has blended with that region's culture, making the certain "Islamic" laws or regulations that rule countries different based on the countries' influences and surrounding areas. There are in fact fifty official Islamic countries in the world and therefore probably fifty different versions of Islam, all with the same underlying faith, prayers, and religious text (the Quran).

The hijab is meant to be a choice, worn out of the love of God and modesty. It is meant to spur your faith in God and to make you stronger when you are doubtful. It is meant to make its wearers grateful for their bodies and to cherish what God has given them. When you force a girl or woman to wear the hijab you are defeating its purposes. Instead of teaching them to love themselves and their religion, it may end up making them insecure and scornful of anything to do with Islam. I've seen this happen so many times with many of my friends whose parents force them to cover their hair.

After three years of wearing the hijab all the time, it has become a part of me. Like some people feel weird without their glasses or hair tied up, I feel weird being out in public without my hijab. My socially awkward self has also faded to a point of nothing, though I suspect it will always be there. My confidence was born out of the hijab and I just hope that other Muslim women will be able to draw strength from it as I have.

WHO AM I?
HADIA SHEERAZI

I wrote about the clash of self-image with the (mis) perceptions of the outside world. Here's to all those who don't fit in a box!

 *Wong, p. 188*
 *p. 73*

Black. White. Asian. South Asian. Native American. Hispanic. One or more.

Other.

They want me to check a box. *"Please check one or more of the following groups in which you consider yourself to be a member:"* But I don't belong in a box. I never have. I've never even thought of myself as anything but a person. Until I came here, that is. Before, I was just me. Hadia. Female. Daughter. Sister. Best friend. Artist. Writer. Dreamer. Sometimes troublemaker and rebel. Mostly Girl-in-Progress. But I wasn't a color. Not till I came here. *Brown.* That's what the boy working in the café called me. A sharp intake of breath. What did he call me? "That pretty brown girl with the long black hair." Brown? I was a color? I looked down at my hands. I just saw my hands. He saw a color. I was a color.

Everyone was a color. White. Black. Brown. Yellow. Red. I thought I was in the melting pot. I guess all the colors hadn't melted, like the crayons I forgot in the backseat of my dad's car when I was eight. They all melted into one big rainbow-colored puddle. That's what I thought New York would look like. Eight-year-old me did anyway. Eighteen-year-old me saw a different world. Exotic. That's what my new hairdresser said as she blow-dried my hair. I stiffened. Why did she say that? "Guys love exotic-looking women." Exotic? I was exotic? I looked at my face in the mirror. I just saw my own reflection. She saw exotic. I was exotic.

The Queen's English. Spanglish. Ebonics. Pinglish. "Wow, you have like, no accent!" I always silently count to ten after I introduce myself to someone and wait for it. They always say it. Always. What does that even mean? No accent. Everyone has an accent. The runner up is: "Your English is really good." For an immigrant, they mean. They mean it as a compliment. I'm not sure it is.

Black. White. Asian. South Asian. Native American. Hispanic. One or more. Other.

The options are still staring at me expectantly. Identify yourself. Classify yourself. Pick a category. A group, a history, a laundry list of stereotypes and statistics. *Asian?* Maybe. *South Asian?* Maybe. *Pakistani?* Wait, that's not an ethnicity—that's a nationality. *White?* Next to "White" is: "including Middle Eastern." Now that's interesting. I never thought of myself as *white*. "There's no place called Persia." That's what the guy in my class said. No Persia? I'm not Persian? I look down at my last name. "Sheerazi." Meaning: From *Shīrāz*. The oldest province of

Ancient Persia. Capital of Persian art, culture and literature. Persian. He said I'm not Persian. I was not Persian.

"Please check one or more of the following groups in which you consider yourself to be a member:"

I'm not this, or not that. I'm not "One of." I am not "Other." I'm just me. I am:

 None of the Above

A CHILDHOOD AMONG GHOSTS

RACHEL ZHAO

Entering the mindset of someone who became a commodity to be sold instead of a daughter, and whose life was bound by the limitations of the upper class, was a new world. The one I live in has so much more freedom than my characters or my ancestors.

 *Agrawal, p. 280*

 *p. 75*

The tattered shirt smelled of the dirt and of the sky and of the storm as I gripped it in my hands. As I waited for the Ghoul-Witch to force the door open, I felt the holes in the worn cotton. Mother had dressed me in them and ran her hands through my tangled hair, in an attempt to get out the tiny grains of soil that had worked their way into my roots, staining the black to a murky brown.

She stood, wearing the finest threads of the prettiest blue I had ever seen, but her face was sunken, wrinkles etched deep into her cheeks, marking her face with time. Her voice echoed with the spirits and naughty children that she had consumed. Her hair was streaked with white because she lived in the clouds, the grey soaking into her ebony hair. Her fingers were just frail bone jutting through a network of blue veins and paper skin; I expected them to pass through me like a ghoul from one of my father's tales.

"Lei," Mother had lowered her voice, as if she were praying, "this is Mistress Guang."

"Lei?" The Ghoul twisted her lips, already adding to the collection of wrinkles. "That is her name? How... distasteful." I twisted in Mother's firm grip, wanting to demand why she had a right to have an opinion about my name. There was a great thunderstorm when I was born, which Mother saw as a good omen from the ancestral spirits—a storm to relieve the drought, and so named me "Lei," "thunder." I was the oldest girl, lording over my two younger brothers and younger sister. Even working in the fields under the rule of the government officials, I was Queen of the Storms. "You will be named Xiaofan, 'little ordinary,'" she proclaimed, "it will do well for you; you will remember your place."

"You are mistaken. My name is Lei, it will always be Lei," I spat out before Mother could stop me.

"Watch yourself Xiaofan," The Ghoul warned. "That will be your name when you come to my house in six years, when you become my daughter. You will answer to that name; you will address me as Mother." She turned to Mother. "My messenger will arrive five days after her 13th birthday. Return to this spot and I will give you your 300 yuan, and I am being very generous with that sum. Most would not even pay 100 for her."

"Thank you Mistress." Mother bowed her head and I couldn't help the surge of revulsion at her subservience, her weakness.

"Six years to discipline her... and stop the fanciful stories. I cannot have her babbling on about witches and spirits." The Ghoul then disappeared in the thick mist, like a nightmare.

We stood there for a minute, feeling the thick dew settle on our skin, until Mother spoke: "Let us go... Xiaofan."

My father never told me a story again.

I was delivered five days after my thirteenth birthday, my mother never looking back, my screams echoing her hurried steps.

I was supposed to be a princess rising from the slums of poverty into the resplendent ranks of wealth. But my mind had not accepted this prison. *We could've been full for days* I would think as they scraped dinner away, *Mother could have sewn that into a beautiful dress,* as they shredded the red fabric apart.

There were no stories here; the "attendants" stared at me strangely before rushing off. My patience was dwindling quickly with the silence I heard, which was only broken by the Ghoul-Witch's remarks of my uncouth behavior at the table, or my inability to dance, or my awkward gait.

A bowl of bean curd ended my silence. It was an accident, my fingers had been too eager. The black stain had caught Ghoul-Witch's sharp eye and her hand had quickly risen. The side of my face prickled with pain as her bony fingers connected with my cheek. The crack echoed through the dining hall.

"Useless girl can't even eat properly!" she snapped. My eyelids fought back against the tears as I squeezed the bottom of my chair to stop my trembling. *Don't cry*, I thought, *Do not be weak. Do not be Mother.*

I pushed my chair back, and sprinted down the maze of hallways, hearing her screech after me. I was stronger than her, faster than her; I was one of the queens in Father's stories fleeing across fields in battle. I slipped into my room.

Splinters scattered across the room as she forced the door open.

"What do you think you're doing, you piece of trash?"

"I am not a possession to be sold and bought." I screamed, willing my anger to beat her down, trample her with its fierceness. "The ancestral spirits blessed me with thunder. I am a queen. You do not sell an empress for 300 yuan."

She hissed, "Your naivety disgusts me. Your family is as good as dead. You will join them in starvation if you do not submit."

She shut the door and locked it, muffling my screams.

RUIYAN XU, MENTOR 2008-2010

At fifteen I didn't yet know that I would be a writer, that I could be a writer, but late at night, with the cheap desk lamp burning and my headphones blasting and my fingers flying across the keyboard, I felt as free as I've ever felt in my life.

strength
TO SURVIVE AND THRIVE

We began to fight
For the right
and control of our lives
not just as wives
But to survive and thrive
as women.

Priscilla Guo, p. 152

As someone with lifelong interests in politics, social justice, and cultural change, I'm an avid reader of those who use their craft to inform and sway opinion. My first forays into commentary—as a high school student without the benefit of Girls Write Now—gave me many things, from empowerment, to precocious pride, to the thick skin to survive some readers' wrath. Later, I found context and community through others' work and learned how far women, particularly, had come in the world of letters.

For some members of our Girls Write Now community, taking a stand means producing journalism about politics, bringing an underrepresented perspective to a larger story, speaking truths about selfhood in a larger context. We discuss and explore social justice movements through poetry, short fiction, or memoir; for others, essays or digital media are the chosen vehicles. My mentee, Brianna Marini, a budding journalist, has written about mental health issues affecting teens. When we mulled this over, she said "I'd rather be controversial and have my opinion [out there] than not say anything at all, be a sheep, and not like it."

Indeed. Because we're not going back.

KRISTEN DEMALINE
2013 MENTOR AND
ANTHOLOGY COMMITTEE MEMBER

WOMEN
PRISCILLA GUO

Reuter, p. 84
p. 35

The story of women
Where do I begin?
More importantly,
Where will we end?

Think back to the days
when we were consumed in those ways.
Ironic how liberty was a lady
That no other lady could meet.
Caged in a cult of domesticity
Where we found utter defeat.

We were the witches
to be burned
and our life embers were to rise up in the sky
to the point of no return.

We were the mothers, the wives, the
sisters, the daughters
And that's all we were for a time.
In the factory drudge
Knee-deep in laundry
We trudged
on.

We began to fight
For the right
and control of our lives
not just as wives
But to survive and thrive
as women.

The woman, sacred vessel she be,
is still robbed and raped
of her rights and her fate.
of the difference between 77 cents and 1
dollar.
of more love than hate.
All for the difference of one appendage
And the ability to create.

See, I'm interested in creating
a whole new world.
Where the old customs and traditions
are unfurled.

Where women aren't supposed to get their

hair curled
dress swirled
body twirled
into a mold.

A woman ain't a car, a plane, a ship, or
domain
that a man can obtain, contain, or restrain.
However much they refer to those things
as she
we can no longer feign that we don't have
a brain
and the household is ours to maintain

we are free.
Cat calls and abuse
Won't stop us from equality
This is a new world and
There simply ain't no apology.
This girl is on fire

KEEP OFF THE GRASS
JESS PASTORE

Paulino, p. 259

p. 57

What does it mean to walk barefoot across
grass
Upon which thousands of women
Have also walked barefoot before you?
We asked, we responded, we kept walking,
and shoes be damned.
Or really, if you like shoes, keep them—
we know you'll still walk with us.
This was not a place where euphemisms
like herstory
made anything but an eye-rolling impression,
but a place where speaking up meant speaking
out
loudly and unapologetically.

Or not,
and knowing you still had a stake.

What does it mean to forget that you ever
felt scared
of anything beyond the protecting embrace
of Pembroke Arch,
to skip diagonally across Merion Green
where the foot-printed track in the mud
eschewed the confines of the sidewalks
because dammit if concrete isn't a
symbol of the Patriarchy?
To run up Taylor steps a changed person,
but one who still is what she was
the day she picked out her first white dress
and checked boxes on forms for the last
time?

What does it mean to learn how to speak
up again,
over traffic and sirens and slamming office
doors?
How to find a place to walk barefoot?
How to speak out without such voices
behind you?
How to remember that you can still walk
confidently,
skip eagerly,
love voraciously,
and are still a Bryn Mawr woman,
and that that changes everything—
where you've come from
and where you are going?

THE TORMENT OF INACTION

JEANINE POGGI

Cindy and I have been fortunate to have never been victims of bullying. However, given its prevalence in both schools and the workplace, we wanted to try to understand its effects. Inspired by Cindy's poem about a girl who is bullied, I wrote through the eyes of one of her tormentors.

 *Caban, p. 156*

 *p. 14*

I laughed when they called her fat. I didn't instigate the name calling. I didn't facilitate its birth. But I laughed anyway.

I giggled when they pulled her hair. I didn't reach out and yank the mousy brown braid myself. I didn't grab her scrunchie and wave it high above her head. But I made a high-pitched squeal as she jumped awkwardly, trying to retrieve it.

I howled when they pulled the chair out from under her. I didn't kick her when she was down. I didn't tip the chair on top of her. But I didn't extend my hand to help her up.

I turned away when they pushed her. "It's okay, she has enough cushion to break her fall," they'd rationalize. I nodded in agreement.

I didn't throw away her liverwurst sandwich. But I didn't offer her the other half of mine as she nibbled on the crumbled cookie that still remained.

I invited her to my birthday, my mother made me, but I didn't say hello. She gave me a friendship bracelet—a heart cut in half—one piece engraved with "Best," the other, "Friend." I gave the "Best" to another girl whose name I can't remember.

The "Friend" still sits in my jewelry box. A reminder of the things I didn't do.

TAKING ACTION

CINDY CABAN

This piece is about a girl who struggles with different forms of bullying, but by the end of the poem, the world filled with cruelty is demolished. The beleaguered girl wakes up to a new world, where torment and hatred don't exist.

 *Poggi, p. 155*

 *p. 14*

Stripped down with nothing,
Nothing but a black cloth tied
To my face, shielding me from eyes
That can't be replaced.
Voices laughing with their high-pitched
tongues,
Now I know they're the conniving ones.
The floor vibrates, ringing along my veins,
As steps walk towards me, they can't be
erased.
They brush past my skin, each
Takes a turn flipping my celestial curve.
Strange hands and lips wrap around me,
Squeeze me until I choke,
Feel me up until I sweat,
Diminish me until I am no longer there.

My body is a rash.
I have the urge to scratch out my skin
And watch the layers, one by one,
Slip away until all I have left is my blood;
Purer than life, purer than me,
Making me no longer ugly.
I am a show to them:
Fast forward me with a toss;
Cut me into shreds and I'll scream;
Rewind me by mocking my past
And I will fall into an abyss of black holes
That welcome me more than the sun;
Press pause, and I will be a figure
For everyone to remember—
That people like me exist.
Press play:
All the blood will wash toward you
At a great speed, faster than a widow's
death.
Fear strikes me, telling me to breathe
When I am not in synch.

I am deteriorating like a comrade in war.
I hear the heavenly sounds of birds
Calling my known name,
Telling me to respond
To filth.

But my mouth is shut.
I am screaming for the whole world to hear,
But no one listens.
No one wants to listen.
People pretend that this cruelty
Will do no harm,
Will not invest in our heart,
When all it truly does
Is break us into fragments
That no amount of sewing
Can ever repair.

All we want is justice,
To clear our sanity,
To give others hope,
To watch this poison
Evaporate like
God is actually watching.
And with the echoes of silence
I hear them succumb to the new era,
The era that makes us all equal,
That makes us all smile
With the wrinkles above our lines
Yelling,
Shouting,
Crying,
That today,
Today has come.

IT SAVES
ARIANA SPATOLA

This piece explores the subject of depression. Someone close to me suffers from it as we speak, so it truly hits close to home.

 *Lopez, p. 199*
 *p. 67*

They're fragile; those who carry darkness
They are shackled and shamed
Shamed to be who they are and who they will
Physically they appear here with you and I
Internally though; isolated and weeping
Their minds a wasteland; exclusive of any light
Surrounded by demons worsening their plight
Oh what lies the demons tell
"You're horrid and insignificant"
"You're unworthy of anyone's love"
"You shall fail in all you do and any effort is futile."
"Leave this world for it'd be better off without you"
This is all they can hear!
Every night they quake in fear!
Rational thought smears!
Deeper into the pit they draw near!
Deeper!
Deeper!
Deeper!
Until...
Their precious wrists and thighs become wet
Just like their eyes
Scarred and red
Oh but I have not reached the full extent of this horror
Hardly. Even. Close.
For this darkness consumes all hope
And without warning they would disappear
Rope, pills, pistol, guns; you name it
And they won't return
They're gone forever
It could have been avoided but how it wasn't!
Society houses such evil
Deeming depression as minuscule
Nonexistent even!
They say it's ridiculous
"Everyone experiences sadness"
"They'll snap out of it."
No.
Absolutely not.

Sadness does not make one question one's very existence
Sadness does not cause one to bleed out
And Sadness is not the reason for suicide
Depression is
I ask that all make themselves familiar with the difference
For it can make a world of difference
Understanding what it truly is can preserve lives
Learning how to aid these troubling souls is so very possible
The answer is simple
Patience and love
If you stand beside those who suffer
Remind them that they are beautiful
That they are shining
That on this dark road they are never alone
Guide them when they cannot see
Help them walk when they can barely stand
Be kind
Be compassionate
And most importantly
Unconditionally love
For I have seen with my own two eyes that love indeed saves
And it's so very beautiful

DON'T FORGET ME

KATHERINE MARTINEZ

M *Flyntz, p. 260*
P *p. 49*

there will come a day
where i'll be too tired and too damn
broken to fight for us anymore.

promise me you'll
pick up the slack.
that we won't fade;
won't disappear.

RUN
IRIS TORRES

My piece wouldn't have been possible without Commissioner of Immigrant Affairs, *Fatima's gripping tale about her father. Her words inspired me to write this poem.*

 *Kristin, p. 166*
 *p. 71*

Today I am seventeen
There are bombs bursting and echoing throughout the streets of Palestine
Mothers sobbing grabbing their hysterical children and putting them to their breasts
Ash rises and occupies the air, making it difficult to breathe
We are dying at the hands of our enemy
From my tiny home I can see the first cloud of debris fill the air
My worrisome mother with her contoured wrinkles comes rushing into my room
Her green doe eyes and her black hair escapes from her red and gold hijab
"My son," she chokes
Her warm hands clasp mine kissing them as she says,
"Flee"
Her light eyes fill dark with tears as she struggles to repeat the word once more
"Leave this war zone while you can"
Our Palestine is no longer home, or our sacred country, but it is a war zone
"I have already lost two sons to this war, and I will not lose another."
I think of my older brother Asar and my younger brother Imad
They too became ash that rises when a bomb explodes
My mother does not give me a suitcase
"Leave our village and find the nearest port. Whatever you do, do not look back at what you are leaving behind. Everything will change"
Her thick black lashes hold her tears like rose petals hold rain drops
She kisses my cheek
The last kiss my mother will ever bestow on to me
I rise and she takes off her hijab
Her most expensive hijab
With her aged yet strong hands she gives it to me "This is all you'll ever have left of

me. Swear to me you'll never come back to Palestine"
Her long straight hair flows freely down her elbows. Her stern green eyes wait for my promise
"Your sister will join you soon. Don't look for her"
I promise to never come back
I promise to never look for Farah like she said
A bomb goes off and woman desperately shrieks in Hebrew
My mother shoves me out the back door
I can't look back at the only woman I have ever loved
Today I am a village boy who must be a man
I reach a port in Lebanon
I slip onto a cargo boat not knowing where I am going
Today I miss Imad
Today would've been his birthday
My mother's hijab smells like orange blossoms
The same blossoms Farah would pick for her
I bury my face in her hijab so I won't be able to look back
I hear gunshots and explosions that are hitting my beloved country
Ripping my childhood to shreds
I must run.

GAW-PO

ALICE SHEBA CANICK

Paldon has introduced me to the world of Tibet. She brought the culture of her native country to the Upper East Side of Manhattan.

 *Dolma, p. 163*

 *p. 29*

In *The New Encyclopedia Britannica*'s fifteenth edition, Tibet is described as an autonomous region of China, and referred to as "the roof of the world."

The struggle to maintain Tibet's unique identity began in 1949, when the Chinese government decided that it wanted to annex the "roof of the world" for itself. After twenty years of fierce fighting, the Chinese annexed Tibet, and tried to submerge the religion and culture of Tibetans. No foreign visitors were allowed in the country from 1963 to 1971, and it is very restricted at the present time, in the twenty-first century. Tibet covers an area of 471,700 square miles, with a population of 1,890,000 people, and was gobbled up by the avaricious Chinese.

The only Tibetan I'd ever seen or heard was the Dalai Lama, and then Paldon came into my life. Paldon is tall and angular in build, with an aquiline nose, which is the description of noble families in central Tibet. I think of Paldon as having a superior mind, character, and ideals. Her parents are agriculturalists without great formal education, but they understood that their daughter would have no future with altered conditions imposed by the aggressive Chinese. They sent her to family for safety when she was seven, and fortunately, she came to the US under the protection of political asylum. Instead of praying in the country of her birth, she is fervent about her devotion to Tibetan Buddhism (since it evolved in the seventh century). Paldon rises early in the Bronx to fulfill the distinctive form of intellectual disciplines and symbolic ritual practices of Tibetan Buddhism, before walking to the subway for her commute to Hunter College High School.

The New Worlds theme is a perfect description of what Paldon has experienced in her seventeen and a half years. It is ironic that because of China's cruel incorporation of Tibet, Paldon has come into my life as my mentee. She is a gift, and has taught me gaw-po, the Tibetan word for love.

DEAR MR. WIESEL

PALDON DOLMA

This is a personal letter to the writer Elie Wiesel. As I get older, I learn the importance of expressing yourself through courageous and interesting ways. I hope this is just the outset.

 *Canick, p. 162*

 *p. 29*

Dear Elie Wiesel,

I am writing this message on behalf of my six million Tibetan compatriots. My name is Paldon Dolma and I am seventeen years old. Last year, my English teacher, Ms. Holmes, assigned us to read *Night*. When I read the book, I was shaken, yet inspired by your persistence and determination through inhumane suffering. I instantly felt connected to your experience and to what has been occurring in my country, Tibet, for the last six decades. I strongly wanted to reach out to you. I genuinely admire you for using your unimaginable experience to become a guide to fight the sufferings and oppressions of the world.

You are not just a prominent figure, but a person of defiance and assiduousness. You are the Liberator of the suffering of the world. You have spoken out for Israel, the plight of Soviet and Ethiopian Jews, the victims of apartheid in South Africa, Argentina's desaparecidos, Bosnian victims of genocide in the former Yugoslavia, Nicaragua's Miskito Indians, the Kurds, and more. In 1986, during your Nobel Prize speech, you stated, "I swore never to be silent whenever human beings endure suffering and humiliation. Neutrality helps the oppressor, never the victim. Silence encourages the tormentor, never the tormented."

Mr. Wiesel, there have been more than ninety self-immolations in Tibet, especially in the Ngaba region. Tibet's self-immolation is listed on top of the untold stories in *Time*'s November/December 2011 issue.

I am left in despair and am compelled to do more than just pray and hope. Just in the month of November, thirty people burned themselves in Tibet protesting against the Chinese government, imploring independence, fundamental rights, and liberty from the Criminal China and the return of Tibet's spiritual leader, His Holiness the 14th Dalai Lama. Most of the self-immolators left poems and messages. Pawo (patrioted) Kalsang Kyab self-immolated on November 27, survived by his final words: "Greetings to my dear brothers and sisters, and especially my parents, the kindest of all in this world. I am setting myself on fire for the sake of Tibet. The long life of Holiness must be assured. It is my wish that the sun of happiness may shine on the land of Tibet."

Self-immolating on August 7, 26-year-old Dolkar Kyi's final message was: "Don't let me get into Chinese Hands. Hit me with stones and kill me with that."

Self-immolation is defined as "voluntary sacrifice or denial of oneself, as for an ideal or another person." In this case, however, the core purpose to the self-immolation would be to sacrifice in hope of autonomy and release from the influence of the oppressive Chinese government. Thupten Ngodup, 60, was the first person to set his entire body on fire on April 29, 1998.

Most self-immolators were teenagers like me. They have missed their innocence and youth. I pondered how the world leaders can stay silent when the Tibetan people are pleading for help.

Is it justifiable for Tibetans to suffer because the illegal takeover of Tibet by China has no effect on other parts of the world? Where have the principles of freedom and justice gone? I think about how life would be much more liberating if Tibetans had lived in America. I feel fortunate to be on American soil.

His Holiness the 14th Dalai Lama, the spiritual leader of Tibet, an advocate of love, forgiveness, and compassion is one of my inspirations. During the illegal Chinese occupation in 1949 and official takeover of Tibet in 1959, he faced great difficulties and was forced to depart from his people and country. His Holiness the 14th Dalai Lama faces undeserved and fabricated criticisms from the Chinese government, but with his steadfast philosophy of compassion, he has always remained calm and pleaded for compromise. The Chinese have lambasted him for inciting the acts of self-immolation in Tibet, and also called the exiled Tibetan freedom fighters the "Dalai Clique." No matter what, however, he always urges and advises the exiled Tibetans to compromise and be compassionate to the Chinese. His prevailing love and altruism helps me cope with my feelings.

There hasn't been any practical international help for this unforgivable crime. Few world leaders have warned the Chinese government about its inhumane practices in Tibet. But are pleading words enough to sway or persuade them to cease the oppression in Tibet? China's status as the booming economy in the world has been put ahead of human values.

This dreadful and horrific event reminded me of *Night*. Mr. Wiesel, you describe witnessing the horrifying scenes of Jews—babies, women, children, and men—being thrown into the blaze of the crematoria as if they were worthless and useless objects. Similarly, in my own country, the Chinese government, just like the evil Nazis, is unreasonably persecuting Tibetans and virtually exerting genocide on our people. The main message you wanted to say was to never let those inhumane incidents reoccur. But Mr. Wiesel, it is happening in Tibet. Please stand up and take action for Tibet.

THE CIVIL RIGHTS ISSUE OF OUR TIME

ALEX BERG

As the fight for marriage equality expands, so does our understanding of the LGBTQ community. Over the past year, transgender news has proliferated in the media, bringing about a new world of exploration and attention on gender nonconforming people.

 *Young Chan, p. 198*

 *p. 18*

After coming out as a transgender woman, Claire Swinford recalled her first time back at the polls as an "incredibly uncomfortable, very, very embarrassing" experience.

When Swinford, forty-one, voted in Arizona's 2010 primary, she was stopped by a poll worker who refused to let her cast her ballot because of her identification documents. While she had an appropriate ID and her name was on the rolls, Swinford, who was early on in her transition from male to female, hadn't yet changed the gender marker and name on her driver's license to reflect her appearance because of the cost, which she said was more than $200.

Despite the poll worker's challenging Swinford's gender, she persisted. "Everyone in the place can overhear the conversation where the person is questioning my identity and calling me 'sir,'" she said. The poll worker finally offered her a provisional ballot, and Swinford asked to see a supervisor who could contact the county elections office. The office said Swinford met the requirements and could vote after all, but "it would have been very easy to walk away from that," she said.

Transgender refers to the broad set of people whose gender identity or expression does not match those typically associated with the sex assigned to them at birth. Many transgender people go through gender transition, though some do not, said Lisa Mottet, transgender civil rights project director at the National Gay and Lesbian Task Force.

At a campaign event on Tuesday, Vice President Joe Biden—who famously got "a little bit over his skies" when he endorsed same-sex marriage earlier this year before President Barack Obama had done so—called transgender discrimination the "civil rights issue of our time," a rare moment in the political spotlight for the group. That statement came after Biden met at his home earlier this year with a conference of LGBTQ activists, apparently marking the first time a president has sent a representative to a conference with transgender people.

Transgender people, though, have largely been overlooked in the national outcry over new voter-identification laws that could pose challenges to people of color, low-income voters, seniors, people with disabilities, and students. But for Swinford and other transgender and gender-nonconforming people, a trip to the polls on November 6 presents a confluence of the legal and cultural barriers they face when changing identification documents, said Jody L. Herman, manager of transgender research at the Williams Institute at UCLA.

What Swinford, now the executive director of the advocacy group TransHaven,, experienced in Arizona was hardly uncommon. Across the country, transgender people face unique challenges when updating gender information on government-issued IDs. Dru Levasseur, a transgender rights attorney for Lambda Legal, an LGBTQ legal organization, said these challenges can include gaining access to legal resources and proof of costly surgery that not all trans people can afford, want, or need.

"We're often asked to show a form of identification wherever we go, whether we're going into a bar or getting on a train," Levasseur said. "Say, a trans guy like me, if I haven't been able to change my driver's license to say 'M,' wherever I go people are going to look at that identity document and say, 'Wait a minute, this can't be you.' And that can present a whole host of problems."

47%
HEATHER KRISTIN

 *Torres, p. 160*

 *p. 71*

When I was growing up in New York, my single mother home-schooled my twin sister and me while working as a nurse and a maid. When her moods took over and she couldn't hold down a job or barely keep the family together, we became homeless for one year. At age ten, my twin sister and I, along with our mother, wandered the city streets and slept in strangers' beds and the subways.

Social Services interviewed us five separate times and not once did they test us (we did not attend school for ten years) or inquire about our mother's mental health. Years later, I learned through a family member that my mother had spent time in a mental institution the decade prior to giving birth to us.

I truly believe if the government or city had been more involved we would never have spent a year homeless, or been on welfare and food stamps. My mother would have received the treatment she deserved and I would not have had to face so many challenges as a kid.

During the last election, Governor Romney talked about the 47% and personal responsibility. I yelled at the TV screen: "I had tons of that." I grew up knowing that if I wanted something, I had to go after it. If I wanted to be fed, I played my violin on street corners for money. If I wanted an education, I went to the library. If I wanted nice clothes, I sang "Tomorrow" from the Broadway musical *Annie* and passed the hat. My entire childhood was spent singing for my supper and slipping through the cracks of bureaucracy.

Luckily, in our teen years, my twin sister inspired me to read books, and I devoured them. I followed her into college, became an actress, waitress, and freelance writer, and today have a loving husband and three-year-old daughter named Daisy. I'd like to brag that "I made it," but the truth is, there's a little voice inside of me that fears that at the snap of a finger I could become a part of the 47% again.

That's why I'm arguing for more government involvement for those at risk of losing their homes and their minds. I'd tell our nation's leaders: "Check mental health. Do drug tests. Have counseling sessions. Don't just fill out paperwork. Make education for all a priority."

But the most important advice I'd tell our leaders and neighbors: "Have compassion."

THE BLACK DEBATE

CHENELLE AGNEW

While writing this piece, I felt as if I were reliving the moments that my grandparents experienced during the 1950s. It made me more appreciative of all the African-American leaders that desegrated the world.

 Hainey, p. 169

 p. 2

The motto is to aspire, to inspire before you expire, but what if everyone judges you by your attire?

Without looking at your inner beauty, it's incomplete, kind of like eating out without leaving a gratuity.

It's like everyone wants to ride the limo with you, yet they can't comply with the work that follows too.

Some may say that I'm exaggerating, but I just think it's facts I'm dictating.

It all comes down to the setting sun; comes down to what we have now become.

Thinking back to the earlier days, when all they did was segregate.

And now you're asking how this all relates but

it coincides with what I call The Black Debate.

When everyone argued whether or not whites and blacks should be together, all the way back in Little Rock where black children saw their education as a roadblock.

Interesting how something as little as the color of your skin determines what your fate brings...

And I understand that everything wasn't sweet like an apple pie, but maybe if there were more Rosa Parks, that much faster racism would die.

But maybe you think I'm unrealistic because I don't know what's going on in their heads but maybe

I could make their thoughts rest a little and go to bed.

I often wonder where the United Nations were, aren't they supposed to keep peace?

But they were nowhere to be found at those fire stations where police dogs had a Southern feast.

Maybe I'm overreacting because I'm black, or maybe it's because I'm afraid that things will escalate.

But I'm positively sure that it's called The Black Debate.

RASHRI SHAMSUNDAR, MENTEE 2006-2007

I always loved to read when I was a little girl. As I grew older, I drifted toward writing. By fifteen, I had a poetry journal. It helped keep me calm and centered. It was as if poetry were my therapist. I could write freely without worrying about confidentiality boundaries.

THE NEW WORLD, ACCORDING TO SHE

EHMONIE HAINEY

This piece was inspired by conversations with multiple African-American women about life following the civil rights movement. Today is a new world compared to the world in which they lived a mere fifty or so years ago.

Agnew, p. 167

p. 2

She says this new world we live in is so different than before. She couldn't hope and dream like we now can. The invisible barriers that held and gripped her tight, like a bear hug from her mother and father after coming home from school, are no longer to be found. Her destiny, so she was told, was to become a maid or something similar; only to serve the descendants of those her ancestors were enslaved to.

She wanted more for herself, but even after all of our nation's fights for equal rights, her high school counselors advised against going to college. "It's not your path," they said. "Do something else," they said. She obeyed, but still yearned for more. On a whim she eventually enrolled and when she finally attended, she was admonished for working so hard, denied points for extra credit, and told to be content with scores no higher than the letter C. Then she was told, "People like you don't become lawyers or doctors; only nurses or teachers."

So she became the latter. She was smart, she was devoted to learning, and she still wanted more but felt forced into educating others. For years she gave it her all, and dedicated herself to teaching the next generation and the next generation and the next, who might one day achieve the things she never could.

She taught them about slavery, and segregation, and civil rights, and Jim Crow, and Martin Luther King, and Rosa Parks, and Malcom X, and Betty Shabazz, and setting their minds to becoming whatever they wanted to be. She wanted them to be free, not in the physical form but in the mental—free from the shackles of the mind. Free from the dashed hopes and dreams of her generation. Free from the segregation. Free from the mindset of an entire congregation of naysayers and hatemongers.

Over time she saw equal opportunities and actions that were affirmative. And the rise of media personalities and political and business powers-that-be who looked like her and me. And black doctors and lawyers—those professions that she was told she could never be. And then, the presidency! She never imagined the day she would see a black president, and pinches herself every time he appears on TV. His success is her personal pride and the culmination of times past, rolled up into a perfect package of the present. He is a representation of the new world, according to she.

REFLECTIONS FROM THE TRIANGLE

CHANDANIE DEVI HIRALAL

This piece relates to experiencing different aspects of life, maturing, and growing throughout a lifetime. On the journey of life we see and create new worlds of splendor and horror as we are tested by fate, while we realize our infinite potential and forge our destinies.

p. 38

You know, the solution to any problem is usually quite a simple one, but emotions hinder one's judgment, making what feels right and what is right hard to distinguish between. It becomes difficult to decide between doing what you want and doing what you should.

But then again, who is to say the "right" thing really is right? We are the ones who decide what is right and what is wrong for ourselves. Even if our decisions turn into mistakes and we start calling ourselves fools, it's because we don't want to take the fall for our actions and we regret we messed up. We don't want to look in. Instead we always try to find some outside justification for what happened and wish we could go back and redo things the "right" way.

To do something the "right way" you would have had to have known all the possible outcomes. The "right way" is really just your true goal; what you really want or what you felt might have been better. With time you will see if it was meant to be, as the silent judgment of the sands is the ultimate test; when the damage has been done, you can either sift through the ruins for salvageable parts and rebuild something defective amongst the charred remains, or let time wither everything to the scar of a memory, and from that faint memory build something better and stronger.

Do people really need to change, or just remember who they truly are at heart? It takes a strong mind to separate emotion and reason and weigh them. It takes a patient mind to wait, observe, and analyze, but waiting in and of itself is difficult, especially if that patient mind is eager to try again but sits alone in silence.

The heart seeks guidance and help, the mind seeks discipline, and the soul seeks experience. An individual must have balance between the three, but balance does not necessarily mean an even distribution of energy and time. Balance calls for focusing and deciding which of the three needs it the most in the moment.

Understanding and knowledge are two powerful tools, as dissecting the past to understand where you stand now endows you with the knowledge—the discriminating eyes—to watch where you step and allows you to pave the path you wish to walk.

Obstacles rear themselves and the strength of our will, mind, heart, emotions,

and thoughts determines whether or not we rush directly in and find the right moment to jump or create that moment. It takes determination and resolve to get up if the jump was premature or too late, and it takes fortitude to continue on and try again.

Never let emotion and desire overwhelm or consume you. If you bear scars and wounds, stop and allow yourself the time to heal instead of continuing to rush forward and get yourself into situations that will inflict even worse pain. In that time you take to heal, arm yourself. Grow stronger in body, mind, and spirit. That way, future trials cannot break your constitution. Take your period of silence to reflect and grow.

The human experience is different for every individual. Who creates it and ends it is up to that person to decide. What people do with their time is for them to decide. Leaving that which is comfortable or remaining there determines their possibilities; deciding to take the first step affects their overall growth or lack thereof as unique entities.

Decisions, decisions... they're yours to make. All of them. Accept all that comes on the path you decide to walk—all the benefits, triumphs, repercussions, and defeats.

It is true that life is unfair, but ask yourself: who and what makes it that way? Adapt to your unique situation instead of bemoaning it. We all are creatures that create and recreate our truths and falsehoods as well as those of others; we live in little worlds of our own because we know not what lies outside and we fear to step out and look or are shackled by limitations both self-imposed and environmental. With time, many learn to see through delusions, but that is only if they seek personal truth and liberation or circumstances cause them to realize it. There are many still who remain asleep and allow everything to pass by in a dream without ever making an effort to observe, ponder, and decide if there's something more or if there's more to them than they know.

It's one thing to be a young fool, but it's something completely different to be an old fool.

Walk the Fool's journey, but along the way master yourself; then The World you create will be yours to command and shape. Paint the reflection of your soul and marvel at the beauty that is you. Create love and cleanse pain; destroy lies and build truths. Be the light you wish to see in the world and let it glow without falter.

family

LET ME TELL YOU A STORY

> *"Siéntate, dejame decirte una historia," she said. (Sit down, let me tell you a story.) We sat on the couch as she drank her milk with her sweet plantains, crossed her legs and began.*
>
> *Sade Swift, p. 195*

It takes a fair amount of bravery to write about people we're close to. As my mentee Rumer LeGendre says, "When you're writing about your family, it can be scary, and you're kind of vulnerable, because your family is connected to you and where you come from, and that can be uncomfortable. But when you do write about them honestly and put the truth out there, it's relieving."

Most of us, when we sit down to write something personal, don't have it all pre-packaged in our heads, ready to type. One sentence opens a road to the next, and all at once something we didn't see before occurs to us. "Writing about my grandmother helped me come to terms with our often argumentative relationship," says mentee Tuhfa Begum *(p. 174)*. Writing helps us to look at people we're close to from a different perspective.

As you read these pieces, you will enter the new worlds our mentees and mentors have discovered through writing about parents, grandparents, siblings (real and imagined), and children (those who are already born and those who soon will be). So turn the page for a treat—a taste of writing that makes art out of understanding, compassion, pain, and yes, joy.

VIVIAN CONAN
2013 MENTOR AND
ANTHOLOGY COMMITTEE MEMBER

TALECRAFT
TUHFA BEGUM

Writing memoir has been a new world for me. Writing about my grandmother for the first time helped me come to terms with our often-argumentative relationship. Now, it has helped me overcome the grief after she passed.

 *Wilson, p. 286*

 *p. 11*

Nanu's room is empty now, except for her hospital bed, oxygen tank, and boxes of unused medical supplies, all pushed against the bare walls and waiting to be shipped back to hospice.

No one ever goes into the room; it's like a ghost town, like the stories Nanu used to tell me about entire villages disappearing because of evil spirits. "Grandma," I would tell her, "there's no such thing as evil spirits." That always started one of our infamous debates. I would defend my ideas with logic and reasoning while Nanu told of a hundred different circumstances that proved me wrong. My grandmother was a firm believer in the supernatural. According to her, she had seen too many phenomena that could only have occurred through supernatural means.

Nanu was born in East Pakistan, now Bangladesh. Her mother died giving birth to her, and her father was killed a few months later, fighting in the Indian Independence movement.

After the British Raj left India, the country was partitioned into two pieces based on prevalence of religion. The Hindu majority became its own country, India. The Muslim minority became Pakistan, which was then further partitioned by language. The people living near Bengal Bay became a part of East Pakistan, while the rest of the country was called West Pakistan.

Nanu grew up as an orphan, living with a wicked stepmother and three half-siblings. Her life seemed like a Grimm fairytale, and, at age seventeen, she married the son of wealthy family friends.

When my mother told me that Nanu used marriage as an escape from her abusive stepmother, I demanded to know why she didn't just finish school and get a job. In my mind, none of her actions made sense because I was lucky enough to be brought up in a world where the people around me supported my dreams and endeavors.

My mother said that my grandmother grew up in a different kind of world. "People back then in Bangladesh did not care much about educating women," my mother explained. "The biggest accomplishment a woman could achieve was marrying and having sons. Any woman who did not marry and give birth to at least one son could be ostracized from the community."

During the months Nanu lived with us, she told me many stories of women who went to see shamans and mystical medicine men to increase their chances of bearing sons. Sometimes I would sit with her after school, propped up next to her in her bed, doing my homework. She would sit up straight and position herself so that we were sitting side by side.

"Nanu, did you ever visit a shaman?" I asked one day. She cackled.

"Of course not," she said. "Shamans work for the devil. The women who visit them end up infertile and divorced!" Her tobacco-stained teeth widened into a grin.

"My best friend Rani went to a shaman once, after her first miscarriage," Nanu said. "The shaman gave her some disgusting concoction to drink. I told her not to drink it, but she ignored my pleas and drank it anyway! Out of desperation, I suppose."

"What happened to her, Nanu?"

"A year later she gave birth to a baby boy."

"Oh, a happy ending, then," I said.

"Not quite. He was born with one leg shorter than the other and six fingers on each hand. When he was three years old he died from a mysterious fever. Rani was never able to have children again." Nanu gave me that I-told-you-so look.

"Grandma," I said, "I hope you know that birth defects are hereditary or sometimes just accidental. That shaman was a fraud!"

"Oh, no," she said. "He was a *djinn*. And he possessed her so that she could never live a happy or fulfilling life."

I rolled my eyes and pretended to study my schoolbook. Genie indeed. Where did she get this stuff?

A few minutes later, Nanu's head gently dropped onto my shoulder and she fell asleep. A light breeze came through the bedroom window and her thin gray curls moved slightly, the last remains of her numerous cancer treatments.

When I was a child, Nanu would put me to sleep just like this. She would make me to tell her some intricate tale until I ran out of words and fell asleep. It's funny how life works, isn't it? That afternoon, Nanu was the child and I was the adult watching over her. I carefully got up and put a blanket around her. I couldn't wait to hear the stories she would come up with from her dreams.

MEETING MARY

KRISTEN DEMALINE

This piece is about my grandparents' meeting in Cleveland, Ohio around 1930.

 *Marini, p. 108*

 *p. 48*

Jim inhaled the onion- and smoke-filled hallway, walking dreamlike toward the battered wooden door. He pushed it open and ducked as the street exploded in riotous sound, but passersby trudged onward. A couple yawned. The morning light was dampened by the oily brown haze hanging over the river. Smudged-faced men shoved by him as he left for work, some grunting in vague familiarity. He'd been lucky when he'd arrived from the farm last winter. He'd been one of them, feeding the hungry furnaces with ore that hadn't had time to be unloaded, a ferocious steel machine. The slowly rising spires of the new railroad tower in Public Square bore the fruits of his labor. One day his cousin handed him a smeared scrap of paper with an address, and a few weeks after that, he was running his own streetcar.

Superior Avenue. The quiet girl with sweet blue eyes always got on here. He'd worked up to a shy smile when she boarded. As he drove up east, he'd sneak glances. Maybe today he'd actually say hello. Before he could do so, a clean-shaven man—so clean—leapt up behind her.

"Mary, Mary, you can't break my heart and leave me," he joked. Mary sighed slightly, her nostrils flared with irritation, but she smiled firmly over her shoulder, and her musical brogue trilled, "But I did, down the street. Don't you have an office to get to?"

"My father says my job is to settle down. Now is it forward to ask if I can meet you for a walk this Saturday?"

Jim gulped as she said, warily, "I suppose... and what is your name?"

"Aha! Patrick!" he crowed triumphantly, bounding off the car at the next stop along Euclid Avenue.

Jim left the car idling for a moment. Oh well, he thought. Of course, she'll want the charming Irishman in a suit who has an office and a clean collar. Not a working bloke. Not me, with not a penny to spare.

Besides, he'd never even said hello.

The next Monday, Jim pulled around the corner to Superior. A few passengers, housemaids like Mary, boarded, and he was just about to release the brake when she stepped on, breathless.

"Thanks," Mary said.

"Well, hang on a second and collect yourself; we've a few blocks 'til the next

stop," Jim said. "How was your weekend?" He turned away quickly, embarrassed at his intrusion.

Mary looked up at him, amused. "Quiet. My sister and I went to the beach."

Jim pulled up to the next stop. Patrick stepped up. "Mary, where were you? I waited on the corner just like you asked!"

"I wasn't feeling well, Patrick," she said. "Now go bother someone else already—

I'm talking to my friend here."

Jim turned to look out the window, grinning, but when he turned around, Mary had found a seat in the back, where she looked pensively out the window.

SMALL THINGS

KATE TREBUSS

It has been fascinating to watch friends become mothers and fathers and enter the new world of parenthood. I often find myself trying to imagine some of the more private and complicated aspects of this experience.

DiFrisco, p. 178

p. 28

Even before her belly grew large, he stopped touching her. At first she did not notice, so mesmerized was she with her body's slow transformation toward motherhood. Each day she watched her skin slowly stretch tighter across her abdomen and felt for the widening of hips that to her had always felt more boyish than womanly. She touched her swollen breasts in the shower, marveling at their tenderness, which seemed a kind of promise, a hint of the future that was slowly unfolding within her. Even the violent waves of nausea that first alerted her to the new presence in her womb and would plague her for most of her pregnancy filled her with awe and joy. And when she focused all of her attention inward and reached for the little fish whose body was slowly forming itself out of her own, she was amazed to find that she could will the noisy world to silence and speak within herself a language at once strange and thrillingly familiar.

She tried to explain this act of magic to her lover as they drove home one night. But neither her mind nor her lips would cooperate. No more than a foot between them, they were as two galaxies caught in a single image though light years apart. She was certain that she could not describe the secret act of communion that took place each time she turned inside herself. And even if she could, what if words—worn, frail things—broke the spell that had opened this new realm?

The man was quiet during the drive. He saw the woman shift in her seat and move both hands over her abdomen. He wanted badly to reach across the gearshift and fold her fingers into his own but felt shy and embarrassed by his loneliness and his need for her. His touch would be an intrusion, he thought, a violation of the private world he saw her tending to each day. And he was sure that should she flinch or tense as his skin made contact with hers, he would die.

They pulled into the driveway. As they plodded up the unshoveled drive to the side door of the house they shared, the man fumbled in the deep pockets of his winter coat for keys. He told her he would clear the snow in the morning, before leaving for the studio. He said this without looking at her, and suddenly she saw this not-looking and her heart was pierced with the same sadness she'd felt once the previous spring, when she was gardening and came across a hummingbird which had flown into the plate glass window of their home, each feather a tiny scale of light, soft and infinitely fragile even in death.

He had found the keys and reached the threshold before her. She stopped a few feet behind him and spoke his name as he opened the door. Together, they went in.

LOST AND FOUND

GINA DIFRISCO

 *Trebuss, p. 177*

 *p. 28*

Crying, echoing back and forth like a bat sending sound waves, mixed with the noise of the passing train. The crying continued even after the train was long gone, after the passing passengers were through the turnstiles. No one in sight, yet there was still crying. Getting up to find the source, he found, behind the machine in a space so tight a grown man's arm barely fit, a child of no more than eleven months, almost a year. A rough estimate of age by sight. He picked up the child as carefully as he could. The crying stopped and wide eyes locked with his. A transparent blue most parents only hope never fades to brown. So placid, one could not tell how deep they went. So wide not even the galaxies together could match the size of one alone. In an instant the eyes were gone and the child was asleep, a sleep so deep not even the next passing train could disrupt it. The child was at peace now and would remain at peace for its next adventure.

The years have passed and the child has grown. No longer eleven months, now eleven years. Middle school years beginning with new friends, teachers, classes, and even a new building. No longer a child, yet not yet an adult, still called a child. No different from any other school, on any other first day of the new year, the child's English teacher asks, "Write about what you did over the summer, and don't forget to include your name." The child, with eyes still the same transparent blue, thinks for a moment before scribbling down what the teacher would most likely expect her students to say about their summers.

The child writes: "My parents took us to a water park in Connecticut. We went with my aunts and one of my uncles and a bunch of my cousins. I went on so many rides and water slides with my cousins. I also went to an aquarium, too, with my dad, and saw some sharks and penguins and tons of other fish. I played in the park sometimes with my friends."

Though this summary of the child's summer fun was not exactly a lie, it wasn't the whole truth either. The child refused to tell anyone of the wedding that took place in late July. Not out of shame but because it was a memory the child did not want to share with outsiders; a private happiness to keep to oneself. That summer, the child's parents were finally married. An ear-to-ear smile fell across the child's face at this thought. The child decided to keep secret this summer fun.

The school day ends when parents come and children retreat to mothers and fathers, babysitters and nannies. The child sees no one familiar and waits. About to give up on waiting, the child feels a slight tap to the right shoulder and turns rapidly to the source, retreating to a father's arms. I thought you'd never come. The father holds his child tight and remembers back to that steaming hot summer afternoon in the train station, looking at an infant, imagining it saying those words. I thought you'd never come.

THE LOST ONES

MARIAH THERESA AVILES

 *Alberts, p. 98*

 *p. 7*

All eight of them.
I guess you can call them my brothers and sisters.
The youngest,
I used to cradle every night
Before I fell asleep.
It brought me peace to know she was okay
and in the right care.
But

One day,
When things got out of hand,
We had to hand them all over.
Our hearts shattered as my aunt held them close to her heart,
During the time we couldn't care for them.
After more than eight years without them,
We gained custody again.
I carried them gently,
My mom warning me every second to hold them the right way,
To be careful with their heads.
And so I did,
Never intending to hurt them or my own mother.
And as we reached home,
she grabbed every single one of the kids.
She bathed them like there was no tomorrow,
Not because they were so dirty,
But because they were hers
And there's nothing like caring for your own.

I have a secret,
A confession.
My mom gave us dolls as siblings.
That night we came home after gaining their custody again,
She snatched off her coat,
Grabbed her dolls,
Stripped them of their clothes and undergarments,
And scrubbed them spotless.
She handled them with care.
She pricked their elastic rubber bands out of their hair
And combed every single strand
Till their brown and blonde hair was pin straight,
The same way she'd comb mine as a child.

Mama spent about an hour
Removing every pair of underwear off her dolls,

Even though no one would ever see them
And know that they were dirty.
I swear she treated them like humans.
But they were her babies.
It's funny, because once I hit the age of five,
I wanted to be a big sister.
Little did I know,
She granted us our wishes
And she had fun pampering her youngest kids.
She didn't have to spend nine months with them in her womb
To provide the unconditional love she has had and still has for them.

I leaked my confession.
My mother gave us dolls as siblings.

EXCERPT FROM THE YELLOW NOTEBOOK

CHANA PORTER

 *Christie, p. 275*

 *p. 21*

Pop-Pop wouldn't look at us, or at Nonna. He wouldn't read. He kept his eyes trained on the television screen as it played soap operas, infomercials, the news. There were no final words exchanged, no tender looks or smiles. Nonna would not speak. She made tuna salad and cut bagels and made sure there were three kinds of cream cheese (scallion, whipped, plain). We ate our brunch in a little room down the hall designed for family members eating awkward meals amongst bad carpeting and paintings of ducks. I think my mother was pushing for some kind of reconciliation, some kind of reckoning, for meaning-making and closure. But Nonna just added this to the long list of Things She Wouldn't Say. Samuel was quickly buried in Florida. She packed a little bag and flew home with us the following day.

Here a kind of happiness was established. Our home seemed to finally have the proper number of people living in it. My parents always meant to have another baby. There just wasn't money; then there wasn't time. Nonna settled into chosen tasks of making the beds and watering the plants. But she put down her spatula for good. "I have done enough cooking, cleaning, and sewing for five lives," she whispered to me, tucking me into bed. My father was now the primary cook of the household, his interests divided equally between health food and ethnic cooking. Nonna would sit down with equal relish to chicken chow mein and beet loaf, Hungarian goulash and lentil balls. All meals were celebrated with the same reverence. "Ah, Larry. You do it again. Very good. A man who can cook is very, very good." My mother lifted her wine glass and smiled her fox smile. "To the chef!" said Sue. Nonna observed her daughter's America, her one lonely child plunking out notes on the guitar, while husband and wife saw each other again and again with new eyes. *Is good*, she thought. *This, is good.*

I wish I could stay in this moment, live in it, in the hopeful peace my Nonna brought to our household, the truce of expectation brokered by my parents' years of compromise. But I am brought back again and again to my grandfather's sneaky smile, the strangeness that permeated all interactions of the last months of his life.

What is cancer if not an alien? I'm not a scientist. I'm truly asking. I want to know. There are so many ways to be devoured, to be eaten alive. By fear. By disease. By guilt. To be consumed, transformed into a sunken husk, then blown away. This is not a poem. It keeps me up at night.

THE BEACH

JENNIFER CODY EPSTEIN

Emily's piece about leaving her mother behind as she goes to college inspired me to think about how I'll feel when the time comes for my daughter to do the same.

 *Ramirez, p. 184*

 *p. 59*

I first registered the fact that my daughter would one day leave me when she was still really a baby.

Though Katie had never crawled, by eighteen months she not only could walk, but could put on her own clothes—swimsuits included. This she did one wintry evening, emerging from her room in a tutu-style one-piece she'd apparently found in her drawer. After shrugging a raincoat over it and tugging on rain boots, she marched purposefully to the door.

"Where are you going?" I asked.

"Beach," she replied, and reached for the doorknob.

My husband and I exchanged glances. It was a freezing February night. The nearest beach was two hours away by car. I didn't know how she figured to get there on her own, but it was clear she wasn't giving up.

"We can't go to the beach right now," I said. "It's nighttime. And cold."

"BEACH," she repeated, rattling the doorknob.

"The beach is closed now," my husband offered.

"Beach! Beach! Beach!" Katie chanted, and proceeded to pound on the door itself. Soon she was hurling herself at it, red-faced and tearful, devastated by this failed attempt at self-determination. As I scooped her up, I found myself teary-eyed too—and not just due to suppressed laughter. Carrying her to the bathroom ("We'll make a beach here," I told her), I also felt a shiver of prescience. Up to that point, Katie's life had been almost indistinguishable from my own: we woke and slept together, came and left together. There was rarely a moment when we weren't somehow connected, and I'd come to take that connection for granted.

Watching her fight so hard to leave that night made me understand something I really hadn't before: that one day, my daughter would don her swimsuit, put her hand on the doorknob, and open that big wooden door with ease. Hey, Mom! I'm going to the beach.

And slam—just like that, she'd be gone.

The image caught in my throat, achingly sweet but painful, too. It was a feeling I'd have often in the years to come: dropping an outgrown dress into the donation box. Passing the playground we no longer went to. Sending Katie to school alone, armed only with a cell phone and attitude (which, I'm thankful, she still has a lot of). I felt it again the other night as I put her to bed. Now twelve, she looked up at me sadly.

"I wish," she said, "I could be little again. Do you wish that, Mommy?"

"Yes," I said, hugging her. And then: "No."

"Well, which is it?" she laughed.

"Both," I told her. "It's contradictory."

For that, I've come to realize, is what parenthood really is: a lifelong, life-affirming and contradictory dance of oppositional moments. Clinging and cleaving, rejoicing and grieving. Putting on your swimsuit, and leaving. Or maybe just banging the door, secretly relieved that—this time, at least—it won't open to let you out.

THE ROAD

EMILY RAMIREZ

My piece explores the road to a higher education for both myself and my mother. It's the path to both of our dreams.

 *Epstein, p. 182*

 *p. 59*

Sitting down on the side of the dirt road, Lalita unties her shoelaces. "Hurry up!" her brother yells. She hands the sneakers they share to walk to school to Gabriel, her brother, who, though one year younger, towers over her.

"You only have them for five minutes. Then we have to switch again." Barefoot for the next forty meters, she tiptoes on the dirt path, careful not to step on glass or the rough, pointy rocks, continuing to make her way to elementary school in Santiago.

As a young girl, my mother strived to be the best student. She was at the top of her class in third grade, but sadly, poverty made working on her family's farm the top priority. By doing so, she contributed to her mother's, father's, and nine siblings' well-being as much as she could. She woke up at five to milk the cows as fast as possible, then got dressed to begin the three-mile walk to school, switching shoes with her older brother as often as she could. To this day, she has always wanted more for herself.

As she sits down with me while I tutor her for her second GED exam, her efforts to learn motivate me to strive for what I want. The road to my acceptance to college has been paved with the same pointy rocks and glass Lalita once walked on, but I walked through it with the help of friends, family, and, most important, my mother. As I enter this new world, where resources to study are at my disposal, I am reminded of the struggle my mother is still trying to overcome to benefit from an education.

I remember, as a child, always asking, "What did you want to be when you were little?"

"A nurse," was always her answer.

Maybe when I begin college this fall, a new world will begin for her: a world where she can pass the GED exam and get an education. And as I begin to walk another jagged road, I will remember my mother's struggle. As it always has, it will motivate me to excel.

SCREEN IN A MILK CRATE

MOIE UESUGI

 *Ashour, p. 234*

 *p. 72*

The ant sashays across the tickets, its shape blending into the standard Microsoft Word font. The tickets are in both Japanese and English, just like everything around me. My mother calls out directions, her arms almost giving a performance of their own as they point to the various things around us—the giant trailer behind her, the handmade screen sitting in a milk crate, the lopsided tents whose flaps fly in the wind.

Last night, sleepy eyes and sore fingers finished stitching the screen together from the densest tablecloths the Internet could offer. In the silent country night of Uno, Japan, one pitch-black screen and one smaller, white screen have somehow been finished. They are really two parts of the same screen, ready to be attached by the Velcro we stuck on with Gorilla Glue and yarn-thick thread. The fruit of the unpaid volunteers' hard work now sits like a lumpy rectangle in the black milk crate.

The crate sits alone in the dusk, its shadow elongating as it reaches the trailer. There are two square canopy tents on each side of our festival grounds, leaving the center space open for the blue plastic tarps (to sit on) and a large projector covered in disassembled black garbage bags (to protect it from the rain). The tents are all set up and ready to be staked to the ground, but they are ignored and stumble around with the wind. Only one is being secured—the closer one, on the right—by a volunteer. I squint through the dwindling light, watching his head bob up and down as he tries to drive a tent stake into the ground. With a brick. The hammer that came with the tent was apparently too flimsy to even dent the stony ground, and it now lies lazily behind the volunteer. The volunteer is a university student, accustomed only to the slim handle of pencils as thick as 6B; nonetheless, he holds a grey cement industrial brick in his right hand, repeatedly trying to slam the wire peg into the ground.

I shift my focus from the unsuccessful construction project to my father, who now stands next to me at the power box—literally a box full of electricity that sits on a metal stick. Each year, we erect it solely for the duration of our film festival. The box is open, its small aluminum door held in my father's grasp. Inside are six outlets, four already filled.

In my hand, I hold the black plug of our extension cord.

"We need light!" I say, trying to mask my desperation.

My father's teeth meet in his mouth. Then, with the intertwined pride and caution of a politician, he says, "If we have outlets left over after we're done setting up, they're yours." He pushes the end of his own extension cord into the fifth outlet and closes the cover. After a last glance that is almost a glare, he turns swiftly back to the trailer.

The trailer's backdrop is the swollen inland sea, along with all of the elegant brushstrokes and various shades that nature has chosen for this exact moment and time of day. It squats like a bull upon the open field, watching the chaos that my family has triggered around it.

An industrial "lamp" (as if it were that elegant) lights up the trailer, eating up volts of our energy and illuminating the bee-like figures of my parents, who buzz around in opposite directions.

I walk back to the ticket "booth," my now-worn flats not quite protecting my legs from the impact of the gravelly ground.

The volunteers milling around at the reception desk all look at me expectantly, waiting for light or guidance. I weigh my options. Do I absolve myself by acting annoyed with my parents, to whom the volunteers have supposedly given their loyalty? I know they might betray the festival the first chance they get. If I complain, won't I be committing a heinous crime, creating a potential revolution?

The last crescents of sun give one final peek over the hill before disappearing. Wordlessly, I reach into the plastic supplies box, pull out a small, battery-operated lamp, and attach it to the edge of the tent. But I fumble and fail to secure it; the clamp won't stay put.

I pause my dramatic life-or-death circumstances and look over to the volunteers once more—only to find their disinterested faces lit up by their smartphone and digital camera screens.

We later sit civilly at the table under the tent and sell the blue tickets, ripping their stubs by feeling for their perforated seams (and failing). We clumsily hand the stubs back to the customers as they glance around like suspicious murderers, trying to find partners-in-crime in the open darkness.

CHANNELIN' MY UNBORN SON

ANNE FEIGUS

Motherhood was a new world, which I entered at the age of forty-eight when my son (now almost seventeen) was born. As Rayhana and I shared stories about our respective families, I remembered the joy (and fear) of impending motherhood.

 *Maarouf, p. 83*

 *p. 47*

Hey, you in there! Don't you know it's nighttime? You just woke me out of a sound sleep with that mighty kick to my ribs. Have mercy on your mama, please! But, I forgive you. I know it's gettin' harder and harder to move around in such a cramped space. My belly is growin' by the day now, like you are. A few months ago, you were doin' a lot of swimmin'—like a happy porpoise. Sometimes, when you did one of your flips, my naked belly bulged up on one side and then on the other. I loved to watch that trick, 'cause I knew you were gettin' your exercise and preparin' to show yourself to me and the world. Even though we can't see each other yet, I feel your presence twenty-four-seven, and I'm beamin' you lasers of love every minute of every day. I talk to you out loud because I want you to recognize the sound of your mama's voice. I also play a lot of music for you. No highfalutin' stuff like that Baby Mozart for my son. You're gonna be a country and western guy. And I'm an older mom so I've been playin' a lot of Kathie Mattea and Tanya Tucker. They sing about real life and the struggles of real people, stuff you'll need to know as you're growin' up. I'm sorry to say that your daddy is long gone. He was a lot of fun and a sexy dude, but he ran away from responsibility faster than a racecar at a speedway. Don' worry, though. We won't need him, 'cause we got lotsa other family—Grandma Bess, Grandpa Sam, and a passel of aunts, uncles, and cousins. The whole gang already adores you. So, little guy, know how much love awaits you the moment you pop outta your mama! In the meantime, rest up. You've got a challengin' journey ahead. But, I promise you with all my heart, it'll be worth it!

MY MOTHER'S HANDS
GILLIAN REAGAN

 *Miah, p. 86*

 *p. 52*

My mother's hands are knobby, like tree roots, like her mother's. Her fingers are stumps, grooved with wounds from digging in soil, mending fences, dog bites. In the winter, her hands peel in layers and molt. Thick shards of skin hang from the chicken wing between her thumb and pointer finger. She uses heavy moisturizers, rubbing cream over the valleys of her finger bones in a nightly ritual. But synthetics are too weak to heal her skin back together. Sometimes in the truck, when she's nervous and driving, she nibbles at her hands, opening the wounds wider and rawer. She rips off pieces of herself and spits them out the window onto the countryside. When I was little, I thought they were seeds that would grow into a rainbow, a weed, another hand. I wanted to jump out of the truck and dig through the dirt to find the pieces and keep them in a jar. Pieces of my mother. Someday I'd bury them in my own backyard. What would grow there?

TINY
CARMIN WONG

 *Sheerazi, p. 146*

 *p. 73*

Tiny. That's what almost everyone calls him and all I've ever heard since I was born. It was either that or "Uncle Chief," or some other crazy name. I don't think people even know his real name is Claxton. Or maybe they do, but I've heard "Tiny" all my life. I guess I figured I'd call him that as well. The word "daddy" seemed like something stuck in my throat. I wonder if he feels just as awkward hearing it. I've tried saying it before, but that was only because my nosey family members thought it seemed impolite that I didn't call my dad daddy. But my two sisters and I agree that it's none of their business. And apparently my dad must agree, too, because he's never questioned us about it or forced us to say it, either. I like that, because to be honest, if anyone else asked, I'd tell them to call him Tiny, too.

My father was born in Berbice, Guyana, which always made me wonder how he met my mom, since she was born in another part of Guyana—Essequibo Coast, to be exact. I'd ask him, but the answer always stayed the same: "Go ask your mom." And my mom, she's no help, either. I don't know why they're so secretive.

Was it just how they were taught growing up? It used to be frustrating. Now the only thing that frustrates me is explaining to people why I have no clue when my parents met or anything about their lives before I was born. Do they think my sisters and I are too young to understand? That doesn't make sense. It's just something I could never fathom. I gave up years ago.

When I was growing up, my father was always on my sisters and me to do well in school and always wanted to know where we were going at all times. It was so annoying. I was jealous of my twelve-year-old friends, who got to party every Saturday night and go outside after eleven. My father was the type to hold your hand when crossing the street and walk you all the way to the school's front door. That's how my friends got to know him. More than anything it was embarrassing. I could never tell if he knew that and just didn't care, or if he really had no idea. I dreaded my pre-teenage life.

In my sixteen years of living, I have never seen that man shed a tear. He was sad when his mother died. Really, really sad. But that was about it. My grandfather passed away a few years later, but that still didn't make a difference. In fact, if he even heard me use the words "passed away," there would be a World War III. But that's my dad for you. "Say it like it is. When you die you're dead," he often says, correcting news reporters on television. I never asked why. For sure, he is a straightforward guy.

However, one thing I've seemed to inherit from my dad is his optimism. He always told me he'd take me back home to feel firsthand what it's like to be in a rainforest. I always smiled when he said that. Then I'd agree and tell him I'd take him to China when I got older and began making money. One summer he even agreed to take me to Niagara Falls. I was so excited. Then the van broke down and we ended up staying home. I was a little upset, but I knew it wasn't his fault. I would have asked about it, but I knew my dad would make the answer brief and blunt as always. I wasn't mad at him that summer, either.

I always knew God had a plan. I think it's safe to say my father knows it too. He took me to church every Sunday. He encouraged me to get involved. I've been an acolyte since I was younger and everyone knows me, though I didn't always like to talk. My dad knew that and never said a word about it when others mentioned it to him. He even encourages me with my writing more than anything. It's nice to have a support system.

It's taken me much of my life to figure out my dad, a line I've often heard people say about me. However, one thing I've learned from him is that love is indefinable. It's something that you must feel for yourself to understand. I love my dad—the same man who has never shown me tears, but has never been afraid to hug me tightly and tell me how much he loves me while we sit and watch movies together. Now I simply refer to his personality as Taurism: the state of being an undeniable Taurus. But I'm a Taurus, too, so I guess it's safe to say I kind of understand the misunderstood of my kind. Or only my dad, and I love him just the same.

TWINSIES
RORY SATRAN

 *Kerina-Rendina, p. 135*

 *p. 62*

The story of Samantha and Anais came to me, like so many others, through the Internet. Probably while I was procrastinating at work. Going from blog to blog as I sipped a late-afternoon iced coffee, taking a self-imposed break. In a nutshell: French fashion student Anais came across a YouTube video of an American actress, Samantha. They were identical. Just like twin sisters.

In fact, they are sisters. Through Skype, chat, Twitter, and Facebook, the girls learned that they had been born on the same day in South Korea and separated at birth. And now they are raising funds through Kickstarter to make a documentary about their story and their first meeting.

It's a modern-day *Parent Trap*. No other narrative obsessed me more as a kid (except, possibly, *Troop Beverly Hills*). The Hayley Mills version, not the pre-breakdown Lindsay Lohan version. Yeah, I'm aging myself. I watched it on VHS.

Why do girls fantasize about having a twin sister? A long-lost other who looks exactly like us? It's pretty creepy, when you think about it. There are probably a million psychoanalytic theories for why we want a double, and to be honest, I'd rather not know them. Likely quite twisted.

I saw my doppelgänger once. We had that weird moment of recognition, staring at each other in the middle of Houston Street. Instead of letting the moment fade into mystery, I blurted out awkwardly, "We could be sisters!" She kept walking.

OUR FATHERS
MARY PAT KANE

 *Ortiz, p. 248*

 *p. 56*

Protective: My father was very protective of me, too much so, I thought. Once when I was in my late twenties and living away in a big city by myself, I came home to visit and was crossing the street to our house when my dad ran out onto the porch frantically waving his arms, directing me to wait, worried there was a car like maybe eight blocks away. I was embarrassed.

There are times now I would so welcome someone caring about getting me safely across the street to them.

Affection/Buddy: My dad took me out of school sometimes to go with him on his "rounds." He worked in want ads—the classified ads for the local newspaper. You'd think he was the editor, the way he loved that paper. We would drive out of the city to small towns and rural areas, chatting away. Whenever we entered an establishment, say, a tractor dealership, everyone would just light up and get real excited and holler out to him, "Hey, Ollie, where've you been, good to see you!" And they'd come running toward him.

It felt so good to be with a man who made people happy just by walking in the door.

Problems: My dad worked in the want ads for many years and after so long, his boss was finally going to retire. My dad assumed he would become the manager of the department. He had, in effect, been doing the job for years. He was real excited. When the new "big guys" who had just purchased the paper called him "upstairs," they told him that they had hired a young man to be manager of the department. He had a "degree" from college. "We love you Ollie, you know that, and we can't be without you. Ooooollie, don't you even think of quitting! We need you to train him."

My father's heart was broken and it never mended. He loved that newspaper and his job. His dignity and his pride were so hurt. Oh, I remember being so mad at those people, and, to tell you the truth, I still am.

Model: My dad would cook huge meals for us. He loved nothing better than feeding a group. When I walked down the street with him, people would come up and tell him the story of their lives. I'd find out later that he often had never seen them before.

My father is not my hero, like my mentee's father is to her. He was more my colleague, my buddy, and, mostly, the person who gave me my values—consideration (I hope), generosity, honesty, faithfulness, love of animals and people, and, most of all, laughter. I can still hear his wonderful laugh.

Happy Father's Day, Ollie Kane, and thank you always.

SNAKES
CHRISTY POTTROFF

 *Bean, p. 110*

 *p. 10*

On the farm, I found snakes under my swing set. Snakes in the dog food barrel. Snakes in the garage. Because I was a kid, I could run. I could cry out. I knew my mother would save me. When she heard me shriek "S-sssnake!" she would grab the hoe by the back door and march toward the beast. Off with their heads!

Usually, I would run into the house and sit quietly on the brown-pilled couch until my mom came back inside. But once, when I was five and feeling particularly intrepid, I followed her to the kill. I watched her raise the hoe above the snake's head. She was barely breathing. It used its tongue to test the air. Suddenly, with unexpected force, my mom brought the blade down. The snake danced violently in the grass. It whipped and coiled from the tip of its tail to the point where it was pinned to the ground. Only when the snake stopped moving did my mother lift the hoe and take another stiff whack. She detached the head completely, scooped it up with the blade and tossed it on the burn pile. It rattled off the tree branches like a Plinko chip as it fell. She left the snake's body for our dog, Suzie.

"Dogs can use the protein," my mother explained. She was a dietician. She knew about these things.

Later that afternoon, I slipped outside and stood by the hoe. I leaned against the wall and looked at the wooden handle looming above my head. I pulled it over to my face. It smelled rich and sweet like sweat and old death.

I lowered the handle onto the concrete and sat next to it. There was still blood on the blade. I put my hand on the rough, warm surface and traced the blade from tip to tip. There was blood and grass and dirt on my hand when I pulled it away. Not wanting to waste it, I smeared the red across the bottom of our back door as a warning: we are protected by mother-goddess.

***

Soon after, we moved to town and my other-worldly mother was subsumed by a heavenly father. I would stand in church with shoes too tight and sing glory, glory, hallelujah. There were hymns of God crushing serpents to protect his children, but my mother could make blood for hers.

The hoe was in the basement and I started dreaming about snakes. They would slink in at night and curl around my feet. They would squeeze me and break my bones. Their teeth would plunge into my flesh. God's heel did not crush them, even when I cried out.

My mother never killed another snake, but the hoe was just below our feet. And every time we would sing or read or pray about God's destruction of the serpent, my mind would return to the days when my mother would march into the wilderness and slay snakes for me.

STILL LIFE
AMY S. CHOI

M Herbert, p. 220
P p. 36

Light spills across the windowsill
Inching longer across the blond wood
About to touch our intertwined feet
Dangling in this puddle of warmth.

If the light stood still
What would we miss?
I wish nothing more than to remain here with you
Before we are lost to age and tiredness.

Yet here is the ticking inside of me
Promising another kind of light
Expansive
Striping across the days unbroken
Without a closing dusk,
Or so it seems.

DAUGHTER'S LITANY
SWATI BARUA

The inspiration for this poem came when my mom fell asleep and our quiet breathing matched. As I watched her, the sentence fragment "living and breathing as the same entity" came to my head, and writing the poem ensued from that.

M Barlament, p. 224
P p. 9

Our breath mixes
Fast and furious
When the fire in our chest
Breathes and brews writhes
curls and unfurls
Into a living breathing entity
That fires through our mouth, our eyes,
our hands

And hurts our tender hearts.

So when our breath matches
Slow and deep
Know our breaths.

While you sleep
Forgive and forget
everything
I have done you wrong for
Everything will
Collide and collapse

When our breath comes as one.
In this moment of clarity let it
last
When we are in harmony
Will shatter
Our words wounds inflicted
And heal
Every bond every wrong
I have done to you
So let it last
Let it last.

TOLERANCE FOR FLIES
LINDA CORMAN

This piece grew out of the family memoir exercise in which we considered a family memory from past and current perspectives. Each time I reflect on my brother's life, I have new realizations about what happened and its impact on me.

 Swift, p. 195
 p. 68

At the time, I thought my brother was being just a little more thin-skinned than I, and a little less obedient.

Our parents were sipping rum punches at the white-clothed tables in the open air restaurant of the Caribbean resort, where we were spending February vacation in 1960.

My brother, writhing in his seat at the table, slapped at the large black flies that had been swarming us since we'd arrived. Despite our parents' angry demands that he remain at the table, my brother, in a crescendoing frenzy, periodically charged out of the restaurant in search of temporary relief from the swarming bugs.

A waiter drew back, protectively cradling his tray.

"Shall I still bring the milk?"

I detested the nasty, biting flies, and I yearned to flee them just as my brother did. But I was determined not to. It was far more important to win my parents' approval and be considered well-behaved by the other guests, waiters, and management than to escape the discomfort.

At the time, it was a little frightening to me that my brother was willing to brave everyone's low opinion; I was afraid, perhaps, that his behavior would reflect badly on me. I was embarrassed, too, that he was complaining about flies during our lavish vacation.

Now, fifty years later, I see my brother's fleeing from the table as a preview of all that followed—his running away from home, his immersion in drugs, his extravagant descent into schizophrenia.

I wonder if his intolerance for the flies wasn't a display of ordinary thin-skinnedness, but an early manifestation of the extreme innate sensibilities that ultimately made it impossible for him to bow to any convention, sensibilities that hurled him into a boundary-less world in which he became ever more unhinged, and which inevitably led to his clashing and increasing misfortune with the demands of living in this one.

FROM DIRT ROADS TO THE CONCRETE JUNGLE

SADE SWIFT

Corman, p. 194

p. 68

I was all dolled up and ready to go watch Transformers. A couple of my friends had invited me, after a long week of work and sleepless nights, to go out and just have some fun. I told my grandmother this but she responded with her usual bitter, no-fun-having answer: "Why are you going to the movies? Don't you have homework to do or something?" At the time, I was annoyed and didn't question her typical response.

One day I sat down and started to wonder what the root of her reactions was. So I decided to ask, "Porque es que nunca me quiere dejar salir?" (Why is it that you never want to let me go out?) What followed surprised me. "Siéntate, dejame decirte una historia," she said. (Sit down, let me tell you a story.) We sat on the couch as she drank her milk with her sweet plantains, crossed her legs, and began.

"When I was twelve years old, my father used to take me out of school early to work in his field, where our four-story house was built. He used to tell me that I didn't need school because it was stupid, and all I should look forward to was getting married into a rich family, but I couldn't disagree more. I loved school and I loved learning new, different concepts. My days revolved around helping my mother in the house and splitting errands with my fourteen brothers and sisters. I remember that my brothers slept on the third floor, my sisters and I on the second, and my parents on the first. Out of all my siblings, I was the only one who cared about school and actually wanted to progress in my education; I just didn't know how. Every time I told my mom, she laughed at me and told me to finish whatever I was doing.

"In the years to come I started to hear about opportunities in America and I thought to myself, Maybe that's what I'll do to get an education. At age eighteen, I knew I wanted to be a lawyer or an engineer, but I knew my parents wouldn't allow it, even though I was old enough to make my own decisions. I loved math and I loved to problem-solve so it was either or—I didn't care which. I got a job and started saving. I hid my money in cocoa leaves and wrapped it with a string of hay, and put it under my bed. Five years went by and I finally saved up enough money to buy my flight. I knew I couldn't buy it in my town because my father was a wealthy, well-known man, and whatever my siblings and I did, he knew about it. So I had to plan a trip to the next town, to visit my cousin and buy my flight there. On a hot August night I went and bought my ticket and planned for the new life I was about to take on in New York City. I decided not to tell anyone, because I didn't want anyone to stop me or hold me back from pursuing something I wanted.

"The day I was leaving, my parents thought I was going to visit my cousin again, but instead I took that taxi straight to the airport and awaited my flight. I didn't know what to expect and that scared me. I had to fight, save, and hide so much to get here. When I reached New York, I stayed at motels and was homeless for a while, but I eventually found a job and a place to stay, saved money, and got my own place. Years later I brought your grandfather here, and so it went. My journey here was hard but finding my bearing around New York City was much harder than I thought it would be, because I didn't know the language and had to make ends meet. It's not that I don't have fun; rather, it's that I still feel that I owe my family something, or have something to prove. They disowned me and felt betrayed because I was following my dream. I want you to follow your dream and get your education, because at one point that wasn't an option."

I now understood her journey and the hardships she went through. For the sake of the dream she has for me, I feel I have to get an education and fight for those things that others think I shouldn't have. Her bitter, no-fun-having responses finally made sense.

courage

I CAN'T STOP NOW

> *Her muscles protested every time she picked up her journey-weary legs. I can't stop now. I have to continue.*
>
> *Samantha Young Chan, p. 198*

Although fears can vary widely—and wildly—overcoming them requires the same qualities: bravery, determination, persistence. Whether fearing depression, zombies, college, or the unrelenting ability to read minds, the women in this chapter dare to take the next step. Sometimes they move toward the fear. Sometimes they back off to recover their energy for another day. But they keep moving.

> *Entering a new world is most likely going to bring fears and uncertainty. We may all have an idea of where our lives should go and what we should be doing, but sometimes life has an entirely different plan for us. During those times I felt completely lost, but I continued to follow my passion, and it never guided me in the wrong direction. So when the time comes to proudly toss your hat in the air, it's best not to worry where it may land.*
>
> *Ashley Rose Howard, p. 201*

WENDY CASTER
2013 MENTOR AND
ANTHOLOGY COMMITTEE MEMBER

TOWARDS THE LIGHT

SAMANTHA YOUNG CHAN

This girl's determination to find a village that was only a legend to her opened up a whole entire world of possibilities.

 *Berg, p. 165*

 *p. 18*

Legend has it that the neighboring forest, which stretches on for miles, houses a mysterious village in the center that has existed since the beginning of time. However, no one's ever found it.

Her small fingers stroked the gilded words on the page and ran over the sketch of the village. She was determined to find it...eventually.

***

She had been wandering in the forest for hours; her footsteps against the snow were the only sounds she heard. The spindly trees reached toward her, scratching at her coat and catching in her hair. She was tired. It felt like she had been walking for years. Her legs ached, her hair was a mess, and more than once she felt like turning back. She wasn't getting any closer to the center of the forest and didn't think she would until the next morning, at the rate she was going.

She dug into her coat pocket and pulled out her map. It was creased and ripped at the edges; some of the words were rubbing off from being wet. She sighed and shoved the map back; there were five landmarks she should have passed by now, but she hadn't seen even one. It was official: she was hopelessly lost.

Her footprints were no longer distinguishable in the snow; it looked like something heavy was being dragged behind her. The sun had begun to sink. It was a blazing orange globe that mingled with the branches of the trees, beckoning her to keep moving and chase it. "But I'm so tired," she half mumbled, half whined. A thought flickered in her mind: Talking to yourself is the first sign of insanity. She shook her head, clearing her mind, and trudged on.

Although the temperature was dropping as the day wore on, she grew hotter and hotter. She hadn't stopped since starting her journey and she felt like her puffy jacket was strangling her. She threw her backpack on the ground and unzipped her jacket, throwing it over her shoulder as she slung her backpack back on. Her heavy breathing came out in white puffs as she continued to move.

It was nighttime. The branches blocked the dim moonlight and she had to grope her way through the forest. Cuts and splinters adorned her palms from clutching the tree trunks. Her muscles protested every time she picked up her journey-weary legs. I can't stop now. I have to continue. As she moved forward, a branch nearby snapped. She jumped and unconsciously hurried forward. Her foot caught on a root, and she fell face-first into the blanket of snow. As the snow covered her,

hopelessness washed over her as she slowly closed her eyes, giving up on her journey altogether.

She woke to the bright sunlight on her face and the sweet chirping of birds. As she pushed herself up from the snow, her gaze fell on a small opening in the trees. Her heartbeat pounded in her ears as she slowly made her way to the opening. As she pushed aside the branches, she gasped: in front of her was a large clearing with a rustic village nestled in the middle. The sketch of the village from the book of myths from her childhood flashed quickly in her mind as she stepped out and into the sunlight.

ON HAPPINESS, TOGGLE SWITCHES, FERRETS, AND FEAR

LUCIANA LOPEZ

Ariana and I have both had to deal with depression in our lives, albeit in different ways. I'm constantly inspired by how much she cares about the people in her life and how much she supports them, no matter what they're going through.

Spatola, p. 158

p. 67

At the age of thirty-seven I've come to the conclusion that happiness is a skill—one that has largely eluded me. Or maybe it's fairer to say that I've eluded it, because I have plenty of reasons to be happy and yet can't seem to bring myself there. For a long time, I thought people were either happy or not, that happiness was a sort of toggle switch that got flipped in us at birth and stayed that way forever. And I just assumed that my switch got set to depressed, and that that was my genetic lot in life, along with frizzy black hair and an overbite that took years of braces to fix. Some people make great casseroles. Some people have a great jump shot. Some people are happy. Me? I make delicious brussels sprouts, if I may be so bold.

But sadness. Wow. Exhausting. It wrings me out. When I'm down in it, I feel like sleep is the only place I can feel light enough to move. The real world becomes the shadow, and yet I still feel too weak to do much. I hate the phrase "struggle with depression," because it makes it sound like depression is an unwieldy carry-on that I'm trying to stuff into an airplane overhead bin. And anyway, that implies that there's a struggle, and sometimes—far too often—that's just not the case.

Well, forget that. Babies can be happy. My boyfriend's ferret goes insane with joy playing with an old slipper. Trees probably do it on sunny days or when they get to eat kites or something. I figure if they can do it, so can I. It's just going to take some trial and error, some experimentation, some practice.

Sometimes I feel my sadness whirring in my skull like a panicked bird, beating its wings bloody against the inside of my head. I want to still that bird. I want to take it in my hands, feel its tiny heart slow, feel its wings fold and its feathers be still against my fingers. I want to hold this frightened bird until its fear passes and its eyes close and it knows how to be quiet again. I'm not sure how to do this. I'm not sure what learning happiness even means. But I think I have to do this.

COLLEGE: A NEW WORLD

KAYTLIN CARLO

Howard, p. 201

p. 17

As a sixteen-year-old junior at Pace High School, the idea of college seems to saturate my thoughts. This is understandable, as I will be applying to colleges in about seven months. I've also had a lot of time to think about my future and where I want to be in twenty years. I have come to realize that high school graduation is quickly approaching and I will be embarking on a whole new experience: college. The thought of college is scary yet exciting. High school and college are two different worlds with two different auras and cosmos. Overall, the new world that I will be sharing my views on is college.

As a young girl I often fantasized about college and how lively it would be. I remember watching *Van Wilder* and *Accepted* and thinking how wonderful it would be to live in a dorm in a huge university with a massive student population, and meet amazing girlfriends that I would know until my children had children. Looking back, I can see that my life will probably not turn out as I had hoped it would. There is no doubt that I still want to meet amazing people and do adventurous things, but what I ultimately want is a school that will benefit me the most for what I want to do with my life. I want to be able to have fun and learn at the same time. I hope my learning will extend beyond textbook pages and lecture halls. The scariest thought for me is coming into a whole new environment and not knowing anybody. Another thing that I find daunting is the work that I will have to complete for my classes. This is scary because in college, I may have more responsibilities than I realize.

Though I have all these fears and dreams, I know that there are many people in my life who will make the college process less terrifying. One of these people is my mentor, Ashley. Ashley is really supportive of my dreams and she truly understands the type of person that I am. During my time with Ashley this year in Girls Write Now, I have grown to be at ease with the idea of college and what it will bring me. Another person who will help me through this time of confusion, wonder, and excitement is my mother. My mother always encourages me to improve on areas of my schoolwork and is always willing to give me advice on anything.

College is a time for exploration, fun, and personal growth. Though college may be a new experience for me, I know my fears will soon subside, and I will ultimately have a good time learning about my writing and myself. I am so excited to embark on this chapter in the book of life.

WHAT'S NEXT?

ASHLEY HOWARD

Carlo, p. 200

p. 17

The crowd is cheering. People are hugging. Everyone tosses their hats into the air and celebrates another successful graduating class. "We did it!" Now what?

No one can really prepare you for the next chapter of life post-college graduation. Your peers warn you and your parents try to prepare you, but nothing is scarier than the idea of entering the "real world."

I'll be the first one to admit it: I was lost. College was over and I had to start putting my journalism degree to use in order to pay back my school loans. None of my professors were there to hold my hand and there was certainly no graduate handbook titled, What's Next? So, what did I do? I got a job.

While I dreamed about graduating from college and moving to New York City to become a big-time magazine editor, reality looked more like an unpaid internship at a regional New Jersey magazine. I was working nine to five and bartending nights to pay my rent. This new reality of hard work and responsibility was certainly an adjustment from afternoon naps and dorm room parties.

The transition from graduation to "working citizen" took some getting used to, but I realized that living outside my comfort zone helped me grow. That first internship turned into an amazing experience working with some of the most respected editors in the publishing world. And those same editors encouraged me to move to Manhattan and become something bigger. Moving to Manhattan helped me manifest the connections that molded me into a successful writer. And becoming a successful writer led me to start mentoring other aspiring writers who may be as lost as I once was.

Entering a new world is most likely going to bring fears and uncertainty. We may all have an idea of where our lives should go and what we should be doing, but sometimes life has an entirely different plan for us. During those times I felt completely lost, I continued to follow my passion, and it never guided me in the wrong direction. So when the time comes to proudly toss your hat in the air, it's best not to worry where it may land.

AN ODE TO PORT JEFFERSON

JODI NARDE

I blended a nonfiction piece into poetry using images from the novel Bridge to Terabithia, *a story about the discovery of a new (and imaginary) world.*

 *K. Daniels, p. 273*

 *p. 26*

in a port town
on a long and lonely island,
we find the beach,
and start.

high tide creates obstacles,
a tight rope balance of brush and wood,
and i can't stop thinking,
this is the bridge to terabithia.

we are children, extraordinary ones,
you with the weighty backpack,
and me, with my shirt around my neck,
looks of elementary determination.

there at last, we stand
bare and bended arm
shoulder-to-shoulder, sandy fist,
my fingers finding refuge in your elbow's
fleshy crook.

THE HUNT
HEIDI OVERBECK

 Dosso, p. 130

 p. 30

It is the quiet of the wood, not
the string slicing flesh from
her finger, that so disarms her.

She had breathed recklessly,
once, before the breath caught
in her throat like a blood clot
that had not bloomed red yet,
that could only wither brown.

A bent bow is no defense
against the sudden rupture
of silence—it breaks her
heart, blurs her vision, makes
her drawn arm quake and
let the arrow loose into the
hollow space that's stalking her.

SECONDS TO MIDNIGHT
KARILIS CRUZ

The meaning of new worlds for me is discovering new possibilities and uncovering what is in front of you. I created a whole new supernatural world for the main character in this piece.

 Faye, p. 204

 p. 24

Running through the forest isn't what you want to do in a dress and heels. The dress was flowing out, getting torn by all of the branches; I already knew my hair was a mess.

I thought to myself: *My night is ruined; I wonder if anybody has noticed I'm gone. Probably not. What am I running from again?*

I stopped in my tracks… I looked around. There was no movement, just the accompaniment of my heavy breathing. I slipped off my heels; I heard small but faint footsteps. I slid off the log I was standing on, with my heart going miles away from me.

A figure came out into the moonlight… I held my breath as the girl from the news—missing for three weeks now—emerged in the red bathing suit she was wearing at the lake when she was last seen. She was only ten years old, the last time anybody saw her. She walked slowly toward me like a panther approaching its prey.

I stayed frozen in place; she slowly raised her finger to her lips and made a shushing gesture.

I started to panic.

She noticed and launched herself at me, baring big canine teeth. I screamed as her teeth entered my shoulder. I continued to shout for help, pleading for her to stop while watching an innocent transform into an animal right before my very eyes. I tried to get free but sharp painful teeth kept me in place, holding me to the ground.

She—no, it!—lifted its head from my shoulder, looking at something beyond me... I took my chances fumbling for a rock and used all my strength to jag the rock into its face, knocking it off at least a little. I started running but then there were claws in my back pulling or dragging me on the dirt ground. I tasted dirt and blood at the same time. I started to have an overwhelming feeling of nausea and suffocation.

I can't breathe; I can't scream! I felt the claws come out of my back then strike again, sending a new flash of pain through my body. Then all at once the claws returned and I heard a pain-filled cry from the horrible creature that was ripping into me.

I saw white lights cross my vision; big hands turned me over. *I can't see—is it 'cause my eyes are closed, are they closed? Please tell me I'm not going to die.*

Probably I already have...

BLOOD RED APPETITES

LYNDSAY FAYE

When I read Seconds to Midnight, *I was fascinated by the young girl turned monster, and I wanted to explore the same world from her perspective. So I asked Karilis if I could borrow her and this is the result.*

M *Cruz, p. 203*

P *p. 24*

She doesn't remember
doesn't
regret
the life she left behind, the way she lived before, a little girl with a big sister and a mom and a dad who all went to the movies together and sometimes made banana floats for dinner and liked sitting on the porch in the evening
sipping lemonade and watching the stray cats do battle in the front yard.

She walks through the woods wearing only her red bathing suit and thinks nothing
beyond
hungry

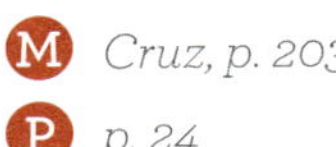

hungry
hungry
and can't recall when human flesh began to
taste like the sweetest red summer apples.

When a week has passed, she
no longer looks at her razor claws
and feels as if they belong on
another
creature
no longer feels fear when she sees her own
bone-white teeth reflected in the surface of
forest ponds
or worries when the teeth cut her lip inside
her mouth and the blood drips like slow
nectar

hungry
cold
alone

After the lake has frosted over with sharp
winter ice
and the birds
fly away south looking for warmth on their
feathers and their small knifelike beaks
she will still
feel hunger
and the pull of the lake
which has become mother father sister now
that the rippling reflections of
her former family
have faded away from its surface
entirely

THE LIVING DEAD

LAWRENCIA TERRIS

 *Werner, p. 225*

 *p. 69*

The grass crunched under my heavy black combat boots. The blazing hot sun reflected heat off my brown skin. There was a slight buzz coming from the electricity running through the fence. I had been constantly surrounded by the sound of gunshots so this was nice, the silence.

I was too hot and too tired.

Tired from walking, and holding a gun, ready to fire and shoot at any given moment. I was tired of waiting to see who the next person to turn would be. I was tired of wondering where my mother and father were and if they were alive. I was tired of calculating when my time to go would come.

I heard the clamorous groan of the walkers from the other side of the town's electric fence. In the beginning, I had felt bad for the zombies. They were people too and it wasn't their choice to turn into flesh-eating monsters. It's safe to say I don't thrive on emotion anymore. Daryl taught me that.

I remember when I first met him. The troops assured us that the disease wouldn't make its way to the Northeast. That was a lie. The disease spread through the country like wildfire and I ran to the woods. After falling asleep on a bed of leaves that I made, and deciding that death might not be so bad, I woke up with a man poking my sides with a stick. His face was friendly. He had brown hair, blue eyes, and a bright smile.

Famished and weak, I wasn't able to walk. After introducing himself as Daryl and promising that he wouldn't hurt me, Daryl picked me up and carried me to a prison with other survivors. Struck with awe, I couldn't believe other people were alive. The temporary feeling of happiness soon left when I started to think about my parents. Daryl sat with me while I cried. He didn't hug me or anything because he didn't know how to handle a crying sixteen-year-old girl.

"You have to stop all that crying, little girl," he finally said one day. "Crying is a sign of weakness and if you keep going with the waterworks, the walkers and the survivors are going to eat you alive."

I wiped the tears from my eyes fiercely. I was angry. Why was this man telling me to stop crying? I had every right to cry! Then, I realized that he was right. I shouldn't cry because it wasn't going to make any of this go away. I wasn't Dorothy, this wasn't Oz, and clicking my Chuck Taylors together wasn't going to make all of this disappear.

The zombie apocalypse isn't something anyone saw coming. Yeah, sure, some people thought it would happen but only because they read too many comics.

This, what was happening right now...would've never been seen as reality.

Everyone in the town had a different opinion about what was happening and when it would stop. The elders kept hope alive, repeating to themselves, "It will be okay." Others thought they would die before the end of the apocalypse came. The rest left their fate in the hands of God.

God.

What happened to my religion? I didn't pray anymore or even think about God until someone mentioned religion. I used to go with my parents to church every weekend. Maybe I still believe and maybe I don't. God could have stopped this from happening, but he didn't. So I wasn't going to rely on him to stop it now.

"The walkers penetrated through the fence! Everyone get your weapons ready!"

Once again, I was surrounded by the sound of gunshots. The cold steel gun in my hand felt like a second skin and I walked around looking for zombies to kill. Sometimes, I would pretend I was playing a video game and I wouldn't feel so bad. After leaping over some steps, I approached a zombie. With my head cocked to the side, I pointed my gun right at the female's head and set off the explosion to her brain.

REVERSED

TESSA LEE-THOMAS

Scheiner, p. 209

p. 70

Jewel was such a sweet kid, always worrying about Kya and the things that were going on. When she got to him, he asked her in the sweetest voice, "Kaka?" (That's what he called her.) "Are we going to be all right?"

"Yes, Jewel, the trouble has passed; we are going to be all right!"

"Okay, Kaka. I love you."

"I love you too, Jewel."

Kya returned to her room and tucked herself under the covers and went to sleep, preparing herself with rest for the next day.

When Kya woke up the next morning, things felt different. She was still in the same room and the sun was shining, but there was something totally unusual. The house was quiet. When you live with four siblings and your parents, life is never quiet. No one was home. Kya thought that maybe everyone had left without waking her. She went back upstairs and entered the bathroom off the upstairs hallway. Kya looked into the mirror and was shocked to see that she looked a few years older. Her face looked more defined, her eyes more almond shaped than before, and her cheeks slightly slimmer as if she had lost weight in her sleep. She screamed so loud that a small crack appeared in the mirror: *"Oh my God, what is happening?"*

Kya ran to her room and pulled out her ID. It still showed her birth date as January 23, 2013. Kya didn't understand what was going on. She was still herself, but she looked older.

It seemed like something bad had happened. Like losing something but not knowing what it was. It was one of those feelings.

Kya sat on the side of the bed, looking out her window at all the people rushing and bustling past. Kya knew that the same people didn't walk past her house all the time, but this group looked strange. There was something off with their presence. They looked like her, confused and worried. Kya turned on her television, hoping that there would be an explanation for the events that were happening.

On the TV, a news reporter was in the middle of her report: *"Due to the planets' aligning, time is moving faster than usual. Researchers and scientists are trying to figure what can be done to reverse the effects. Stay tuned for more information after these commercials."*

Kya dropped the remote. She couldn't believe what she was hearing. How could time be speeding up so fast? What was going to be done to prevent the time from forwarding? Kya went into her closet and pulled out some clothes and quickly threw them on. She wanted to see how the rest of the world was coping with the news that time had sped up.

She saw that the city was full of chaos and people were moving quicker than usual. Some people sat on the edge of the curb, looking into convenient handheld mirrors, perplexed by the images that were reflected back at them. Kya walked through the streets, making her way to the college where her mother worked. When she arrived, all seemed quiet and deserted. She walked to her mother's office. The name on the door read Harold Jones. Kya went in anyway and found her mom sitting behind her desk, hair long and gray, bags under her eyes so it looked as if she hadn't slept in days.

"Mom, why is your name not on the door?" Kya asked.

Her mother looked up, surprised. "Kya, baby. I don't know."

"Mom, are you okay? Where is everybody? I woke up this morning and everyone was gone. Where are they?"

"The kids should be in school, but I don't know where Daddy is."

"What do you mean?"

"When I woke up, he wasn't there."

Kya could feel her heart stop and then begin to speed up a little faster. Where can my father be? Everything was changing.

"Ma, we need to find Daddy. I'm going to go get the kids and bring them home. Please meet us there."

"Okay, Kya."

Kya ran out of the building as fast as she could, going to Cirus High School to get her sister Kyra. When she walked into the building, nothing looked any different from the days when she had attended. She strolled into the main office.

"I'm looking for Kyra Middleton."

The lady behind the desk went to the PA system and made an announcement.

"Kyra M. please report to the main office."

Within ten minutes, a thin teenage girl wandered into the office wearing a miniskirt just covering her behind and a top that looked small enough for a toddler to wear.

"Kyra, what are you wearing?"

"Kya, all my clothes are too little for me—just the other day I was twelve."

"I know, time is progressing really fast. We need to go get the rest of the kids, quick."

GRAVE OFFERINGS

KATHLEEN SCHEINER

Lee-Thomas, p. 207

p. 70

I got my dream journal out of my bag and sat at the kitchen table, pen in hand, waiting for something to grab me. I've always been a very vivid dreamer—it's part of the gift—and sometimes I can make sense by writing dreams down straightaway like a story. If it's too weird, though, I'll drift with my pen levered over the page and see what pen strokes accumulate. Sometimes I get written messages this way; other times little sketch pictures are left for me.

I don't do this for my paying customers. I stick to tarot cards and astrology when I'm giving a reading. People are cautious the first time they visit a psychic—they want to get bang for their buck, but nothing too crazy. I like cards and charts because they're something solid and tangible that people can see and point to as guideposts for their lives. Rather than taking responsibility for what's going wrong, they can push it off on having the devil in their readings or a badly aspected Saturn on their charts. This also distances me somewhat, giving me something else to focus on rather than the person right in front of me, burning like a lamp.

I'm porous and can pick up another's feelings and moods just like that, especially if they're distraught, which many are when they come to see me. People are looking for higher guidance when consulting a psychic. All churned up, their thoughts hit me like barbed wire: *I'm going to die! No money, maxed out, can I file for bankruptcy? Money, bills, rent. Is he cheating on me? I'll kill him, kill him. Put arsenic in his stupid coffee drink and see how he likes that.*

That's why I took this dog-sitting job out of town. While New York City is great for business—I can go to the boardwalk on Coney Island and make two hundred dollars on a summer afternoon—it leaves my nerves jangled with the millions of sensory impressions that I pick up daily, going through my regular life.

And this last year has been particularly rough for me. I think either people's moods are becoming blacker because of all the years we've had a bad economy, or I'm getting more sensitive as I age. So I welcomed the chance to take the train upstate and stay alone in a rambling farmhouse all by myself except for an animal who oozes nothing but loyalty and love.

I see people unzippered all the time, and it's frightening. You might think it's the homeless or the crazies who have the scariest insides, but that's not true. It's the beautiful and most put-together who frighten me most; the people who have built walls to keep themselves from this world.

PROJECT GIRL
ROBERTA NIN FELIZ

Burrell, p. 213

p. 31

Roberta Yadira Nin Feliz
I am an immigrant
Who has lived in America
Since winters lasted months
Not weeks
But I am not American
I wonder
Why no one ever asks me
For my green card

Although my color is whisked away in the season's snow
I was raised under the sun
There I am in my skin
guiltless

I am a writer
Who has scribbled down
Threats
Curses
"I wish you wouldn't handcuff my brother"
"Don't leave crack next to the kids"
My fingers are bleeding
But my blood ain't red or blue
I'm writing so fast
I can't read what I'm writing
But I hope that you can read my heart
I hope that the ink bleeds
Through the paper

My Mami
Said I would be great
She did
And she told me to stick up for what I believe in
"Don't ever tell on folks though"
But how she expect me to sit around
And let the 'hood get destroyed
"Mami, I wanna be great"
Believe me
But sitting in a cramped office
Miserably making money
As the gunshots echo
Or yet another baby gets thrown out the window
Is not my idea of greatness
I'm going to be great
And Imma take the 'hood with me

I stopped eating meat for a month
Because I thought it would cure
A loved one's breast cancer
Now she has a wig

Her nails are black
Chemotherapy calls
I couldn't heal her
Now
Unhealed and broken
Healthy and broken
We join hands
Accepting fate

I am from the 'hood
Too many times
I have succumbed to its embrace
Laid on its chest
Let it sing me lullabies
Braid my hair
Each time its long arms enshroud me
And I dwell there
Surviving on the scraps it feeds me
There are lost souls there
Some doomed to an endless cycle of
shooting up
Into collapsed veins
And they cry
Shout
Kick
When they waste their dope
Some doomed to covert birth
No epidural
The babies squeeze out of them
Landing with a splat
I sit there and sway
To a phantom melancholy melody
I close my eyes
And just let it take me
Do what it pleases with me
I am high off the 'hood
I'm floating
Groping
I fashion a ladder from needles, condoms,
dead babies
I climb out
I can breathe

I reach out
To get ahold of pain
Failure
Tragedy
Cause I have a hard time
Believing in happiness
It doesn't last long
From where I'm from
Tragedy kisses the tip of my middle finger
It stings
But I wait till it's done to retrieve my hand
I look down at my hand
I have a purple burn mark
Satisfaction tickles my fingertips

I'D LIKE TO WRITE A POEM BETTER THAN THIS

JALYLAH BURRELL

M *Feliz, p. 210*
P *p. 31*

The regret I got accustomed to
blistered my toes this morning.
At the river I rested.
I hummed home.
The hymn was you.
And come dawn
I will do it all over again.

HOPE
NATHALIE GOMEZ

This poem details the inner battle between the forces that want to keep me down and my own internal reserves that keep me standing strong.

 *Berlin, p. 294*

 *p. 33*

You're the prisoner in my mind
Stuck in the cell you made for me
you think you could've taken over,
but you underestimated my strength.
You underestimated my power.

I am not your prisoner.
You are mine.

You came to me as a stranger.
You came to me as a friend.
But you became my enemy.

With you I felt happy.
With you I felt sad.
With you I felt emotions I didn't even
know existed, Emotions I didn't know I
was capable of feeling.

I trusted you.
I showed you my one weakness and you
took advantage of that.
My trust was the only thing I had left.
And you thought you could take it.

Your plan was flawless in your eyes.
But you forgot one thing.

Hope.

Hope set me free from your grasps.
You filled my head with dark thoughts and
fears.
And Hope untangled the chaos you made.

When I was all alone in the dark, where
you left me to rot,
Hope gave me a flashlight.
Hope gave me direction.
Hope showed me the bright side.

Hope was your weakness.

Hope is my strength.

release

THIS LETTING GO

This is a strange summer. This letting go.

Jessi Hempel, p. 217

We all have something we've held onto. Something that follows us, haunts us, weighs heavy upon us until we unclasp our hands and let it go. Sometimes it's a notion, an experience, a grudge, a moment that wasn't meant to hang around. But we fold it up and file it away, and it possesses us until we can free ourselves to move down a different path, where we can see there is more around us than the thing that we won't let go. It's accepting that it happened, maybe even for a reason. These stories show how we release things big and small—a parent, a child, an expectation. These stories are about letting go of the things that keep us.

HEATHER GRAHAM
2013 MENTOR AND
ANTHOLOGY COMMITTEE MEMBER

두근두근 (DUGEUN DUGEUN)

SOPHIA CHAN

In January, Siobhan invited me to a performance choreographed by Michelle Dorrance. It was described as a contemporary tap dance piece. I was expecting a tap dance show similar to others I've watched, but it was an incredible, unexpected fusion of various dance styles. Inspired, I made this creative documentary of it.

 *Burke, p. 256*

 *p. 19*

The room basks in darkness, echoes vibrantly of footsteps, stomps, and scratchy gliding all around, up and down. Are they calling out to each other? Blindly reaching out for each other?

Onlookers' eyes adjust to the silhouettes of bodies swept to the center. In a moment's breath, light.

Dance erupts. Stiff bodies move, blocked; bodies, fluid, twirl. Feet tap; feet slide. Beat pulses change in time. It's a waltz greeting breakdance. Arms graceful; arms flailing. Mellifluence flows around the sharp kicks. Variation has never slid under such smooth covers rolling and rolling into itself again and over and under again.

Vibrations and thuds in the dark. Smooth sailing in stockings on a slippery ground. Strenuous tap dance solos with varied interjections in between. Darkness dawns again and the forest is filled with sounds. With shoes, with socks, and bare feet. Pounding body beat boxer filled with stamina. The replying stationary dancers clap in complements. A grave swallow of the strings sliding against the thread of a bow controls the movements of the emerging dancer and the tempo of her taps. Squeaking faster, more desperately as time passes, the bass jerks dancers' fancies, jerks their feet into blurs. Suddenly, it's an orchestra of bodies and a bass. The fused styles and the all-mighty bass make sense, forming a beautifully functioning society.

JACKIE O.

JESSI HEMPEL

I had two fathers. In 2009, we lost Ron after a twenty-two-year fight with HIV. Living without Ron meant living in a new world, in which all guiding principles had to be reorganized. A year later, I wrote this piece, which Ava helped me pick out to share.

 *Nadel, p. 283*

 *p. 53*

This afternoon while everyone was downtown shopping for shoes, Dad and I waited behind for the two ladies with the thick-rimmed glasses who work for an AIDS support group in town. Every year, they hold a silent auction, and they came to collect Ron's stuff.

They started in the kitchen, marking a green-clouded glass pitcher with a small bit of tape. "This will sell," the shorter lady told me. Then she told me all about her twenty-two-year-old cat. It had recently died. I asked too many questions about the cat, hoping to distract all of us from the fact that she was packing what we had left of Ron into auctionable lots.

Ron was a collector and the house had become a shrine to all of his varied passions. Dad and I lumbered clumsily into each room behind the ladies. After an hour, I got everyone ice water.

The Virgin Marys went. The JFK commemorative plates. The broom collection. The glassware. The antique ashtray collection. I kept the framed *LIFE* magazine covers; wouldn't you?

This is a strange summer. This letting go. Last year, there were the firsts. There was the funeral and there were the ashes. First trip to market. First day of summer at the Provincetown gift store. First Christmas. But this year, there's only what is left—and my father nesting within it.

Next week the house will be still, the walls empty. By September, the store will be closed. Dad will be on his way to Oregon to play house with a man I have met once, hiding from the fact of his own mortality. I will hang the framed *LIFE* magazine cover from 1964 in my office, the one in which JFK gazes steadily off to the left while Jackie O. fixes her stare on the camera.

NOAH AND ME

KIRSTIE PLASENCIA

 *Wolas, p. 268*

 *p. 58*

When I get home I start dinner because Noah will be hungry. I put the pasta to boil, and I'm halfway through my Algebra homework when Noah runs in. She throws her Barbie backpack down on the floor, and props up on the wooden stool across from me. The way she looks makes me laugh: covered from head to toe in green and pink paint, and her pigtails, which I did this morning, are out of whack.

"Wow! Someone had fun at school," I say, and Noah tells me that Tracy the Gerbil escaped from her cage and ran all over the school. She tells me about art class, which explains the mess. She shows me her painting and I hang it on the fridge, along with other paintings of me that always look like different vegetables.

I've gotten good at not overcooking the spaghetti. Ladling the long noodles into bowls. When I mix in the hot tomato sauce, my meal looks actually edible. Noah is a good sport about my cooking and never complains when I burn the grilled cheese or put too much mayo in the tuna. Soon, she's added sauce to her painted face.

After dinner, Noah fills the tub with her toys. She's old enough to bathe herself. But I still help and wash her hair. I give her a soapy Mohawk. Then a George Washington flip. She laughs at herself in the mirror. When she's ready to "dry herself like a big girl," I clean up the kitchen. While she wears her favorite yellow monkey PJs, I tuck her and her stuffed animals into bed. Usually, she has books for me to read, but not tonight, so I know she wants to ask about Mom.

Our mom died when I was ten and Noah was three. I'm the only one who remembers her. Every few months, Noah asks me questions, which I like answering. It's the only time I let myself think about how much I miss her.

Tonight, she asks, "Did Mom think I was a boy?"

"Trust me, she knew you were a girl. That's why you have so many dolls!"

"So why'd she give me a boy's name?"

"Well, her favorite story to tell me at bedtime was Noah's ark. She'd say, "No matter the storm, Daniel, when you have faith, there's always a rainbow waiting." She lived by that, you know. When you were a baby, before she got sick, Mom would play old records, and sing and dance with you and make me pancakes shaped like dinosaurs. When you came along, you made her extra happy, like you were her ark."

"Wow!" Noah says, excitedly. "I'm gonna tell everyone at school on Monday!" After I've kissed her goodnight, I watch TV in my bedroom until I fall asleep. I

never hear our dad come in. The last time I remember him not working late was when Mom was sick.

He's gone when I get up. His note says, *Have a good day, Love Dad*. There's a crisp twenty dollar bill on top. It's nothing unusual. Sometimes we don't see him all week long.

Noah has left a puddle of milk on the kitchen counter. I follow the trail of Fruit Loops to the living room. She's munching away, watching cartoons. Her mouth is full so I have to decipher her words. She wants to set up her lemonade stand.

"Go for it, squirt," I say. Noah runs to make a pitcher of lemonade.

I clean up after Noah's new mess and make myself toast. I watch her get ready for business in front of our house. She sells lemonade every weekend so she can buy the karaoke machine at the toy store. Her few customers today grimace; I'm guessing her lemonade must be too sour or too sweet.

I go outside, and I'm about to say I'll make her a fresh batch, when the prettiest girl in eighth grade rides up on her purple bike.

Sarah smiles at me and I freeze up with the pitcher in my hand.

"Hey, Danny," she says to me, and my insides jump.

"Hiya, kiddo," she says to Noah.

"Want some lemonade?" Noah asks. "If you and everyone else keeps buying my lemonade, I'll be able to get a karachoki!"

Sarah's pretty laugh makes me sweaty.

"Wow, that's awesome!" Sarah says, and she holds up one of Noah's Dixie cups.

My face gets hot. I want to ask her out, but if I give her the nasty lemonade, she'll wonder if I'm trying to poison her, and if I tell her the lemonade is awful, I'll hurt Noah's feelings, and then Sarah will think I'm a jerk.

Sarah wiggles the cup, and says, "Danny?"

Suddenly, I'm chugging down the lemonade. Definitely not enough sugar! The yellow juice drips down my chin and onto my blue shirt. They both stare at me, shocked.

"I guess your brother was thirsty," Sarah says to Noah.

"That'll be twenty bucks!" Noah tells me, and holds out her little chubby hand.

I look at Sarah and we both start laughing.

SLEEPING BEAUTY

AMANDA HERBERT

 Choi, p. 193

 p. 36

She looks across her daughter's room with boxes planted at every side.
She can't believe she is leaving this all behind.
Her husband is putting the boxes inside the car.
All she can hear is the countdown inside her head.
One moment is all that remains, and she knows
Even if she leaves she can't push the memories aside.

Her laughter, as bright as day. Dressed in a yellow sundress
With her brown long hair dancing in the wind.
She saw the car come around a little too quickly.
No words escaped her when the car struck her from behind.
She ran outside and held her in her arms, her body fell limp
As she said the last word. "Mom."
Faith died a few days later, after being in a coma for several days.
She wanted to move out of this house to leave all the pain behind.

She smiles sadly out the window,
remembering the events of the past year.
The white flowers that were laid upon her coffin, the smell of sweet potato pie, her daughter's favorite.
The day she was laid to rest it looked like she was sleeping. She thought she saw her breathing.
Dressed in the yellow sundress one last time. She couldn't bear the goodbye.
Nothing could compensate for their daughter's loss.

She takes the picture off the dresser of her four-year-old Faith smiling.

The edges are rough. Just like the pain
implanted in her heart.
Her husband comes up behind and holds
her tightly, and she knows it is time to go.
She looks across the room one more time.
A countdown: ten-nine-eight-seven-six
She turns off the light in what once was
Faith's room. Walks down the steps into
the car.
A final farewell.

LETTING GO

ELAINE STUART-SHAH

 *Chin, p. 222*

 *p. 20*

Her ponytail swept the nape of her neck as she trotted toward the steps.

"Do you want to carry one of these with you?" I called after her but she was already out of earshot, opening the glass door to her dorm. It hovered a second after she slipped through, framing an empty space just her size, then clanged shut.

I glanced down at the suitcases and boxes full of toiletries and groceries bought in bulk. But instead of starting to unload, I closed the trunk and leaned against it. All around me students and siblings streamed between the parked cars and through the campus. I looked up at the bright, Downey-blue sky and imagined the scene from above, an elaborate ant farm.

Hadn't it been just as sunny that day so many years ago when my mom moved *me* in? I had spied the imposing Gothic spires of the school while driving over the bridge. It had seemed like a fairytale castle we were approaching, not a college. We'd pulled into the parking lot, the maroon paint on our old Mitsubishi gleaming from a fresh wash, and my mother had patiently unpacked my belongings while I fluttered about collecting flyers and introducing myself to my floormates.

It had been different. I'd left home before.

A cluster of kids in matching orange T-shirts started announcing an event in the student commons. I tried to catch the details but my mind was too clouded.

Someone else would tell her. I had more important things to relate in our final moments together—practical advice, life lessons, woman to woman. I thought of her ponytail bobbing again.

I popped the trunk and surveyed the stuff, mildly envious that it would remain with her hours later, after we'd made her bed and organized her closet and set up her computer and hung posters on the walls and hugged tight and promised to talk weekly. After I'd climbed back into the driver's seat and started the ignition and watched her wave as I backed out.

She reappeared at the door, clutching an orange T-shirt, and began walking toward the car.

GLASS CAGE

MONICA CHIN

 *Stuart-Shah, p. 221*

 *p. 20*

I tell myself to be strong. I force my welling tear ducts to squeeze shut, but they are not dams and they cannot keep the sudden throng of salty tears from seeping through. My hands flush pink, fingers puckered red as I strangle them with the loose threads of my sleeves. I am forced to turn away from my family and set my eyes on the plain view of my campus from my dorm window.

This is where I will be living for the next four years. A dusty room with an old darkened carpet lining the floor, stained in every corner. How many memories have already been made here? How many more will it hold?

My pop beckons for me; he must sense something is wrong. Grudgingly I twist my head and—oh no, his face has started to melt. The soft crinkles around his eyes crease and his cheeks blush. He gives me a big smile and holds his arms up for a hug. I stop in my tracks. The smile in his eyes is transparent. I feel like a young girl again, irresistible to my parents' open affection, and wrap my arms tightly around him, encircling his neck. After a quick second I retract my arms. He rubs his eyes gently underneath his wire-rimmed glasses, leaving a watermark at the corner of his eye. I look up and I see this and crumble. The white vacant walls of my new room close in on me. The pressure in my chest builds like a hot kettle left too long on the stove. The rhythmic thumping of my heart echoes through my ears and my throat tightens. I am about to say something to him and then...

My mother and brother burst into the room, carrying my belongings in a cardboard box. The door hinges creak faintly. The glass cage surrounding the two of us shatters. Pops gets up from the mattress and helps my mom unpack.

THE MIND-BODY PROBLEM

ROBIN MARANTZ HENIG

I've long been aware of how the mind can affect the body, but not until I met Brooke Hopkins did I think of the relationship differently: how the mind can exist apart from the body. It gave me a new way of thinking about how we interact with the world.

 *Civil, p. 80*

 *p. 22*

Last February, I met a man named Brooke Hopkins, who looked from the outside like the poster boy for assisted suicide. Like the characters in films like *Whose Life Is It, Anyway?* and *The Sea Inside*, he was a fierce intelligence trapped within a paralyzed body. But unlike those characters, who were pleading for help in ending their lives, the experience of actually living within that paralyzed body was different for Brooke, not at all what he would have pictured from the safe remove of mobility.

Brooke had been paralyzed from the shoulders down in a bicycle collision four years earlier, when he was 66 and newly retired from his job as an English professor at the University of Utah. He was an intensely physical man, six-foot-five and a lover of adventurous vacations—trekking in the Himalayas, backpacking in Venezuela. He skied, biked, or hiked the mountains around Salt Lake City whenever he could.

Is there a deeper tragedy when quadriplegia strikes someone so intensely physical, whose athletic prowess is an essential part of his emotional self-image? Maybe. But maybe it's only a person with a particular grit and steeliness who ends up in this situation in the first place. Not just because that's who is most likely to have been in situations where these injuries tend to occur—out there on a mountain bike or on horseback or doing back flips on a trampoline—but because decisions are made again and again after the injury about how hard to fight, and the most physical people might be the ones who fight the hardest.

For many people the challenges of life as a quad, especially a quad trying to regain some motion or some breathing ability, are just too hard, or not worth the incremental reward.

Those with less stamina might crash on the first rocky shoals and say this is enough. For Brooke, though, this new stage of his life is something that he has managed to think of as yet another physical adventure, a variation on the backpacking and trekking and skiing adventures that were an essential part of his adulthood. It helps that he's a Buddhist, too, and willing to think of the mind as separate from the body. Today, Brooke Hopkins is living his life almost entirely in the mind, and experiencing it—on the good days, at least—as a period of creativity, calm, and occasional transcendence.

AT DUSK
LAURA BARLAMENT

The birds in my nearby Silver Lake Park have always fascinated me, but before joining Girls Write Now and meeting Swati, a gifted poet, it had never occurred to me to find words to describe my observations. These lines came to me on a November evening.

Barua, p. 193

p. 9

At dusk, the feeding ducks' busy ballet
Inscribes on the still lake
A lyric I long to read—
Unheard music,
Etched in light,
A hieroglyphic of survival.

At the water's edge, a heron
Poses an elegant question mark
Against the rosy horizon.
Quietly I draw closer.
The curved neck unbends into an alert arrow
And wings, like two paths diverging,
Beat the air,
Disappearing into darkness.

THE PULP AND THE BEAN

JULIET WERNER

I wrote this piece with Lawrencia. We had just been rejected by a previously-booked interview subject and processed this blow together by trading my notebook back and forth. I'd write a little, she'd write a little. It was a liberating experience for me to write something and then immediately turn it over to be read.

 *Terris, p.. 206*

 *p. 69*

I let my eyes wander across the coffee shop's chalkboard pastel. Hot Apple Cider in yellow caps. Ginger Bread Syrup in script. Many sweet options. Only two tables.

This is awkward. This is really really awkward. His blue hat keeps making reappearances in the coffee shop and that's okay, but this is awkward and I feel awkward.

The blue hat belongs to Amar. Amar, son of Tony. Not that Tony has introduced himself to us. But he has lined the coffee shop with newspaper clippings and autographed headshots. "Dear Tony," and "Thanks, Tony." Apparently there are some customers Tony will speak to. He barely addresses his teenage son, who, with his slight frame and eager eyes, mans the counter with proprietary pride.

Last week, Saturday, I came here and did what I usually do: look at the painting on the side, brick wall. Something about the sight of an empty Franklin Ave. "back in the day" made me feel as if I were watching a movie that I was a part of. As comfortable as the painting made me, the owner did not.

The Pulp and The Bean has been here since 2009, long enough for the decorations to show signs of decay. The two baristas clean nervously as the afternoon deepens. Maybe it's the coffee that's made them jittery, or maybe it's Tony. Even when he's not here, he's here.

I've never seen anyone darken a room so fast. Juliet sat across from me, talking about the basics of journalism. I was listening, but his presence was so distracting. He stared at his phone with the same frown he entered with. How can someone with such a successful business feel so threatened and mad? The picture frames that lined the wall told of his friendships with famous and or important people. And his son was so friendly. So what exactly was Tony's dilemma?

Lawrencia and I thought his son would talk to us. It seemed like a good bet ever since we changed our order one day from a bagel to a muffin and he launched into a lecture on how "the body craves salt and not sugar." He was so animated and spirited. But when we followed up with him, prepared with a list of interview questions, he shyly stated that his father "disapproved" and that was that. Should we be surprised given that the cafe door has one message posted four times: "Watch your step."

The plant matter remaining after a process: Pulp.
The edible seed: Bean.

Lawrencia and I now know The Pulp and The Bean. And if they know us, it's as the two writers who fled their coffee shop, confident we'd find other people more willing to answer our questions.

WHY I GO TO THE YMCA

KATE JACOBS

The YMCA is a completely different world for me. I've been going for nearly six years, but my relationship to both working out and the other gym members is constantly evolving. Going to the Y is something that Mandy and I have in common, although our experiences there are quite different.

 *Nervais, p. 226*

 *p. 54*

The best thing about belonging to a YMCA is the confidence boost it gives you. This is not because the exercise helps you lose weight. Or because cardiovascular workouts condition your heart so it's easier to go up and down the stairs in the subway. And it has nothing to do with endorphins. No, the confidence boost the YMCA gives you comes in the locker room.

Don't believe me? Let me explain. Most of the women in the YMCA locker room are old ladies. The first thing you need to know about them is that they don't have an ounce of modesty. They walk around the locker room with their sagging breasts, round abdomens, and flat, drooping butts for all to see. The second thing you need to know is that they talk and talk. "How was your daughter's bat mitzvah?" one woman calls to another. "I brought the latest New Yorker for you—I'll put it in your locker," another woman announces with a broad New York accent. "You're getting married! Let me see the ring!" This last exclamation comes in the shower when everyone is completely naked with the curtains drawn back so they can chat while they scrub.

I close the curtain on my shower stall. I wrap a too-small towel around my body even though it's not really hiding anything. ("Oh, aren't you sweet," exclaims one old lady when I tug at the edge of the towel that barely covers my ass.) I just want to get dressed with most of my dignity and very little embarrassment. But the old ladies are neither humiliated nor ashamed and their good cheer extends to everyone in the locker room, including me. "That's a beautiful dress!" one woman declares. "Did you get a hair cut?" another might say. And they love to ask: "Have you lost weight? You look so great!" Not a pound, ladies, but I'll take the compliment anyway.

Life often has a way of battering you around, of kicking you when you're already down, and seemingly delighting in watching you struggle to get up. This is why I work out: To condition myself for the struggle, to learn how to summon my resources and stand squarely on my own two feet. But this is why I love the YMCA: Because after the workouts there's a bunch of old ladies with enough years padding their bellies to laugh at life's attempts to trample their spirits, and with enough generosity to pass on the tools—the encouragement and optimism—to help me survive.

SWEATING OUT STORIES IN THE SAUNA

AMANDA NERVAIS

Writing this piece helped me realize that the gym itself has become a new world for me to explore. Ever since I decided to become healthier, I've been visiting the gym and meeting all kinds of people. The sauna is just a snippet of some of the stories I've encountered.

M *Jacobs, p. 227*

P *p. 54*

In the sauna at my gym, there are stories to be told with every drop of sweat that comes out of our systems.

None of them involves me; perhaps because they know I'm not 18, the minimum age to enter the sauna. They ignore my existence in order to discipline me. Or they somehow know my lips were born closed and I wouldn't utter a word even if directly addressed.

Instead I just listen silently in the background. Even when there are no more than five allowed in the room at a time, there are so many views and opinions to follow and retrace. I listen silently in the background, making my own judgments and decisions.

"Americans are slaves. We work and go home and work and go home and in the end, at least once a year, we have to pay back to our 'masters' with the tax system. It's a never-ending system that keeps repeating itself because we think that's just the way it is," one African-American lady said. She referred to herself as a conspiracy theorist.

"I wanna run the marathon one day, and do it cuz I wanna breathe, I wanna fly, you know? It's gonna take a lot of pushing and shoving but I know I could do it. This little southern belle can do it," another woman said. She was actually really slim, but I knew it took more than that to run a marathon.

There are stories that range from a mother and daughter's troubles with HIV to what another woman is going to prepare for her family for dinner. And even though nobody knows anybody's name, we all trust each other, we all stitch up each other because we are all just one long strand of thread.

Leaving the sauna, you always say, "Everyone have a nice day/weekend/evening," and smile before showing your back and walking out. It is a unique level of respect that is rarely found in our country and probably in more proper places, like Britain. I am usually the very last one to leave, not only because I love to watch my sweat have derby cart races to the bottom of my foot, but also because I have to let each and every story told slowly sink in and stir around inside my head.

Now the only story that hasn't been told is my own, but after all, I haven't even reached the minimum age to use the sauna room. My story of growing into the mature realties of life hasn't even begun yet, has it?

DEBORAH BLUMBERG, MENTOR 2009-2011

Writing was scary. Essays graded by my no holds barred Southern English teacher were blanketed in red. One day, she gave me an index card that read: "Every sentence must connect to the next and carry the piece forward." Something clicked. I still keep it with me when I write.

GIVING VOICE TO THE UNSPEAKABLE

PAMELA BAYLESS

All year I've hoped that Suleyma would find release in writing about the traumatic episode that triggered a devastating depression when she was 12. I imagined that someday she would weave it into a memoir. She surprised me when she chose to write about it for this anthology.

Cuellar, p. 230

p. 25

"There is such a thing as absolute power over narrative. Those who secure this privilege for themselves can arrange stories about others pretty much where, and as, they like."

—Chinua Achebe (1930-2013), Nigerian novelist

This chapter starts, and may end, at the Barnes & Noble café on Eighty-Sixth Street. Toting a yellow legal pad, an extra pen, and something good to read if I have to wait, I snag a table and a couple of chairs. Suleyma appears, eager to put her thoughts, her fantasies, her inner workings on paper. She is prolific: poetry flows easily from her pen. Stories take shape as we sit quietly, her hand moving steadily, stopping only to search for a better word.

Early on she told me she'd never been able to write about a cold night in September, that late evening six years ago when her innocence was so abruptly stolen—not unlike losing a limb, she hadn't given it much thought until it was gone. She'd been able to talk about what transpired in a matter-of-fact way since then, but feelings were harder to express than facts. Suleyma couldn't put into words the emotional devastation she carried inside for so long. Giving voice to it was just too wrenching.

That horror-struck girl, on the threshold of adolescence, is a full-fledged young woman now. Having seen the world at its worst, she has matured and faces her future with joy and excitement. Now, finally, she's ready, planning on college and a career in which she'll offer wise counsel and deep understanding to help others heal. She's come to grips with terrible trauma, navigated a fraught family situation, kept up with her studies and made honors, and won the heart of a boyfriend who thinks the world of her and is always there when she needs someone to lean on. And she's found a way to transcend the wounds and injuries of her childhood with a powerful pen.

Suleyma's writing now offers her catharsis, a reckoning, empowerment. Not only can she write about that unspeakable evening that changed everything, but through her writing she gains the power to tell her story in her own words, not holding anything back as she creates a new ending to that episode and enters a world where she will determine her direction and find nothing too shameful or impossible to tell. This newfound power can change her thoughts and steer her in new directions, perhaps never to forget, but to put her knowledge to a positive end, for herself and others.

Te felicito, Suleyma, al verte reclamar tu puesto en este mundo nuevo.

SADNESS FILLS MY HEART

SULEYMA CUELLAR

I am currently working on a story about what happened after I was molested by a cousin. Originally I wrote an essay, but listening to a fellow Girls Write Now mentee read her poem about depression touched me so deeply that it inspired me to write this poem.

 *Bayless, p. 229*

 *p. 25*

Sadness fills my heart, emptiness makes place
Hopelessness invades my mind, not letting me escape.

All I see is the face smiling
And licking his lips, savoring
The moment that he took

My innocence away, not wanting to look
But only feeling his dirty big hands all

Over my breasts. He has a lot of gall.
I want to scream, kick, or even shout.
My body becomes still with the doubt
Is this real or a dream? Or a fantasy

Created by my mind? But now the sad reality
Kicks in, when I wake up to see the sadness I am living.
But what is worse than that is feeling

Disgusted when my own father
Uncle, cousin, friend, and brother
Tries to talk to me and hug me or

Get close to me, I head for the door.
Wishing to be alone, not wanting their company
All because of a sinverguenza who took the key
And opened the door and let the depression monster

Come inside me. Taking my body on a
rollercoaster

Where I no longer had trust in guys.
All I wanted and thought I needed was to
buy
A ticket to a fast ride to eternity.
My wounded heart pleaded for tranquility.

Day by day my thoughts took over.
My shattered innocence cried every night
Pleading to get healed, knowing it might
Take forever to let go of the pain inside.

My body feels betrayed, defiled and broken
It wishes for one thing, just a simple token
To be able to ride to an Ecstasy world
Where all my pain could be hurled
to the side

Letting every other emotion die.
My world is darker each day
I feel my God vanishing far away.

My hope is quickly disappearing.
Now I let my murky thoughts consume me
I open my mouth and invite death to enter
my body.
It takes a few seconds for my mind to lose
Its balance. For my brain to quickly send
notes

To my heart letting it know how to beat
My body feels heavy but it feels no heat
Just coldness running through my bones
Within minutes my heart is hard as a stone.

All I see is darkness everywhere.
I start to become dizzy, the atmosphere
Begins to spin. My body loses control,
Gravity pulls me down this pitch-black
hole.

I can't see the depth or where it will end
I just fall down and down. But I don't
intend

To stop myself from falling. I fall deeper and deeper
I am almost touching the ground. I can sense my time
Coming to an end. Yet my mind begins to scream, "climb!"

That's when my heart decides to change its mind
And my brain wakes up from approaching the end of time.
My eyes feel heavy but want to see the world again.
I sit up feeling dizzy, hopeless, lonely, and dull pain.

My mind begins to shout that I am a failure.
Tears fall down like rain drops from the sky
Just when my life and my hope seem to slowly die.

Yet suddenly a unique boy comes into my sight.
Within months I trust you and you begin to brighten
My days with just a simple laugh. My brain is confused.
It doesn't know what to do or what emotion to choose.

The first time you held my hand electricity went
Through every one of my bones. My mind right away sent
Pictures to replace the time my cousin's hands were all over my breasts.
I am confused because just a few days ago I felt so oppressed.

But now that you are holding me I feel ashamed.
Just a few months ago I wanted the end. I

can't blame
My mind for the thoughts, because I wanted to end it so badly.
Now that's not what I want. You showed me I can also be happy.

You taught me a new way to let my pain go away.
Replacing it with contentment, my days are no longer gray.
My body doesn't feel dead; somehow you made it feel alive.
Now that I look back a year has passed and I only want to strive

For a better tomorrow without any darkness invading my mind.
All those times that sadness filled my heart and emptiness made a place
Where hopelessness invaded my mind, I was trapped, it didn't let me escape.
All those times my heart was cold and my thoughts took control are behind.

RABBIT VALLEY

SAVANNAH ASHOUR

I wrote this piece as an elegy to a lost place—the new world here, America, is present only as a shadow, an unfathomably sticky place where people eat peanut butter.

 Uesugi, p. 185

 p. 72

My brother's cheeks were ripe and soft and perfectly tinged with rose. Ten, twenty, thirty kisses a day I planted there. He was a wild little boy, but I was wily and strong-willed.

There was honeysuckle down there, in Rabbit Valley. No rabbits, but frogs that croaked all summer long. From our gorge we looked up at our village, whose lights sprinkled the sky at night and whose church bells hailed the hours by day. Our village was old, older than time, and so were the men who played boules in the square, and so were the waiters in the Café de la Place—they had always been there.

The old women wore nightdresses and smoked cigars and drank beer with the men in the late mornings. The village doctor, Veronique, was drawn and tired and smoked constantly. I was her favorite patient; she liked to hear stories about California. Joel Stratte McClure, an American journalist, would offer me all the money in his pocket for a proper word spelling, never more than a few centimes. Bill and Joan got drunk at their going-away party and jumped into our pool in their fancy clothes, and a man in a Speedo and bowtie followed them in. My best friend Emilie had the longest blond hair anyone had ever seen, and Anne-Marie ate lemons from the courtyard trees. It snowed once, and we rode down our long, steep driveway on garbage-can lids.

"The States" were far away and sticky. They ate strange things like peanut butter and jelly there and celebrated holidays that didn't exist, like Halloween.

We were a busy little clan. My brother had a miniature broom and liked to wield a garden hose as well. He rode his bike in frantic whirring circles around the pool, singing songs at the top of his lungs until he fell in and screamed for help. He climbed trees in the field across the way with a secretive gang of Algerians, always whispering and plotting. I had all the volumes of Sweet Valley High and the complete works of Marcel Pagnol to read. There was ballet and swimming and an ongoing parade of homemade costumes, mostly in the gypsy vein. There were walks with my mother and run-ins with the lively shepherd and his endlessly defecating sheep. There were strange, forbidding houses to be passed by in a hurry. Once, we were surrounded by a rabid pack of wild dogs, foaming at the mouth, some of them cut and bleeding from a recent fight. My mother scared them off with a stick.

There are new Americans now, and Germans and British and Saudis. The busloads of tourists have multiplied, their presence so commonplace it evokes

only the barest hint of derision. The English of the waiters at the Café de la Place has improved, if only superficially, along with their manners.

When we left they painted our house an awful yellow, easily spotted from the village ramparts on the eastern side. The valley is crowded. There are hundreds more houses down there than there used to be, it seems, stretching out all the way to the sea. Out to that glittering blue-green water, where the planes take me to, where home is now.

identity

I EMBRACE THE EXPOSURE

As I hold here, head dangling upside down between my arms, belly reaching for the sky, I embrace the exposure.

Samantha Carlin, p. 255

As our intrepid writers strike out on unknown paths, they often find themselves exploring that most intimate of topics: identity. Who am I? Who do I want to be? What makes me who I am? It's a quest both thrilling and scary, powerful and painful.

In this chapter, yoga becomes both a metaphor for stretching into new relationships and a medium for meditation on memory and meaning. One mentor questions the manufactured "honesty" of a celebrity facade, while her mentee describes the searing pain of true self-exposure. Others waltz with confidence while rejecting social norms and the limiting expectations of others. In these pieces, we meet alternative selves and ponder the slipperiness of the very notion of "self." We reject easy labels; we discover new aspects of our selves and our purpose in new places; we negotiate identity within communities that both restrict and support our selves. Finally, we create entirely new and perfected identities, in a fantasy where we cut all ties and leave the past behind.

As my mentee, Swati Barua, observed while we discussed the pieces in this chapter, "'I Embrace the Exposure' makes the perfect title for this chapter because through each piece, the reader will embrace the writer's new world."

LAURA BARLAMENT
2013 MENTOR AND
ANTHOLOGY COMMITTEE MEMBER

A QUERY, MS. T-SWIFT
CHRISTINA BROSMAN

 *Newsome, p. 239*

 *p. 55*

Hello, Taylor
Thank you so much for joining me
I'll keep this quick and painless, but—

T-Swift, what's your story?
Your real story
Not love story, baby just say yes
Fluttered eyes and lullabies

And all your sing-alongs to breakup songs
While he rehearses his new play
Blocks away
And your army chants against him
In the plaza down at *GMA*
I'd guess at least, I'd venture
From your cheeky little overture
Because your not-so-secret secrets
Aren't so very hard to see through

No but after, later
Once you exit the elevator
Away from your
Agent, manager, publicist, stylist,
assistant, business manager, lawyer,
security guard, hair stylist, makeup artist,
manicurist, roadies, back-up band, and
fans
Et al.
Et al.

After the one-thousandth "thank you guys
SO MUCH!!!" of the day
And the crowd has gone away
The doors have all locked tight
You'll be your alias tonight
Maybe, just maybe
Does your patience wear a little thin?
Knowing when you get groceries the next
morning
That the whole world will weigh in

Or do you, baby, just say yes?
And step out into the gloss and glimmer
Flashes and fashion
And tip your hat to normalcy

And all the things you never got to be

And lead the same chorus
The throngs know down to each and every letter
And resign yourself to
We (eeeee!) are never ever ever
Getting back together

BREAK UNTIL IT'S BROKEN

BRE'ANN NEWSOME

 Brosman, p. 238

 p. 55

It's beating against my chest
Thrusting, cracking my rib cage
Pulsing, beating, breaking
Whatever is in its way

Cracked, fracturing, breaking, broken
Chipped bones puncturing tender flesh
Forging a hole that only gets deeper
Red, hot, liquid life

Creating a pain I can feel with every draw of breath
A pain I can feel with the calloused pads of my rough fingertips
Creating a black and blue bruise
Creating a another blemish

But the blemish doesn't stop it
But the pain doesn't stop it
The thing's still thrusting against my broken rib cage

Now working to split the fragments and opposing flesh in its way
Now it's on fire
Burning a hole through layers of taut flesh
Surfacing
Baring itself for all to see

They see it above them
Still pumping against thick air
Almost as thick as blood

Rivulets of red turn into
Pitch black cursive
Dropping to the floor
Climbing the walls
Increasing their font size
I stand attached only by a thin vein
Pulsating with pain, a throbbing hurt
Swallowing the boulder in my throat
The cursive is on the walls they see it
Try to read it, but no one else understands,
sign language

No one understands instructions of which
ways to contort your hand to understand

Two fingered, gun sign

Upright fist, thumb extended

Thumb up wedged between the index and
middle finger

Loose fist claws baring

H-A-T-E

Thumb extended, index finger upright

Index finger and thumb touching followed
by other fingers making an O

Index and middle finger creating a "peace"
sign, colored side facing the crowd

Baring claw, like a loose fist

L-O-V-E

But they are all incompetent
Can't understand the silent language
Lights burst
Like an old star creating a supernova!

And then it falls to the ground
My heart falls to the ground
Riding the vein that connects us all the way
back into the gaping hole in my chest

I repair my rib cage
Stitching the ruptured flesh back into dark
perfection
Then it continues to trust, throb, thrum with
life
But I still pulsate with pain
And they still watch

TAKE THIS WALTZ

RACHEL KRANTZ

 *Joseph, p. 243*
 *p. 41*

Last night

I danced with a man from Pakistan.

His face was close to yours
except for the recognition behind the eyes,
which as it turns out
is the most important part of your face.

I taught him how to waltz.

We stepped on feet and beige carpet
he told me to maintain eye contact
It would ensure our concentration;
balance.

It was difficult.

This should be harder for me than it is
for you
he scolded me
I've never done this before
and you
you waltz all the time

I most certainly do not.

Not to mention
we don't look each other in the eyes here
we're just a bunch of introverts, masked as
extroverts.

In the corner
his friend from Berlin
with that Aryan sharp, young-old face
massages my roommate Colleen's feet.

Is this really happening right now?
she keeps exclaiming
cracking up
neck arched back
booty on carpet
leg in air
foot in attentive hand.

Earlier that night
she was sent flowers
and a box of chocolate-covered
strawberries
and a note
by a man apologizing
for saying he'd marry her
if only she lost some weight.

She read his groveling
and laughed.

Sticking his card on the fridge with a
magnet,
she put the flowers in water,
shared some chocolate strawberries,
and invited me to meet some new friends.

MY OWN CONFIDANT
KIARA JOSEPH

 *Krantz, p. 241*

 *p. 41*

Confidence. According to *Merriam-Webster's* dictionary, confidence is a faith or belief that one will act in a right, proper, or effective way. It's a seemingly simple definition, yet today, a plethora of teen girls find themselves without it. Why is it that so many teens have trouble believing that they will act in a right, proper, or effective way?

I believe the answer is a combination of the facts that teens are too critical of themselves, and that society is too critical of teen girls in return. It is easy to decipher why a girl would be hard on herself. In every commercial and on every billboard, a thin figure is glorified and put above all else. When we are exposed to these images all the time as teenage girls, it becomes programmed in our heads that we should want to look extremely skinny. Since the ideal figure portrayed by the media is thin and tall, it's no surprise that girls criticize themselves if they are anything but that. Most models seen on runways or on billboards are not "plus-size," and the result is that not having a thin figure is seen as almost obscene by many people. The media and society work in conjunction with each other to create one tough situation for young women.

As a teenage girl, I can of course directly relate. I'm five feet and two inches tall, and I am not thin. Sometimes, I find myself in the mirror picking out things I don't like about myself. I wish I were taller and thinner, but since those traits don't seem to be on the horizon for me, I often find myself feeling little confidence.

As a result, when I found out about my obligation to perform at the first CHAPTERS reading for Girls Write Now, I was anything but confident. Rather than being nervous about tripping over my words, what I was really scared about was the audience looking at me and criticizing me for the way I look. I was afraid people would consider me to be obese or too short, even though I knew that I was really just picking myself apart.

After I finished reading, I was surprised by the applause that I received, as well as all the compliments I was given after the show. People didn't see the flaws that I saw in myself; they just saw me. At that moment, I realized that as humans, we have the privilege of being different sizes, shapes, and skin tones. We are all different and we should embrace that instead of denouncing it. Some people will be tall and thin, while some people will be short and thick. When I realized that, I had a sudden burst of confidence. I realized that there is nothing wrong with not having an idealized look. I also realized that society shouldn't decide what is right, proper, and effective. We as individuals should make that decision, and that is what will build confidence in girls like me.

Girls Write Now is a program that allowed me to read at the CHAPTERS reading series. Without this program, I would be looking in a mirror right now, critiquing my looks. Instead, I'm here writing this. I look at myself in a new light. I may look the same, but now, I accept my differences and value them. In that small way, I find myself feeling more confident in the way I look. So that is why I am so grateful for the opportunity this program has given me: to have the confidence to know I can write or look a certain way without being criticized. Instead of feeling powerless, weak, and feeble, I feel strong, confident, and empowered. And that feels freaking great.

THE SWEET ESCAPE

TATYANA ALEXANDER

I imagined a new world a person might build when they don't feel accepted, and thought about drugs and alcohol as a way I've seen people look for acceptance. In the end, the happiness and perks that come from substance abuse are only temporary. And so are the imaginary worlds we build.

M Gallagher, p. 247

P p. 3

Turned necks and rolled eyes.
They're coming at you while you hide
From the truth and the hate.
Hide from the fakes.

Go home.
In the cabinet.
Jack Daniel's on the shelf.
Thoughts cannot contain themselves.
The bottle pops open.

You take a sip.

Those necks turned reveal.
Faces flex their cheeks
Spread their lips
All you see is teeth.

Must be the fakes.

How real are the feelings felt from
imagination?

The truth LIES, when you take another sip.
The necks turn to you.
Happy faces.
Possessing parting gifts.

Uninvited.

They come in numerous amounts.

Another sip.

The parting gifts they consist of.
Reality, you crept away from.
Love, that you never received and
desperately desire.

Take another sip.

You desire more.

Take another sip.
Now you find something to argue against.

Those same happy faces
Turn into raging hatred.
Razor-sharp curse words slice your face.

The last sip in the bottle.
It's ending.
Everyone hates you.
They start to leave.
Bottles are empty.
Cabinet is tapped out.
You submit to life.
Tap out.
Those faces remember you no longer.

Pop a pill.

Those same faces that once despised you,
hated your guts.
Are drawn to you.
The drug makes itself at home.
In your body it settles.

The pill sparks your fascination.
You start to do things
the fake faces don't like.
They are aggravated.

Clouds cover the sun.
Darkness of the night sets in.
Be aware of the company you let in.
They let themselves out.

The few that stay are real or raise Doubt.
Abuse you like a drug.

You inject yourself.

The door opens and you have company.
It's all fun and games.
Do you see?
The stares blink revenge and pain
As the drug runs laps in your veins.
You regain
Consciousness.
Fully aware.
The company you let in
Isn't There.

There is no reality to your imagination.

You take fascination in the gun
Hidden in the basement.
The Metal feels cold against your temple.
One bullet.
Russian roulette.
Rush and cock it.
Imagination is the trigger.
Bullet is reality.
Your imagination triggers reality.

Reality kills.

You wake up and your lungs take in a gust of air.
Heartbeat is too fast to feel.
Panic rushes into your thoughts.

A figment of imagination.

How far can you escape before life sniffs out your tracks?

Our only escape to another world is our own imagination.
That same imagination that ignites a good feeling inside you.
Rejects you.
Your self can only run away from its own

body so far
Until it turns the corner and trips right
back into its body.
The human body subconsciously
Creates new worlds every day
What a shame
We could never stay.

THE SHE
JILLIAN GALLAGHER

 *Alexander, p. 244*

 *p. 3*

She's close enough to be a sister.
Or a cousin. Or a niece.
Maybe weathered more, or less
A stranger with my face

She could be my better. My idol.
Or my thorn.
The object then of jealousy.
The object now of scorn.

She could be my vindication.
She could be the one that stayed close.
She could be the one that hoped to leave
Or the one that they miss most.

She could be a smaller girl
Part of a smaller world.
The big splash in the smallest pond
A bright face among the old

She might feel so much less guilty.
She might feel much more at home.
She could be the one with all the buzz
The one never alone

But I turned left when she turned right
I went east when she faced west.
And so, I guess we'll never meet.
And I wonder.
Is it for the best?

She isn't coming back.
And I guess now, neither will I
I kill her more with every choice
But hear her laugh in every sigh.

YOU'RE PERFECT TO ME

KATHERINE ORTIZ

 *Kane, p. 190*

 *p. 56*

Her eyes surveyed the image in front of her. She'd seen herself so many times before. Her emotions varied from dulling shame to a sharpening disgust. *This isn't me.* She gathered the satin fabric in her hands and gnawed on her bottom lip to such an extent that she began to taste the metal of her own blood. Hot tears pushed against the backs of her eyes as her gaze became fixed on her legs that were greatly exposed in the attire.

Her heart wrenched at the thought of Harry's broken expression at the sight of her in a dress different than this one. She could vividly see the way his emerald green eyes had brightened when he'd seen her. He'd demanded she twirl in the dress, exposing her body at every angle possible. He'd been mesmerized by the sight of the beautiful specimen he called his.

Hayley began to pinch at the fabric as it reluctantly rose further up her thighs and rose until the hem reached her waistline. She continued to pull it off before she suddenly felt a pair of hands land on her bare skin.

Harry stood behind Hayley, his hands gently reaching toward the hem of the dress and pulling it back downward over the curve of her bum.

"What's wrong?" Harry asked. He towered over her petite frame, quickly noticing the red outlining her eyes and the flushed appearance that had come over her pale features. "Please say something."

"I'm sorry," she mumbled as her hands slowly traveled up the length of his arms, her figure distancing from him. Harry allowed his finger to rest beneath her chin, guiding her gaze toward his. He sensed her apprehension before he slowly traced the contour of her jaw, his fingers gracefully dancing across her skin.

"Hayley," he whispered breathlessly. "What's wrong?" She turned away from

Harry as she boldly slipped the dress off in one swift motion, exposing all of the imperfections she'd hidden so well. Harry's gaze burned on her flesh as he took a step forward, his figure looming above her. Hayley's fingers slowly rose, grazing the marks that signified the stretching of her skin on the base of her legs. She then slowly gathered the accumulated fat stored in the inner fragment of her thigh. She continued to painfully analyze each and every one of her imperfections as if Harry weren't there. Hayley became numb to the pain-riddled emotions electrifying her entire being. She no longer cared whether Harry acknowledged the things she worked toward keeping hidden.

He watched as she observed herself, the emptiness in her eyes frightening him. His fingers grazed the skin on her shoulders, distracting her. A thick layer of tears had caused her eyes to resemble glass, translucent. He felt the need to comfort her and remind her that he'd fallen in love with her so deeply that he could hardly feel the surface any longer. He adored each and every one of her features and wished to remind her that she was more than what she thought herself to be.

"Hayley, don't do this to yourself," he whispered. His fingers traced her spine as his hands enveloped each of her hips. He couldn't believe the amount of hate she held toward herself when all he could do was love her. "You're beautiful." Although he'd overused this term of endearment toward her various times before, it seemed as if this might be what would mend her broken state. Her eyes remained dull and lifeless, not managing to find any amount of truth in his words.

"I love your body," he whispered as his forehead grazed hers. Her gaze became lost in the depth of his eyes. "I love your freckles." He smiled as he gently held onto the sides of her face, his thumbs continuing to gently poke the skin that held the markings. "I love your lips." His thumb grazed over her bottom lip as his lips gingerly molded against hers. "I love *you,"* he finished.

Her heart thumped wildly against her chest as she looked toward this boy—this boy who managed to secure her heart and hold her close when she became desperate for acceptance, exorcising her demons.

Harry slowly pulled away from her before leaning down and gathering the fabric she'd disposed of earlier. She watched him in curiosity as he directed her to raise her arms. She smiled in spite of herself as Harry slowly led the silk fabric down the length of her arms and the curve of her breasts. Harry's arms enveloped her, which caused her to lean against his chest, her hands encircling his waist. Hayley kissed the outline of his jaw as he intertwined their fingers.

She sat on the edge of the bed as Harry knelt before her, guiding her foot delicately into her shoes. He couldn't help wondering how such a beautiful person could find such hatred toward herself.

"I love you," he whispered against her lips, his breath fanning against her. "You're perfect to me."

RED HERRING
MONICA HERNANDEZ

 *Reach, p. 277*

 *p. 37*

Today I am someone I was not yesterday.
Tomorrow, then, I will be someone I was
not this morning.

Tonight the moonbeams will destroy me,
How your scent haunts me.

Today, this morning and tomorrow at
dawn
I find and found comfort
Because I didn't know who I was.
I shall wander.
I am lost.
Will I wonder why I'm lost?

In the intervals between seconds
It seems I linger.
And in your motionless gestures
I so gaily wither.
Your sight I do not dare meet in dreams.

I was not found.

Only when lost seconds turn back,
When the shards of a broken teacup come
back together again,
Will I understand (will you understand?)
That in this blessed twilight I have not
lingered.
Because our (my) seconds are still not,
They will never be, nor should they ever.
Saunter lost as you will, my fading star, for
I am not
In a long way gone. I was meant to be,
For not do I exist.

MORE THAN A LABEL
TEAMARÉ GASTÓN

 *Nero, p. 282*

 *p. 32*

We as people categorize all that we do, from growing up to growing old. We space each year of our lives into labeled Tupperware holders in our photo albums. So if that's the case, then let's take a look at human existence from the only point of view I know: my own. The story begins in fourth grade, when I had just learned what the term *goth* was. It was all new to me—the appreciation of black, old literature, and all things that go bump in the night. I would not have known what any of this was if it were not for emulating Sam Manson from *Danny Phantom's* quirky lifestyle.

Fourth grade was the year when I thought I knew it all just because I could read at a sixth-grade level and could name all the phases of the moon. I thought to myself, "If I can do that, I can so pull this look off," and there was the beginning of my understanding of the word ego. Lucky enough for me in fourth grade, kids didn't waste their time trying to pinpoint who the most pretentious person in their class was. This was before the digital age, when a computer was still used to just paint and do line art. That saved me the trouble of worrying that people would see right through my Morticia Addams act. That feeling in the pit of my stomach that stemmed from the worry that someone would say, "You're such a faker" should have been the first clue that the front I was putting up was going to fall hard and soon.

Now fast forward a few years to my seventh-grade year, and you can really see where the line was drawn between eco and my ego. Most kids are excited to share their first locker with their friends; I know I was. Yet it could have gone over way better if people weren't so afraid to share a locker with me. It was by this time in my adolescence that I had let the goth thing run a bit too long and found that it was playing itself into everything I did. I went from being "witty" to "cynical" to just a plain callous ass. I was "The Undead Reject" thanks to a few boys on the basketball team, one being an old, old, old ex-best friend. I know what you're thinking: I totally deserved it for letting my life be run by this label, and you are right. Yet I didn't learn my lesson there.

There's this thing that people love being; it's called a martyr. We make ourselves the victims in order to say that we are the heroes of our own little dramas. But that's just tragedy upon ourselves that we sadly play along with. I learned this the hard way when I got to eighth grade and my knowledge of the dark was tested. Her name was Lola and she was the gothest (if that's even a word) person in Mett Hill Middle School. She could rock the look and afford all of the fancy, flashy grunge boots and torn Black Veil Brides sweaters. When she came along, I went from being "The Undead Reject" to just another kid going through a phase.

That's when the panic set in.

I was so caught up in being noticed that I ignored the fact that I had morals that I wanted to follow. I went from goth, to grunge, to emo, to teenybopper, to straightedge, to the Molly Soda wannabe. I was desperate to stand out until one day, when I was over-caking my eyes with liquid eyeliner, I got a good look at myself—one of those deep get-swirled-into-another-universe looks that you do at the mirror. What was I doing? I was a good kid. It was just all of the hype placed on being different that led me astray from what I wanted: being accepted while being myself. And trust me, I doubt sporting green highlights was really helping me come into tune with my inner Tea.

What is the difference between ego and eco? In our lives we are told that there are categories for every moment of our existence. Yet when we truly look at life for what it is, we begin to wonder what it all really means. Are we truly here because we are destined for a greater purpose, or are we as individuals the outcome of years of stardust build-up? With each passing day, I found that the "secrets" to life were no more than small fancies and life lessons that have served as the basis for children's tales. The stories that children distract themselves with, the tall tales of wolves and little girls in red hoods, served as more than just a kindergarten pastime. I find that by looking back at events and phases in my own little world I created while growing up, I understand myself as a person a little more now.

MARIE ANNE K. BALTAZAR, MENTEE 2007-2010

At fifteen in a new country, I had a very hostile home life. My writing became what I had to hold on to. It wasn't just an escape, it was hope. It was my confidant and my tears. With every sentence I penned, I grew so strong, joyful, and proud.

THE MANTRA
AMANDA DAY MCCULLOUGH

Last summer, I embarked on a service trip to Nicaragua. My journal from the trip is teeming with written memories of the friendships and places I encountered in that new world. I dove into one of those memories in this piece by exploring another new world: meditation.

 *Carlin, p. 255*

 *p. 50*

"Regulate your breathing," Mr. Gaudenzi instructs. I'm lying on a foam yoga mat in the cafeteria. I breathe deeply. In through my nose, out through my mouth.

"Now think of your mantra. Your mantra can be a pleasant thought, place, or experience. Something that makes you feel at peace. Close your eyes, and escape."

Mr. Gaudenzi turns on the music. *Whoooshhhh*, the sounds of a waterfall fill my ears.

"Breathe in, breathe out. Breathe in..."

Even after half a semester of yoga classes, I still have to focus on the breathing exercises.

As my stomach rises and falls, I let the music consume me. The waterfall becomes a water wheel, churning gallon upon gallon of water, dumping it down a makeshift waterslide. The waterslide empties into an artificial lake. Mr Gaudenzi's voice fades.

I'm in Kilimanjaro, Nicaragua's most famous coffee plantation. I see Don Andi and Doña Emma, the owners of la finca. They smile and call out.

"¡Amanda! ¿Qué tal?"

I open my mouth to answer but someone behind me is already responding.

"¡Bien, gracias!"

I whip around and see—myself. I'm treading water in the lake, waving to Don Andi and Doña Emma. Other teens on my service trip are splashing in the water as well, but no one notices me. I'm not in Kilimanjaro at all.

I'm navigating my memories.

The sun is setting on the hills of la finca and I follow myself out of the lake and down the hill to the cabins. The rest of the service group is lounging there. I want to wander off to the rustic stable where my white horse, Gabelon, is tied up. I remember shaking like a leaf when I rode her, grasping her mane for dear life as she wobbled up the rocky incline. But when I try to leave the cabins, the plantation blurs. I don't have power over the memories I visit; I must stay within the confines of this one.

Night is fast approaching. Everyone is eating s'mores around the bonfire that our counselor, Dave, built. We called him "Chaparro," or "Shorty." Though small, he had a passion and strength unrivaled by anyone else on the trip. The fire hisses and spits at me and I retreat, knocking into a picnic chair that's been dragged to the fireside.

"You ready?" I hear Eric's voice. He was one of the first friends I made on the trip.

"Yeah, as soon as Sophie starts playing," I hear myself respond. I'm sitting between Eric and Sophie in muddy shorts and a Nike T-shirt, absently twirling a wooden stick in my hand for marshmallow roasting.

Sophie strums the guitar and Eric clears his throat. "All the, small things..."

"True care, truth brings!"

"I'll take one lift..." We sing together, laughing and stumbling over words. The sounds of crunching graham crackers accompany our music.

When the song finishes, I see my friends Ginny and Emily drag me back up the hill with counselors David and Michelle to stargaze. I follow them and hear myself squeal.

"Wait—that's the Milky Way? This is insane!"

"Cool, right? And something else—we're seeing these stars as they were hundreds of years ago. That's how long it takes for their light to reach us," David says. His bright blue eyes twinkle, or maybe that's just the reflection of the stars.

"I feel like a time traveler!" I chuckle—I'm such a New Yorker.

I lie beside Amanda, who's six months younger, and study the sky with her. I can actually tell that the world is a sphere. The edges seem rounded where the sky and ground meet. Kilimanjaro is a snow globe and I'm lying in it. It's a million times better than The Museum of Natural History's planetarium. It's real.

"Look at the stars, look how they shine for you!" we're singing again. This time, it's Coldplay's "Yellow." Ginny, Emily, and I don't remember all the words, so we just sing the same three lines over and over until we become so entranced by the stars that we forget to keep going. I smile and watch myself marvel in the discovery of this new world.

"Take a few more deep breaths..."

Mr. Gaudenzi's voice shakes Kilimanjaro. The singing stops and I'm alone on the hill. I look for something to grasp, something to ground myself in this place. But the lights in the sky sputter and extinguish one by one, and I can't see the hill or the lake or the stable.

"One last breath, make it count..."

Everything is black.

"Okay, everybody, you can open your eyes."

I blink and see friends stretching and sitting up around me. Kilimanjaro is thousands of miles away from my high school on Park Avenue. All I have is the memory.

MELT THE HEART

SAMANTHA CARLIN

When Amanda started her new worlds piece about meditation, I thought of the journeys I take within myself on my yoga mat.

 *McCullough, p. 253*

 *p. 50*

Bend your back to melt your heart.

Barb's voice leading Vinyasa is like tea with honey. She's moving the class through backbends, also called heart-openers, for they way they expose the chest and core.

This is my favorite of her mantras, but today it's not soothing. I'm thinking about an e-mail I received that morning from a new guy I'm dating. He revealed that he went running and was near my apartment. He almost stopped by, but didn't, choosing to respect my time and space.

On my yoga mat, I remember my knee-jerk reaction to his letter—*That would totally freak me out, your bursting my privacy, exploding my routines.*

No bending back there...no melting heart.

The yoga class is preparing for *urdhva dhanurasana*, wheel pose. The pose looks as it sounds: the body contorting to imitate a wheel. I'm at my most vulnerable and sensitive in this position. My arching back exhibits my whole body; every curve and crevice is visible. And it's painful—my wrists always ache, despite years of practice.

This is exactly how I felt reading this young man's e-mail. Like he was asking me to do wheel pose when my wrists were already stressed. All my past relationships had only resulted in hurt. Just thinking about dating, with its necessary process of laying myself bare, exhausted me. Recently, I'd been actively avoiding the practice, with scattered and shallow exceptions. So by the time this beautiful, open-hearted e-mail floated into my inbox, I thought protecting myself was just "who I was." As if my back were paralyzed, my heart solidified. In my reply, I thanked him for choosing respect over romance, telling him I needed my "alone time" to have energy for my relationships.

Wheel, averted.

There's no avoiding wheel in class, though. At Barb's prompting, I must hoist myself up. I send all my positive energy and breath into my wrists, silently telling them that they are stronger than they imagine. As I hold here, head dangling upside down between my arms, belly reaching for the sky, I embrace the exposure. My bending back expands my ribcage; there's new space in my chest. My breath overflowing my lungs deepens my heartbeat.

My wrists are straining; in each moment I swear I'm about to collapse. I breathe through the discomfort. As Barb lets us release down to the mat, I feel exquisite.

Recovering, rolling my wrists, I suddenly regret my e-mail. The truth is I'm falling for this guy, harder than I've fallen in ages. I pine for romance, *his* romance. And he's standing in front of me, my heart butter in his hands. It hits me—I'm psyching myself out. I'm not paralyzed to emotional backbends, I'm just sorely, sorely out of practice.

Later that day, Barb's voice in my head, I write him back again, and, wrists pinching under the weight of my vulnerability, the total exposure of new love, I admit my misgivings.

This is my bending back...this is my melting heart.

Wheel, accepted.

EXIT PLAN
SIOBHAN BURKE

M *Chan, p. 216*
P *p. 19*

For a while I'd been trying
To escape the grey fluorescence
That swallowed up the length of every day.
Only the right combination
Of certainty and risk
Could resist gravitational pull.

When I finally found it,
I landed in this room, lit mostly by the sun
(And a desk lamp, if I want)
At the outer reaches of the chaos.
A far-flung urban orbit,
Where I pay a little money every month
To choose between the quiet
And the quieter quiet,
To determine when I come and when I go.

Where the silence lies adjacent
To the clean communal space,
With the meticulous signs
That urge us to work together.
This is where you eat your lunch
From the deli across the street.
This is the hook where the hand towel goes,
And if the garbage overflows,
Don't just stand there. Change it.

Out here things are slower,
But never slow enough.
The planet reliably glides through its rotations.
What happens at eleven a.m. on a Wednesday?
What do the streets look like at three?
You really get to know the length of an hour,
A friend once told me, of his morning meditations.
I am getting to know the length of a day,
And it's not as long as I thought.

A CHANGE OF PACE

VALENE MEZMIN

 *Lippman, p. 114*

 *p. 51*

How much longer? My pulse is racing, I'm tired, and my legs are aching from the distance I've already traveled, and yet I keep going. I'm sweaty and tired and my stomach sounds like Chewbacca, and I'm starting to think that wearing my Converse was probably the worst decision I've ever made... EVER, but still I keep pushing on. Because this isn't about me; this is about something greater than my aching feet or my growling stomach. This is about helping others and fighting for a cure that could save the lives of millions of women around the world. This is about striving to end breast cancer.

"Two more miles to go," I think, and because I don't have the energy to talk anymore to my friends beside me (liar—I've just run out of things to say), I start to closely observe all the other people around me. Most of them are wearing pink stickers on their backs stating, "I'm fighting for______." But I'm not wearing a sticker, and I start to really think about why I'm doing this. This isn't just a bonding time with friends, even though they do make good company. Years ago at a family reunion, my distant cousin gave an emotional speech about her fight with breast cancer, and because she found out about it early, through the good grace of God, she was able to fend it off before it could take her down with it. But what about people who are diagnosed too late? Whose options become more and more limited as the disease progresses? And then I start to speed up because I just found my greater purpose.

"One more mile to go," and my mind starts to wander. Prospect Park. I don't come here often. The sweet melodic sounds of nature and all that inhabit it call out to me. I notice the soft dance of the trees dancing to the sweet tunes of nature, picking up rhythm and then slowing back down in the most graceful of moves. With every movement, a few crispy brown leaves fall from their branches, undergoing the natural process of autumnal changes. But every once in a while I still see those random tall, vibrant green trees with most of their leaves still intact. They're fighters, I think. I admire that about them.

I walk past a large, bulky, billowing tree. Its bark is as dark as fresh mud after a heavy downpour. The leaves are a rainbow of colors: green, brown, red, orange, and the others a brilliant combination, all living harmoniously together on the branches of the tree. Just when I think it can't get any more beautiful, I spot a small lonely bird. Now, I don't know much about birds, but I can tell you this bird is small, capable of fitting comfortably in just the palm of my hand, and it is blue, the same dusky blue color of the sky enveloping the world around me. It looks lonely. Doesn't it have any friends or family? Or maybe it just wants to escape; it wants to be alone. I mean, it is a New York City bird, which has to deal with all the chaos that defines this city also. On my journey over to Prospect Park, the subway was crowded with people bumping into each other left and right. I wonder, is there bird traffic in the sky? I feel an odd connection to this bird. There's a reason the bird chose to come here. There's a strange sense of freedom here. Earlier I thought, with so many people participating in this walk, it would be crowded and I would feel suffocated. But it's just the opposite. Amidst all the people around me, I feel a sense of isolation, like I'm in my own little bubble. It's such a refreshing feeling; I had never felt quite like this before.

I'm free here, I think again. Free to go deep inside my mind, to relax, to escape from the hustle and bustle that is New York City. The city that never sleeps? The city that never takes a moment to breathe. Here I don't have to think about the pressures of school and life. I like it here in Prospect Park, and I know that I will be back here again. Soon.

All of a sudden my thoughts are disrupted by loud applause. Other walkers and onlookers are clapping for me! I did it! I finished the Breast Cancer Walk. This is a major accomplishment in the story that is my life. I blend myself back into my group of friends, and together we go off in search of the promised free bottles of water and rumors of free ice cream traveling around.

IMPROPER UNIFORM

EMELY PAULINO

Since Jess and I have both been to a single-sex school, we knew this was something that we could both write about. My poem discusses what it's like to be in this environment, how it has shaped my way of thinking, and what it means to be a woman today.

 *Pastore, p. 153*

 *p. 57*

what does it mean to be among the first
to wear a navy blue sweater
with an emblem ironed on to the acrylic
that itched you while you waited on the
lunch line?
they asked you, at age ten, "do you want
to be here?"
and you shyly nodded your head.
this was not a place where you could go
unnoticed,
unless you wore improper uniform
which seven years earlier, would have
earned you a call home,
but that rule crumbled under our opinions
and stylish shoes
because whether we wore white knee-high
socks or not,
we were still TYWLS girls.

what does it mean to have a voice
that took centuries to be heard?
at birth they immediately loved you,
protected you,
protected you to the point where you
could not make a choice
without asking for permission,
or thinking about somebody else first.
you were bound, but not unaware
of those before you who abandoned the
etiquette you were expected to follow,
and those around you
who invited you to follow their footsteps
who supported you, for taking off the
emblem
for cutting your hair and wearing makeup
if you wanted to,
they supported you
for being you.

what does it mean to walk down Steinway
when the sun was warm,
the wind trickled through your hair
and you slowed down your pace because
you didn't want to go home?

inhaling the smell of smoke and kebabs
burning in the corner,
you knew this wouldn't last for much
longer.

what does it mean to be a woman,
who from a young age grew to understand
the language that only eyes can speak?
in the two seconds it takes them to
measure you
you already know what they are thinking,
but that doesn't change
where you come from,
or where you are going.

FOR GILLIAN ROSE

AMY FLYNTZ

After being fortunate enough to spend some quality time with my nine-year-old niece lately, I was inspired (and humbled) by her fiercely loyal, independent spirit, and boundless capacity for joy.

 Martinez, p. 159
 p. 49

They call you *princess*
But I know the truth:
You were baptized into this family of
women—
Not royal, but noble, still.

When they ask for your tiara
Go ahead
And tell them this:

You were raised by the Three Sister Spirits;
And your Mama is a medicine woman—
Those freckles are made of cinnamon
Placed with care by Grammy's knotty
hands
And your dreams are the clouds
Hand-woven by Auntie K.

Your turret is a tree trunk—
Your kingdom is the world;
The weight of it doesn't make a dent
On your tiny shoulders.

There is an army of little brothers

Awaiting your command
And when you make up your mind,
There is not enough fury in the Universe
That can change your point of view.

Your legs are strong enough to carry you
Without waiting for a white horse
And should they ever give out
You will call upon the recesses of your
mind
To come to your rescue.

When they call you *princess*
Ask them this:

Should you settle for *princess*
When you have the
Grace
...of Nanny May
Kindness
...of your Grammy
Strength
...of your Mama
Fire
...of your Aunties

And the Heart
of a
Warrior
?

DEAR KRISTOPH

TEMA REGIST

This poem is addressed to my unborn nephew.

 *DeLuna, p. 263*

 *p. 60*

Dear Kristoph,

*"Is solace anywhere more comforting
than in the arms of a sister?"*

The echoing cries that penetrated her tired ears,
Swaying me back and forth in her adolescent arms,
Her angelic smile that rose above her ears,
Allowing her divine cheekbones to protrude and consume a rosy vibrant color

She sang:

*"You can own the Earth and still,
All you'll own is earth until you can paint with all the colors of the wind."*

She gave me my treasures,
My canvas and my paintbrush.

While life gave me the paint filled with the brightest colors for the sunniest and fruitful days
And darkest colors for the hurricanes that pass me by.

With every moment we spend together, my paintbrush
Swirls and twirls and twists and spins,
Elegantly dancing across my canvas.

My canvas tells our story.

My unfinished painting can never be completed,
For we have more memories to be created.

Kristoph, your mommy is as beautiful as the stars that glisten at night,
As strong as the roots implanted upon this earth,
As elegant as a blossoming tulip,
And as benevolent as our mommy.

She is powerful.

In time, she will give you your canvas,
But now, I pass my paintbrush on to you.

CHANCE
JOANN DELUNA

My poem was inspired by Jonathan Reed's poem "Lost Generation," which has the opposite message if you read the poem backwards. Tema and I delved into a whole new world trying to write our own backwards poems.

 *Regist, p. 262*
 *p. 60*

Take a chance
Don't
Be afraid of success
Embrace failure
Ignore
Insecurities
You can't succeed
If you don't try
Forget what they say
"Leading a stable life"
No more
Every day the same
Looking at spreadsheets
You'll get paid
But knots in your stomach
Scream
"Set me free."

EXCERPT FROM
QUICK KILLS
LYNN LURIE

 Sandino, p. 264

 p. 65

I dig the soles of my feet into the clay that covers the bottom of the lake, opening and closing my toes. The water clouds and from the waist down I am missing.

I carry the clay in the apron of my bathing suit to the boulders that separate the lake from the woods. Stanchions of birch trees hide me. Autumn is coming and some of the leaves are already turning color. I spread myself on my back across the warm flat rocks, rubbing clumps of wet clay into my legs and arms. I peel it away after it hardens and cracks. My skin is parched and wrinkled. With the still wet clay, I roll arms and legs and connect these to rectangular torsos and flattened heads.

My family begins to dry.

Birch bark peels horizontally. I use it as paper and list the names. When I am done, I tie the scroll with the vein of a leaf and at the end of the day I stash the list with the dried figurines in the crook of a rock. When summer is over, I bury us deep into the soil, posting no marker.

NO THANKS, I LIKE THE WAY THINGS ARE
ASHLEY SANDINO

 Lurie, p. 264

 p. 65

It comes down to knowing how to get where you want to be. In this new world, only knowing what you want is not enough. Everyone is dealt a hand of cards, which tells you your destiny. First you have to agree to play. Few people know how to do this and no one can teach you. If you had the chance to see the cards you're about to pick up, would you still pick them up? Here, in this new world, you have to find the right time to pull that intangible from the air. You have to know how to align your chances. If you decide to play, you are in control. You are the head designer. Here's the creation of a girl who realigned her cards in a way that became right for her:

She is a film student currently traveling and documenting her experiences. She meets new people who think she is interesting and develops lasting relationships

with them. Her sophistication and style charm them. And of course, why wouldn't they think she's interesting: a young artist in high demand but at the same time humble and modest. Her friends, many from college, help her with her projects and use this as an opportunity to build their resumes. Every chance they get, they do something new. During a break from school, they take a road trip through the entire Southwest, finding inspiration in the dry and warm desert air. They organize charity events, attracting funders from agencies simply by providing great music, food, performances, and showing films and artwork. They'll travel to beautiful, remote landscapes to host photo shoots, and use the photographs to get hired by advertisement industries and fashion labels. That's what she is about: knowing how to cherish the moments and savor the memories she has with her friends, people that help her in her career and well-being.

Her admirers look toward her independence, which seems so difficult to master, but she has no problem offering guidance. She is giving. Though she concentrates on herself, she is not isolated, but rather gives everyone a chance to get to know her and allows herself to open up to others.

She has an outgoing presence and a headstrong, witty attitude. She beats the odds. She faces challenges unafraid. She is stubborn when she needs to support a cause or a friend. She won't back down but she will compromise. She is a smart negotiator, supporting her opinion. She will have you questioning your own positions. She does not just settle for what she can get; she fights for what she wants. She is outspoken and makes a statement.

She is always in the social scene. From her home in New York City to anywhere across the country, she familiarizes herself with every environment she encounters. She walks on the sidewalks of these cities as if they were concrete runways, owning the attention with no remorse and not an ounce of insecurity. We see one vibrantly colored heel being placed in front of the other in her signature walk. Her brown eyes are focused forward but acknowledge those who greet her. She smiles back, and her bright lipstick accentuates her subtle, sweet expression. Her long, wavy, auburn locks flow as they are caught by the wind. She'll be a fierce fashion supermodel. No longer staring into the windows of stores featuring fabulous fashion brands that she could not have while growing up. She breaks the stereotype of what a model is and sets a new course. No one takes advantage of her, and she is not deprived of food. Next to the people in her life, food is her best friend. She absolutely loves to eat. She is respected and acknowledged as a beautiful, intelligent woman who knows what she is doing in every move she makes.

As for romance, occasionally she accepts the invitation, but she never gets overly involved because she is completely self-aware and careful to protect herself. She doesn't have time for the jealousy and stressful demands that come hand in hand with being in a relationship. Her relationships don't constrain her or hold her down; they make her happy to be alive.

Her life is demanding: juggling a career, a social life, and personal time is not easy, but she loves every moment. She embraces who she is. She is a force to reckon with, even though all her struggles and hard times are still a part of her.

In this new world, whatever abandonment she experienced, tormentors she had to face every day while growing up, the shame, the embarrassment, the pain, the exhaustion from getting by every day is part of the past. Once she has unlocked the secret of the cards she is someone new. It would not have happened had she stayed a moment longer in her old life, or had she clung to the familiar. The girl mentioned has given herself a new life, one she would have missed if she had clung to the familiar. Now, her life is a marvelous dream that she will never wake up from. The horrible past that nearly crushed her no longer defines who she is. You too should join in and play. You will not regret it.

ERIN BAER, MENTOR 2008-2009

"I'm better written than I am spoken," I'd say to classmates, family members, fellow AOL Instant Messengers. I needed a way to sift through the over-analytical anxious inner-workings of my developing mind. Writing was not about journals or class assignments or even school newspapers. Writing was the channel between my head, my heart, and the world.

exploration

ADVENTURES AWAIT MY ARRIVAL

Allow me a moment
For my fantasy and reality to finally meet
I land feet first into a cobble-stoned land
Just a hop across the pond
Where rare adventures await my arrival

Najaya Royal, p. 290

With writing, the possibilities are endless. We escape from our daily lives to explore places we've never been, places we've always dreamed of, and create new worlds. Most importantly, we learn something new about ourselves.

Each of the following pieces takes us on a different adventure. We'll travel back to the 1920s and imagine what the world was like for our ancestors. We'll explore new, magical worlds different from our own. Alexus Colbert *(p. 289)* will take us to her secret paradise: "the perfect place to relax and discover your inner self." On the other hand, Mennen Gordon *(p. 287)* will transport us to a place she hates: Florida. Through the pieces, we'll discover what we can learn about ourselves in unfamiliar places.

When Xiao Shan Liu immigrated to New York from China, she found herself, realizing that the "...little Chinese girl who spent her childhood in a small town had grown up. In New York, she has become a young woman who is taking responsibility for her life and is starting to fight for her dreams and goals." *(p. 284)*

Through our written adventures we've learned a lot about ourselves and hope you will learn something about yourself as well.

WHITNEY JACOBY
2013 MENTOR AND
ANTHOLOGY COMMITTEE MEMBER

SIMON TUCKER

CHERISE WOLAS

This piece is an excerpt from Words of New Beginnings, *my nearly complete novel. For twelve-year old Simon Tucker, stuck in his room while his body heals, creating new worlds might be how he is healing his mind.*

 *Plasencia, p. 218*

 *p. 58*

I have written in these pages about the Russian prince living in a tent outside his dacha; the English lord contemplating a move to Las Vegas; the breeder whose dogs meow, furious as cats in heat; the linguist and his ability to speak of love in ten different countries; the hemophiliac who communes with his ghostly suffering ancestors, his published accounts of their conversational feats. I have written about the mailman's Panama hat; the milkman's hazelnut milk; miniature Consuelo and her Guatemalan nachos. Of course, the truths of my boyish life are white caps on a rendered sea.

You read the truer tales about Simon Tucker, narrated by those perhaps more honest, certainly less ingenious. My father is Jack, not Harry, and he weighs catastrophes, not an inherited fortune. My mother is Susan. Unlike Pearl, she mans no charity, just the reception desk for a surgeon who breaks original noses, reforms them at will. My sisters are cheerleaders and a shortstop; none has a boyfriend named Virgil, his lip split by the wishbones of chickens. Guatemalan Consuelo is unwieldy, resents fetching, burns all my afternoon snacks. Hercules is actually Scooter, a mongrel I named before I was bold. Our grand house with rolling grounds, silvered birches, an ancient koi pond crusted with algae the gardener ignores, is just a house in a development with other houses just like it, coated in paint-can individuality. Ours is in a shade whose name promises more than it should. The small tidy lawn is hand-mowed, spindly trees rise along the back of the fence, not hand-built from stone but rather thick planks. But there is not much more to see for miles and miles.

I am twelve, room-bound, broken, plastered, casted, and wrapped. I lie on my bed and read the books my mother lugs home from the library. Through the window, the summer shimmies away. When I grow tired of reading the words of others, I follow Deo, and Abel, and Icarus, and Theo, and Zed around with my mind, write their stories down, think of how to live. Always, when I close my eyes, I return to those soaring seconds of flight through a pure blue sky, a cotton ball cloud cornering my eye. Such wonder and awe before plummeting. The old toddler pool, inflated and filled, could not sustain the impact of a high dive. When I hit, the water was warm, sunlight bright.

Some may tussle with my disclosures, the righteous, certain that I have fabricated, that I am passing along deliberate mistruths to the naïve. Who can say, when all of life filters through personal stones. My own experience has taught me that there is no golden ticket at birth; the richest life is stitched with thievery. Take what you need from everyone—just do right by those stolen gifts. Exhaust all to ashes. If you are brave, you too may experience what I, Simon Tucker, have experienced: a transformed life that might still be extraordinary, miraculous, and singular.

HIDDEN IDENTITY

CHANDRA HUGHES

This is a short memoir from a time at camp when I really connected with the character whom I was role-playing.

 *Parsons, p. 292*

 *p. 40*

I stare at Matthew Johnson with his embroidered cape. We are inside the dining room, the room that is now the empty banquet. Matthew is no longer Matthew, he is Talion: the leader of our group, the warrior carrying the sword. And I am Rune: the healer, wearing a purple velvet dress. My mind rushes, trying to balance reality with the role-playing. I hear Rachel's voice as Fiona, her seducing voice calling Talion's name. I am Rune, the one who decided to protect Talion, the one who's secretly in love with him. My mind is pulled into the game, fading from reality.

As Rune, I push Talion down onto the table. My mind is racing, frustrated, annoyed, in love. Passionate feelings to protect Talion overwhelm me. "Talion, she's not her. You need to stay away from Fiona! She's not herself!" I scream at him. Talion looks at me. His eyes sadden in pain.

"I know," Talion says, his eyes averting from mine to his lover. He gazes at Fiona as I bite my lip, unsure what to say, what to do. My fingers loosen their grip on Talion's arms and begin to relax. Then I feel a shadow lurking behind me. Fiona leans into my ear.

"Charm," she whispers. I am knocked out of the game, back into reality. Charm? I think. In all of the four other games I've played at camp, a spell has never been cast upon me. I waver, unsure of what to do. I sigh and decide to play as Rune again. My body relaxes, my frustration ceases, and I sit down next to Talion, almost in a trance. My eyes follow Fiona, entranced by her blue flowing dress. I crave to follow her, wanting to help her. Two seconds later, I hear the chanting words of Runhildia, my teammate. "Sleep!" she says. Fiona crumbles to the floor,

the sleep spell overpowering her. My brain hurts; my respect for Fiona tells me to wake her up but my heart tells me not to. I am again knocked back into reality. *Is charm still in effect when one is asleep?* I think, forgetting the rules that we had covered at camp earlier. *Crap, what should I do?* Pushing my thoughts back into playing Rune, I lower my head, my hair covering my face. I stare down at Fiona's sleeping body. *Should I wake her up? No one cares about me. No one wants to know what is wrong with Rune,* I think. I clear my thoughts. My mind lets go of all my worries of how to act. I no longer care anymore. I let my heart be overtaken by the feelings I've created as my character. I let go of myself, and I become Rune.

I kneel down and approach Fiona. My arms automatically touch her arm and my voice lets out a soft scream. "Fiona?" I say. My heart tells me to stop. That this is wrong. That I am not me. That I need to save Talion. But my mind ignores it. I give in to the power of charm. "Fiona!" I scream, shaking her. "Fiona! Wake up!"

"What's wrong with her?" Talion asks to no one in particular. Talion's words rush to my head. My heart reminds me of the love I have for Talion. I let go of Fiona, sitting there. Unsure of what to do. "Take Rune away from here!" Talion shouts to the people around. Nadia grabs me by the arm and leads me out of the room.

I hit the floor, leaning against the wooden wall. My arms hug my knees, my head is in pain, my heart aches. Tears roll down my eyes and I begin to cry. My cries of pain, my thoughts of Talion, my heart telling me to defeat this charm cast upon me. I peer into the other room. I look at Talion, and then realization hits. Talion didn't come to me. *He didn't care about me enough to take me away,* I think. Charm begins to kick in again, and I let it overwhelm me. I struggle to get up, screaming Fiona's name. Nadia and her group hold me down. I put up a fight, trying to wriggle out of their grasp. Charm becomes more powerful and I feel as though I hear Fiona herself asking me to wake her up. I scream her name once more. Nadia holds me tight, telling me that everything will be okay.

Her words knock me out of the moment. I am no longer Rune. I am me. My eyes look around the room. I recognize the main space, and I see Anna looking back at me. I feel the watery tears down my face. I am shocked. Shocked by the fact that I was so into character. Shocked by the fact that Rune's feelings of love towards Talion, the ones I created, the ones that I told myself to think about, absorbed me, sending me out of the realistic world into the fantasy life. Totally thrown out of the moment, full of shock and eagerness to tell people what had happened, and annoyed that no one noticed that a spell was cast upon me, I go on acting as Rune, but no longer being her.

TIMES SQUARE TURN BACK

KAADIANA BARNES

This piece is an excerpt from a story I started during the Historical Fiction Workshop. It's about a teenage girl who has to adapt to the 1920s before getting back to the future.

 *O'Dell, p. 141*

 *p. 8*

Ten, nine, eight...

People are screaming the numbers and counting down backward. We have waited outside for many hours in the freezing cold with our coats and scarves around our mouths, waiting for the ball to drop.

Seven, six, five...

We are standing tightly together and there's barely anywhere to move. There are tall people, short people, big people, and little people.

Four, three, two...

BOOM.

What's just happened? It felt like I was flashed into another dimension. I know this is not a dream because I was just standing with my friends and it looks like a ghost town now. I can hear a pin dropped. This is reality, but not my reality.

There are small black cars that look like carriages on wheels driving where the tourists would stand. When I turn around, the Times Square towers are very short and thick with big bright white lights. The Forever 21 store with the huge number 21 that stands out doesn't appear.

I notice that a lot of men have Michael Jackson's "Smooth Criminal" suits. The flappers are walking around with high heels and short dresses and furry coats. The people are staring at me as I walk down the street with my sneakers, jeans, and marmot coat. All of sudden, a tornado wind is pushing me around until I trip over a package. It says, "To: Isabella Wilson." A letter inside reads:

> *Good Afternoon, Isabella,*
>
> *You became a new victim of "flashing back." Today is December 1, 1922 and it is your duty to learn something new from the past. The golden watch here is to tell you how much time you have left in 1922. If you disobey any of the rules, more time will be added to your stay here.*
>
> 1. *You must wear the 1920's outfit.*
> 2. *You cannot take anything from this era.*
> 3. *Don't talk to any strangers.*
> 4. *You can't fall in love with someone from 1922.*

You will go back home more quickly if you obey the rules.

- Good Luck

I have to follow rules to get out of here. I come across an amazing jazz club from which I hear loud music. I go inside and start creeping toward the ladies bathroom before people notice what I have on. I go inside the stall and open the bag that the package came with. The clothes appear as if there were a magical spell on them. I put on the gold high heels that are six inches high with a short gold dress. There's a wig that is identical to my hair color, brunette, and it is very short with big thick curls. I put on the wig and some makeup. I look at the reflection in the mirror, and I see that I don't look like myself, but like my 18-year-old great-grandmother.

As I leave, my heart is racing inside of me. I have to try my best to blend in. The music is very loud and with many musical instruments playing at once. I decide to sit down while couples are dancing the swing. A boy starts to look toward my direction. I look away fast because I check my watch, and it is counting down. I try my best not to get his attention, but he keeps looking right at me. He is wearing a "Smooth Criminal" outfit. He starts to walk toward me and reaches his hand out.

"Would you like to dance?" he asks. I am so nervous I don't know what to do, because I keep thinking about the rules.

"I am sorry, no thanks," I answer nicely.

"Why not?" he asks. I am trying to look around to think of an excuse.

"Umm...Um... I can't dance the swing; it is very hard," I answer. I mean, it is bad enough to wear heels that I can barely walk in, let alone dance in.

"It's easy—come try," he asks again. I think if I came to this era to blend in, then I should be able to dance with someone. In the '20s people would dance the swing together, which is culture. He takes me to the middle of the dance floor.

"So, you step your front foot forward and then step your back foot back and jump."

He is teaching me how to swing and this dance is not bad at all. I am used to my kind of music and this kind of party is very new to me.

"You are such a great dancer," I tell him.

"Thanks; what's your name?" he asks.

"My name is Isabella. What about you?" I ask.

"My name is Jake," he tells me. Meanwhile, I notice that my watch is moving forward quickly. It went from "two days" to "four days." I have no idea what I'm going to do for the next few days. I am wondering if talking to Jake is going to help me or hinder me. Is he a start for now?

MOTE IT BE

KRISTASIAH DANIELS

This piece explores Wicca, an ancient religion still practiced today. The protagonist in my story discovers a new underworld of religion through a vision of her past.

Narde, p. 202

p. 26

I ran to my bed and threw myself down onto my pillow. The school day was long and miserable, like most days. The others harassed me—they mocked my hair and eyes and size because I am different from them, and yet, are those not the usual rules of high school?

As I took off my shoes, I felt something behind my heels, under the bed. It was a package with my name on it. With excitement, I tore into it, shredding the soft, blue wrapping. It was a book. The cover was black and hard, with an encircled five-point star embedded in it. *I've seen this symbol before,* I thought. *Grandma had a necklace just like it.*

As I opened the book, a vision came to me like a sudden dream. A crowd gathered as a woman stood tied to a stake, in the midst of a fire. Her flesh melted off her bones and the crowd, as witness, cheered in glee. Their joy mocked human nature so much that I could weep. STOP! STOP! my thoughts cried, but no one heard. Through their squeals of pleasure, I heard a whisper: "*You shall live on and become what you were born to be.*"

The book still in my hand, I began to feel watched in the crowd. Then, I saw her: a young girl looking right through me. Her eyes were wide and her hair black and short. She stood, emotionless, at a distance from the crowd. She was clutching her necklace, a necklace that resembled my grandmother's. I couldn't help noticing how much she looked like me.

Everything became blurry and faint, as I slowly came to my senses. I was back in my room. I looked down and the book was in my lap. Running my fingers down its spine, I felt a familiar feeling, as if the book were mine. As I opened it, a note fell from between its pages.

Dear Nivea,

This is your grandmother. I don't know what is going on in your life. If you're reading this I must be dead and gone. It is time to learn that you are not what you seem. My dear, you are a witch, a Wiccan I might say. It has been practiced through generations. You have the power of wind, water, air, fire, and spirit. Read this book and you shall enter the world of the Wicca.

Merry ye meet and merry ye meet again.

Grandma had just died last year. How did this get here? I thought. Who sent it? I thought of my mother. She had been in deep denial since my grandmother's passing and had since emancipated me. The last time I saw my mother, she was complaining that the moon was not at its peak and that she must leave to prepare herself for the ceremony. A month ago, I did not understand what she was talking about. She was neither an unfit parent, nor mental—just grieving.

My mother was always a talker and loved taking walks in Prospect Park. She had told me every day since I was ten to write in my journal about everything I did and learned throughout the day. *"Journals are magic and can be the best of listeners at times. One day they will talk back,"* I remember her telling me. Now my dead grandmother was sending me mail and claiming I was a witch—and here I thought I only had to deal with the harassment of my Neanderthal classmates. At least now I could add "freak of nature" to the list of my oddities.

I opened the book again to discover on the first page a handwritten poem called "The Wiccan Rede." I began to read it, trying to make sense of the words, many of them foreign to me. *What does it all mean?* I thought.

"You never were that good at remembering," a voice said.

I knew that voice. I turned around. "Grandma..." I stammered.

"Hello, sweetheart," she said, her ghost standing before me. *"The book has found you at last. A young witch such as yourself needs to remember the rede in order to understand the full capacity of your power."*

She pointed to the rede and said, *"Sweetheart, open your mind."* She touched my head and it felt so real, almost as if she were alive. The tip of her finger left a faint linger of sage: white sage. She was gone. I remembered a game we played when I was young where she would draw a star on the ground and light candles. There was an altar where we would put our happiness and joy. Then, my grandma would speak poetry while she burned the sage. She called it the purifying of our heart.

EXCERPT FROM
THE COLOR BLUE
ASHLEY CHRISTIE

This piece was inspired by The Color Purple *by Alice Walker. It's set in Brooklyn in 2009.*

 *Porter, p. 181*

 *p. 21*

July 4, 2009

Dear Mommy,

Happy Independence Day; it's the Fourth of July. Last night Ms. Candice took D'quaya who's seventeen just like me, Tyrique, who's nine, and Devonte, who's eight and I out to Manhattan. We went to Forty-Second Street to M&M World and walked around. Then she took us to this cool movie theatre that brought us meals while we were watching the movie. What a way to welcome me! We didn't go to her house yet; we're in a hotel. I don't think we're going until tomorrow but I don't mind. I'm enjoying this. I think we're going to watch fireworks tonight in DUMBO, right under the Brooklyn Bridge, or Coney Island. I'm excited about either one. Maybe I was wrong—maybe this will work out just fine. None of the kids and I spoke much, we just exchanged names and ages and some small talk about how excited we are school is over and it's finally summer break. Nothing too revealing and I'm glad. There's something a little strange about D'quaya though. She doesn't seem so excited about anything. It's like she's just here to be here.

July 5, 2009

Dear Mommy,

We got back around two this morning to her house, and it's not really what I expected. I don't have my own room. It isn't such a big deal to me, but I guess it wasn't what I was expecting, that's all. The house was a little messy, but I think it was because everyone was in such a rush getting ready to pick me up and show me a good time that they forgot to clean. D'quaya doesn't say much; she's been on the computer and phone. She talks really softly so I can't make out what she's saying; it's something funny about her. Anyway, Tyrique and Devonte share a room and Ms. Candice has her own room. The neighborhood isn't that bad. We're in Flatbush and I've heard a lot of negative things about this place, but it seems quiet so far. There's lots of kids and they all seem to know each other, so I doubt it's anything serious out here. I'm going to unpack and get ready to go out with Ms. Candice and D'quaya again. I think she's going to take us shopping and get our hair done. I could get used to this.

July 6, 2009

Dear Mommy,

She bought me tons of new clothes and shoes. My hair has never felt so healthy—it's like it bounces when I move. I thanked her about a million times and she just tells me it's no problem. D'quaya didn't seem so happy and again I don't know why. She just watched me, not in a bad way, but in a sorry way. The social worker is supposed to come today. I guess to check on me and the others and see how things are going so far. I helped Ms. Candice clean, and so did Tyrique; he's a little sweetheart. Everyone's out in the living room watching TV, waiting for dinner and the social worker, and it sounds like a calm day. I'm going to join them. I love you, Mom.

July 7, 2009

Dear Mommy,

This morning I went outside by myself to walk around. I got back inside after about two hours and there were four men inside the living room sitting down. I walked in so confused, and didn't know what to say. I just looked at them. They didn't say anything to me, but they looked at me like I was a piece of meat, especially the guy on the small couch. He broke his neck to look at my butt. Mom, something's wrong with this woman, and wrong with this house, and I'm going to find out today!

D'quaya got home at like ten o'clock. I told her what I saw today, then she gave me that same sorry look. I asked her what was wrong and I needed to know and then she told me everything. Ms. Candice is a front mom. She is a drug dealer, a huge one, which explains where she gets all her money from. She doesn't do much work but she has men do it for her, and those were some of them that I walked into today. D'quaya told me I did the right thing by keeping it moving and to make sure I do it always. She told me all about her life story, too, and how she ended up here. Her mom was a drug addict and left her outside and someone called the cops. That happened to her when she was around Tyrique's age, and she's been with Ms. Candice since. She told me Ms. Candice isn't violent or anything towards us, but she is money hungry, and every month she does the same thing: pays us no attention, and when it's around time for the social worker to visit, she takes us out and stuff so we won't have anything bad to say. D'quaya says that during school, she helps Devonte and Tyrique with their homework and gets them ready because she really thinks of them as little brothers and she doesn't want them on the street like the men that work for Ms. Candice.

I need you, Mom.

EXCERPT FROM

TEMPEST FOR TWO

NANCY HOOPER

I like throwing characters into challenging circumstances to create new worlds for them. This piece is an introduction to a story, Tempest for Two, *which I'm currently writing.*

 *Hossain, p. 95*

 *p. 39*

In seventeen years of marriage, my husband and I engaged in our most titanic battles aboard our twenty-six-foot sailboat. Sure, we bickered on dry land like other couples, but there was something about being afloat on Serena that brought out the worst in both of us. My genial, even-tempered partner turned into Captain Bly, and I, the queen of calm, morphed into chicken-bitch of the sea. Only once was our predictable maritime combat averted—when Mother Nature tossed us about in a great storm at sea and beat us to the punch.

DINOSAUR WORLD

KIRSTEN REACH

On a snowy drive to Nashville in January, a sign on the interstate caught my attention. I interviewed friends and strangers for days, but no one had visited it. We had to investigate.

 *Hernandez, p. 250*

 *p. 37*

The entrance was straight out of *Jurassic Park,* complete with a pterodactyl soaring over the words DINOSAUR WORLD. OK, *Jurassic Park* with just a hint of *The Flintstones,* set in Kentucky, on a rainy Monday morning in late January.

Oddly, ours was the only car in the parking lot.

A purple dinosaur beside the door held his jaw open, proffering a mouth full of soil and cigarette butts. Barney for smokers.

The main building of Dinosaur World is a cement-floored gift shop the size of a small warehouse. Busts of velociraptors line the walls, available in three sizes for those on the hunt for roadside merch. Glass cases snake through the room, overflowing with arthropods, claws, and resin. Bowls of key chains line the counters. Sadly, the shirts featuring "beach bum" dinosaurs in sunglasses on the front, their tails on the back, only come in a child's small.

A book on the children's table caught my eye. Dinosaurs & the Bible. Beside it, a sign: "For more information about Creationism, please ask the front desk."

An older man by the back door sold us tickets and kindly offered us an umbrella.

Dinosaur World was all ours!

The first dinosaur sculptures emerged from the mulch pile on our left. We took a hundred photos them: a green, short one with a face like a frog; a tall, mohawked one with long, pointy teeth; a blue-gray one with little points along his spine who cocked his head to the side like a dog. They were outrageous! They were brilliant!

Two rolls of film later, we realized we'd never heard of any of them before.

The only details given on the placards beside each species were what they ate. Even animatronic exhibits I'd seen as a kid offered a little information about the etymology of the species' names and when they had roamed the earth.

In fact, we began to suspect there were no dates on the placards at all.

The rain evolved into freezing rain. I balanced an umbrella and two bags over Eugene as he reloaded his SLR. Our enthusiasm waned as the temperature dropped.

It became clear there were only a few dinosaur molds at work in this park. To compensate, an artist embellished each with imaginative designs: polka dots, neon stripes, bright blue cow print.

We followed a weak path about a quarter mile to our left. There we came face-to-face with the forty-foot dinosaur on the side of I-65, next to the billboard for the park.

The placard informed us that "Photosaurus" had never actually lived.

So be it. There is no Latin root for "Photosaurus."

We turned back.

Behind us, the interstate roared.

JUNGLE MORNING
ALYSSA VINE

In this short piece, I attempt to capture the experience of an early morning sunrise I saw while traveling in the Amazon.

Liu, p. 284

p. 46

My yellow poncho flickered in the dark as we motored away from the dock. The revving engine cut through the stillness of the Rio Solomon and the early morning, churning out a measure of privacy for all aboard the small boat. Three days in the jungle is plenty of time to settle in and befriend fellow tourists, but there's something about heading out to watch a sunrise, cloaked in plastic, dripping sweat and rain and DEET, that demands a little solitude. Hunched under umbrellas, we were all silent as the boat cut across the river, which is boundless in the wet season. We weaved between treetops, peaking out of the mind-bendingly high water, their trunks fully submerged and branches reaching skyward.

Aboard the boat, our guide cut the engine and gestured eastward. As the boat bumped the muddy shore, we quietly stared across the dark water at the monstrous clouds guarding the horizon. A timid glow mounted in the clouds' thinnest spots, softening the hue of gray slightly. The raindrops dotted the river water, reverberating outward in small circles.

I felt vaguely cheated—up at an ungodly hour, watching a non-sunrise in the rain, on my last day in the Amazon. But as darting birdcalls and the far-off squabble of howler monkeys pierced the thick air around me, I focused on the shrouded skyline. Slowly, almost indiscernibly, the clouds seemed to drift a bit, revealing a sliver of light above the distant tree line. The softened gray stretched up and out, changing shape as the equatorial sunlight burned through weakened patches.

The sky above remained dark and the moisture hung thick in the cool air as the raindrops tapered off. Around the boat, people were halfheartedly pulling their cameras out from within the folds of their rain gear. I fooled around with the manual settings on my camera, experimenting with light exposure and shutter speed to maximize the grandeur of the sprawling river and clouds and light. This was hardly a magnificent sunrise, but it was a beautiful setting and I wanted to remember it.

The backs of my thighs were stiffening against the boat's wooden bench. I began to think of breakfast and the long day of travel ahead, back through the winding turns of the river all the way to Manaus, past thick stretches of wilderness and clearings where lean-to-style homes stood high on stilts in deference to the rising water. Just as I started to feel antsy and wish that the guide would restart the engine and whisk us back across the water, the breaks in the clouds shifted and the sun's true light cracked through in earnest, fiery and bright. A belated but

true sunrise shimmered across the water in streaks of pink and orange. This time, I didn't bother taking out my camera. I just watched.

CHAI-SPICE MACAROONS / NON-JEWS CAN BE GOOD PEOPLE, TOO

NINA AGRAWAL

Both the subject matter and genre of this piece represent new worlds to me. As an Indian woman whose boyfriend is Jewish, I hoped to capture our exploration of each other's cultures; as a writer who takes solace in the objectivity of journalism, I pushed myself to write more personally.

Zhao, p. 147

p. 75

"What I've come to realize is, it's not just about the religion... Non-Jews can be good people, too!" exclaimed the woman to my left, sounding genuinely surprised. I, acutely aware of my non-Jewish status, envisioned myself shriveling up and disappearing, lest someone at the table ask that I demonstrate there and then the truth of her statement.

It was late, five hours into a Passover seder with no end in sight. Until that moment, I had found the dinner and discussion to be refreshingly progressive, even enlightening. I was there with my boyfriend, Joshua, who had been raised as a Conservative Jew. Normally we spent Passover with his parents, which consisted of perfunctory—albeit faithful—readings of the Passover story and four questions, and a rousing rendition of "There's no seder like our seder" (sung to the tune of "There's No Business Like Show Business") by Josh's sister, an aspiring playwright and actress.

This year, though, we thought we'd try something different—something new, something that might challenge our previously held notions about the holiday. For the most part, we had succeeded. We were invited to join a Reform rabbi and his family and friends at their home on the Upper West Side. During dinner we discussed personal and universal definitions of freedom, the significance of the Emancipation Proclamation, and even *The Life of Pi*. One couple took the Passover story to a whole new level using images and phrases culled from social media.

Now we're getting somewhere, I thought. *Here are people who can think critically about their faith and their identity, and still make them come alive in a modern context.*

So I was wholly unprepared for the demonstration of narrow-mindedness by my fellow guest. Why did she sound so surprised? What happened to all that talk of beets on the seder plate for vegetarians, and oranges for gay people?

I decided to ignore the comment and appreciate the evening for what it had otherwise been: thought-provoking, welcoming, warm.

Fast forward to Night Two of Passover, which we spent with my boyfriend's extended family. Though I had known them for years, in some ways I felt more out of place at their seder than I had the previous night. Theirs was a family with fixed traditions, histories I had no place in, and memories that stretched across maps of Brooklyn, from one grandpa's soda factory to another's toy shop. I was a first-generation American who harbored a preference for alu gobhi over latkes and demanded explanations for rituals. I oozed otherness.

I decided on this night to keep quiet and avoid bringing attention to these differences.

My plan failed quickly. Josh kept interrupting the usual proceedings of the seder to say, "Well, last night Nina and I discussed these different meanings of freedom; what do you think about that?" And, "Nina thought this passage from the readings yesterday was really meaningful, so I'd like to have her read it again tonight." As if that weren't enough, his contribution to the meal was macaroons he had made using all my Indian spices. These include things like ginger, cardamom, cloves—not exactly ingredients you cook with if you're trying not to stick out.

Again, I started to contemplate the vision of me shriveling up and disappearing, but then I started to hear the conversation around me. "What a great new perspective you two brought to Passover this year," his aunt said. "It's amazing to see all the different ways people celebrate Passover," reflected his cousin.

And from my boyfriend's mother, notorious for her aversion to strong flavors of any sort: "These macaroons are delicious! What is that in there...one of your tea spices?"

Turns out non-Jews can be good people and good cooks... doesn't that make you an honorary member of the tribe?

MORE THAN A LABEL

KATHERINE NERO

I love traveling internationally, and Teamaré's memoir inspired me to explore the assumptions we make about people from other countries and vice versa.

 *Gastón, p. 251*

 *p. 32*

"What do you call a person who speaks three languages? Trilingual. What do you call a person who speaks two languages? Bilingual. What do you call a person who speaks one language?" The taxi driver glanced at me in the rearview mirror and he said, "American!" Then he roared with laughter at my expense. I gazed out the window, wishing to be anywhere else. After years of looking forward to attending the Pan African Film Festival in Ouagadougou, the capital of Burkina Faso, I found myself longing for home after only three days.

I didn't mind being labeled an *American*. After all, that was and is true. What I found objectionable were the assumptions that went along with the classification, such as being entitled, a big spender, pushy, dismissive of other cultures, and linguistically challenged. As a result of those stereotypes, I was overcharged for taxis, derided when attempting to communicate in French, and constantly accosted to buy this, that and the other. I labeled Burkina Faso hostile and acted accordingly. For the remainder of my stay, my interactions, though polite, were brief and impersonal. I also double-checked all charges and fees.

While strolling near the hotel on my last day in Ouagadougou, I was suddenly approached by a teenage boy. He frantically pointed in the direction of one of the nearby vendors, a middle-aged woman from whom I had purchased a gown the day before. The woman smiled and beckoned me. Cautiously, I walked towards her. The woman handed a head wrap to me made of material that matched the gown I bought for my mother. I hesitated taking the head wrap and asked how much it was. The woman's smile grew more radiant as she said, "For your mother. My gift to your mother."

"How did you know I was shopping for her?" I stammered.

"Because of the care you showed. Just like my daughter."

The woman gently placed the head wrap in my hand and kissed me on the cheek. I was deeply touched by the woman's gesture and told her so.

Labels like American and hostile are useless and limiting. We miss out on so much when we act on preconceived notions. When tempted to draw quick conclusions, I will remember how frustrated I feel when assumptions are made about me. I will also recall the kindness of the woman in Burkina Faso who made me feel at home in what I had perceived to be an unfriendly place. One does not

have to travel to expand one's horizons. An open, non-judgmental mind is all you need wherever you are.

LOVING IN NEW WAYS

AVA NADEL

I traveled to Ecuador with a group from my high school. We took part in a homestay in Pucará, a small village of about 200 people. This experience helped me to see that relationships, especially familial ones, do not need much foundation to sprout.

 *Hempel, p. 217*

 *p. 53*

"¿Cuantos años tienes tú, Norma?

"Dos."

Dos? I thought. *That's odd. Norma had to be older than 16.* Later that night, after dinner, my homestay mother told me that Norma has an intellectual disability: she is twenty-eight and doesn't know how to read or write.

Because my Spanish wasn't entirely perfect, I was unsure of how I should go about communicating with Norma. I had tried conversing with her using my Spanish, but even then she seemed not to understand basic phrases I was saying. So I sat there, at the dining table, shelling the lima beans for dinner. I could feel her staring at me, smiling as I plopped the shelled beans into a bowl. She then stuck one of them in front of my face. I had put the unshelled lima bean into the bowl with the shelled ones. She started laughing both with her mouth and eyes, and I did the same. We may not have been communicating using words, but using our emotions was enough.

For the next four days, I didn't feel so nervous around Norma anymore. I found that just by smiling and laughing, we could read each other's minds just fine. The next few mornings, I would be applying sunscreen in the bedroom and she'd come in, freshly showered, combing her silky, long black hair. We'd sit there in silence, taking care of ourselves separately, but fully aware of the other's presence. Much as I had when peeling the lima beans, I found that if I pulled off humorous actions, we'd improve our communication. I would play around with the stray dogs and cats and have her try and throw food in my mouth. One way or another she'd burst into a fit of giggles.

Through forming this sisterly bond with Norma with hardly any speaking, I learned perhaps one of the most valuable life lessons that any teenager could learn at my age: relationships don't need to be built on much. Norma and I surrounded each other with smiles and laughter and I came to realize that positive energy and emotions were all we needed.

The last morning of my homestay, my homestay mother, Carmela, was cooking us breakfast. Norma turned up the radio, humming along to what I assumed was her favorite song. She took me by the hands and started dancing with me. I could feel the tears welling up in my eyes—the tears I refused to let fall because I knew that if I showed her how weak I was, I wouldn't be able to explain it.

I miss her. I miss her cooing at the stray cat underneath the dining table. I miss her combing her wet hair as she watched me spray sunscreen on my mosquito bites before I left to weed the garden. I miss the dimples in her cheeks from when she'd get herself into a fit of giggles and couldn't stop laughing.

Sometimes the best love is the one that can exist without words.

THE FIRST 1,578 DAYS IN NEW YORK CITY

XIAO SHAN LIU

Vine, p. 279

p. 46

Right from the minute we got on the plane in China, my mother and sister depended entirely on the poor English I had learned in school. This never happened to me; I had never used English in China and I had never been around people using English.

After landing and the long process of immigration, I officially became a resident of New York City. My father came and picked us up outside the airport, telling us we would live with my aunt's family. Before I arrived, it was hard to think that an apartment can fit almost ten people, but we managed to make it work.

The first American culture that I experienced was Thanksgiving Day right after I arrived. It is similar to the Chinese New Year: family will come together and eat. But the food was different from what I had tried before. In my first American dinner, I ate turkey with some of the nuts stuck in its stomach and the sauce. The skin was crispy and tasted awesome with the spices, but the meat tasted unflavored and made me think that the turkey hadn't exercised for a long time, compared with the chickens we raised in China. It was a very interesting dinner for me.

I went to school right after Thanksgiving. MS 131 was a bilingual school where everyone spoke Chinese and English. The students came from different places,

such as Fuzhou, Guangzhou, and Malaysia. We were what people called ESL students, or "English as a Second Language" students.

Outside of school, since I was the one with the most education in the family, I felt like I had the responsibility to help my mom and sister adjust to New York and learn to communicate. For that, I had to learn more, know more. The school work wasn't enough for me, so I practiced at crowded restaurants like McDonald's and Burger King a lot, trying to use English to order food and listen to people next to me.

I also went around and watched the New York lifestyle: seeing New Yorkers walking, talking, and yelling in the street with all kinds of languages. Seeing different cars pass by, rock music was so loud blowing through the windows to the street that sometimes it spurred the passerby to dance and sing with the music.

After I arrived, New York showed me that my old view of the world was like that of the frog in the well, knowing nothing of the great ocean. It was the first time I realized that the world is so big, and I was just a country girl from a small town of China. Knowing this, I became more active in my life. I joined the school activities and outside programs, I became more social and more determined with the things going on around me.

This is New York, a place that bubbles with enthusiasm and freedom. It is a city with plenty of opportunities; here I have become a more gung-ho and proactive person than I used to be. I am no longer a country girl who couldn't understand what others were talking about. I want people to know: that little Chinese girl who spent her childhood in a small town has grown up. In New York, she has become a young woman who is taking responsibility for her life and starting to fight for her dreams and goals.

CAN YOU DIG IT?

JOSLEEN WILSON

Sometimes discovering new worlds means uncovering old worlds. We can all do it and be rewarded in innumerable ways, including college credits!

 *Begum, p. 174*

 *p. 11*

Out near what is called Agate Basin in eastern Wyoming is a sheep ranch sprawling over thousands of acres under heavy storm-filled skies.

I crouch down next to John Steeger, a student from the University of Iowa, who is digging up dirt with a hand spade and tossing it into a shallow square box. He pours a bucket of water into the box and starts kneading the mud with his bare hands until it washes through the sieved bottom, leaving the tiny fragments of artifact and bone so dear to the heart of archaeologists.

"John, isn't the first thing that attracts people to archaeology the fun of playing in the dirt?"

"Certainly not," he says, waving a muddy hand at me for emphasis. "I hate this. It's disgusting. What I really like to do," he continues, gazing wistfully toward the center of the large excavation site where a dozen other students are working, "is dig in that big dirt hole over there with a shovel."

Like most kids of my generation I grew up with the movies, so very early I knew there were people called archaeologists. They wore funny helmets and were always defying some ancient curse—it was heady stuff and I longed for a shovel of my own. I've learned that I'm not alone in this. Perhaps there's a bit of the scientist in every child, and a little bit of child in every archaeologist.

Aside from its vital role in the discovery and interpretation of human history, archaeology is romantic. I said as much to a professional archaeologist who was working like a mule one muggy ninety-nine degree afternoon in southern Georgia. "You must be kidding," he said, sweat streaming down his forehead and into his eyes. But he smiled as he said it.

Archaeologists insist that the work is hard and painstaking and often dismally unrewarding. True, but there's also no denying it: archaeology is fun. It's traveling to remote places and playing in the dirt. It's meeting interesting people, some of whom have been dead for centuries.

Visiting an archaeological site or joining a dig also provides an almost mystical experience. You needn't view the great gold baubles of Tutankhamen to experience this. Consider the mysterious American deserts of the Southwest, where lost cities are hidden like jewels among the gold bluffs.

Archaeology in the United States is called a living science because descendants of

a single prehistoric race of people, Native Americans, still live here in the pueblo villages of New Mexico and Arizona. Although most modern Americans today come from all over the world, we are also people of this land, and so we are bound strongly to those who lived and died on this soil in centuries past. These ancient people are in a very real sense among our spiritual ancestors.

Here's the best part: In every state, students and amateurs of all ages can participate in summer digs, ranging from the great burial mounds of the Mississippi Valley, to the Marching Bears mounds in Iowa, to the shell heaps of Florida. College students can sign up at their schools. Plus, almost every state has a State Archaeologist or an active amateur archaeological society that welcomes volunteers. So, what are you doing this summer?

DON'T SAY I DIDN'T WARN YOU... HALLANDALE, FLORIDA

MENNEN GORDON

This piece came about in the Travel Writing Journalism Workshop, where we were asked to write about our favorite place. I turned to Florida, a hodgepodge of all the things I hate–hot weather, chain restaurants, and something called "New York Style Pizza."

Roland, p. 100

p. 34

Florida is made for a specific kind of person. If you're a beach bum who loves the feeling of hot sand between your toes and ninety-degree weather on Christmas Day, you will love Florida. In Hallandale there are beaches and pools everywhere, so you would never have to visit the same one twice. But if you are a Yankee, like me, I would not suggest Florida. Even if your favorite place is Coney Island and fish is your favorite food, I suggest you start in Coney Island. If you're planning on vacationing in Florida and hoping you'll fit right in, don't bother—it's a place where no one seems to belong. The old people complain about the young people and the young people complain about the old people—no one can win in Florida.

Hallandale, Florida is hot and humid, even in the winter, but it's not the kind of heat you would feel on a crowded subway in August. Florida is Southern hot. You can feel how close it is to the equator, and it burns. Supposedly, after a week or two of having your blood boil, your body gets

used to the heat, but I didn't stay long enough to find out.

While Florida is right on the water, its own little peninsula that's always first found on a states puzzle, the seafood isn't the best you could eat. Florida is also packed with buffet restaurants where you could purchase every food item known to man (and woman). They have meats and pastas and frozen yogurt and ice cream and a whole section with a myriad of pizzas—thin crust, deep dish, pizza made on focaccia (which may sound good, but keep in mind it's not Italian focaccia; it's Floridian). Most horrifically, you can always find some strange food called "New York Style Pizza." I'm not quite sure what it's meant to be, but it tastes like a bastardization of the city itself.

The state of Florida gets 1.5 stars, half of a star for being bright out for a long time and one star because the word "Floridian" is really cool.

Go there if you'd like, but don't say I didn't warn you.

ANOTHER FACE OF THE BRONX

DAHLMA LLANOS-FIGUEROA

Tired of hearing about all the ills of the Bronx, I wrote this piece about City Island, one of the many undiscovered treasures of the borough.

 Colbert, p. 289

 p. 23

When people think about the Bronx, it seems all the images elicited are negative—burnt-out buildings, crime, menacing teenagers, and homeless men. And all those do exist, as they do in many cities all over the world. But there are many other faces of the Bronx that are never seen on the evening news.

Did you know we have a fishing village here? There are tiny cottages that are hundreds of years old, with gnarly fruit trees in their backyards and a profusion of lush flowering shrubs in the front. There are boat yards and marinas and a tiny yellow submarine in someone's front yard. There's a Bed and Breakfast Inn just as you cross onto the island. It's called City Island and it has some of the best seafood restaurants anywhere. The island is full of white linen and restaurants that overlook the water and the boats that dot the water. And right in the middle of these fine dining establishments is my favorite restaurant, Seafood City. It's nothing like its elegant neighbors. Seafood City can be loud and tacky and way too crowded, with crowds of people who love the well-seasoned food and low prices as much as I do. And their children feed all their change into the penny arcade machines that line the side of the huge room.

But if you go there during the cooler months of the year, in the middle of the day when most people are working or in school, you will find my Seafood City—a cavernous space where silence reigns and the sensuous scents of delicious delicacies fill the air. I pick up my tray and walk right past the sea of dining room tables and onto the terrace overlooking Long Island Sound. I settle down to watch the boats sail by like gentle swans on a tranquil lake. I listen to the caw, caw of the hungry birds overhead and stretch out in the warm sun. Finally, unable to resist the aromas calling from my table, I turn to my king crab legs dripping in garlic butter and fragrant herbs. I suck out the tender, moist meat, and let the juices drip off my fingers. I let the flavors fill my mouth and abandon myself to the pleasure of a well-prepared meal. It takes a long time to eat this particular dish but I am totally happy when, a half hour later, I throw down my last greasy napkin.

So when you are tired of the hustle and bustle of Manhattan and want to kick back and just delight in good food and a quiet seaside afternoon, head north to City Island and don't forget to tell your friends about the wonderful fishing village you found one day—in the Bronx.

CAMILLA, GEORGIA

ALEXUS COLBERT

Travelers may be familiar with the attractions of Atlanta, but few know about the charms of small, rural Georgia towns like Camilla.

 *Llanos-Figueroa, p. 288*

 *p. 23*

"You don't have to live forever; you just have to live," was the last line in the film *Tuck Everlasting*, based on the novel by Natalie Babbitt. This can be taken to mean that you should enjoy life and exploration while it is in your grasp. You can do this in the town of Camilla, Georgia. Although Camilla is a quiet place, it is also very exciting because you never know what you might stumble upon. Maybe a small garden snake in your backpack. Or a frog that sits like a statue, blending in among the blades of grass waiting to capture your attention. You may even come across a small creek in the forest, occupied by a variety of colorful fish enjoying the shaded water.

Camilla, Georgia is a calm place. You can simply rest in the grass under a tree and dive into an interesting book without many interruptions. The grass goes on for miles under the beaming sun and bright blue sky. Sometimes the weather can become very hot and humid, maybe even to the point where you require some sunscreen, or you might even be better off not going out at all. Depending on your preference, this can be a positive or a negative aspect.

Camilla is a great place to escape the city. The city is flooded with people rushing to get to different destinations. The streets are packed with cars pushing up against one another, creating never-ending traffic. The bright lights and constant chatter will surround you. Pollution will hang over the city streets. Camilla, Georgia, on the other hand, is the complete opposite. There aren't any crowds, traffic, or much noise. The air is clean and the only smell is the scent of freshly cut grass or newly opened flowers. One major difference is the fact that here, you can walk barefoot in the front of your home.

Camilla, Georgia can be the perfect place to relax and discover your inner self. Enjoy Atlanta, and then come to Camilla for the real deal.

LONDON

NAJAYA ROYAL

This piece was a challenge, but I'm glad my mentor talked me into stepping out of my comfort zone. I always said I wanted to go to London. It's a new world to me, but I never really thought to write a poem about it. Thanks, Anuja, for opening my eyes yet again to something new.

 *Madar, p. 291*

 *p. 63*

Allow me a moment
For my fantasy and reality to finally meet
I land feet first into a cobble-stoned land
Just a hop across the pond
Where rare adventures await my arrival

London

The setting of my dreams
Air full of mist
The scent of fish and chips dancing around me
To a Spice Girls soundtrack
The melody maneuvers its way through a mix of classic buildings and modern-day homes
Mingling with the most wanted of accents

Let's take a trip to central London
Where the night still has its innocence

No longer dreaming
I'm living within the now
A mild breeze caressing my face
An introduction to an adventure waiting to be pursued
Where my fantasy and reality finally meet

LONDON CALLING

ANUJA MADAR

Najaya has dreamt of London since she was a little girl, and it's a place I've been going since I was a little girl. In writing this piece I discovered my adult view of the city to be a lot different from that of my youth.

Royal, p. 290

p. 63

Let's take a trip
To a place I know well
Where I lost the emphasis in my last name
And those who were overtaken are now taking over
Where various patterns create the same quilt
And what were once new additions now claim there is no more space
Where American is not just a nationality, but an accent
And Indian was the wrong word for what I am
Where my father got an education that put three letters after his name
And I put a hole in my nose for the equivalent of $8
Where my family celebrated love and mourned loss
And I finally understood the bond between branches on the same tree

SAILING AWAY

CLAUDIA PARSONS

My husband and I recently moved aboard a boat. We're getting used to life afloat and spend a lot of time thinking about what the future holds.

 *Hughes, p. 269*

 *p. 40*

I've been reading a lot lately about sailing away. I picture myself, not too long from now, waking up to the sound of waves lapping against the hull of our boat in a lonely bay off some little-known Caribbean island. I would wake up early and get to work on the book—of course I will have plenty of time to write then, when I don't have to go to work every day. Perhaps Rick will be fixing the engine or a water pump. There's always something to fix on a boat, lest you think I have rose-tinted spectacles about this dream. I fully intend to learn how to fix water pumps myself, as they seem to be the most frequent source of trouble. I even downloaded the first chapter of a book on marine diesel engines and read about compression chambers, cylinders, and camshafts.

Another favorite download (no room for real books onboard) is The Boat Galley Cookbook. Who knew there was so much you can do with canned chicken and tuna? I like to think we'll be grilling fresh fish straight from the ocean, but I guess it's good to know how to make yet another meal from canned food. And then there's the whole pressure cooker debate. Love them or hate them, most boat cooks have strong feelings and I assume I will too.

What I am really addicted to, however, is anything and everything that's been written about babies on boats. If there's a blog out there by sailing parents, I want to read it. How do you stop them falling overboard? Where do they sleep? How do you keep them busy? What happens when they get sick? Don't they miss other kids? What about school when they're older? It turns out hundreds of families find the answers to these questions and lots of them are blogging about it. Most of the kids look ridiculously happy in the photos on these blogs, though I suspect the bloggers don't have a camera handy when little Joey gets seasick on a stormy night.

As I sit writing this on a chilly March day in New York, these dreams—boat and baby—seem just out of reach. As it turns out, the dream of sailing away may be the one that is actually possible.

LEIA 2.0

LIZZ CARROLL

This is my first attempt at fan fiction, Luljeta's absolute favorite style of writing (with a focus on characters from DC Comics). As a mini-homage to her passion, I decided to give it a shot, using one of my favorite sci-fi sagas, Star Wars.

 *Zenka, p. 127*

 *p. 74*

A voice called out to her in her dreams. It was familiar, but distant...

"Leia... Leia... Leia? Hey sis, wake up!" Her twin brother's voice vibrated through her skull.

"Ok, ok, ok, Luke! I'm up!" she shouted back without moving her mouth or opening her eyes.

"It's time to get going... I'll meet you at the usual spot in thirty minutes," he said in his usual Zen tone.

"See you soon," she replied with an internal yawn. This whole telepathy thing was definitely going to take some getting used to. But it worked out well for not waking up her husband, Han, who was sleeping peacefully beside her. Getting getting up before the sun rose didn't mean that the whole household had to be disturbed.

This was an ungodly hour, but it was the only way she could get in a full morning of training. The dawn's darkness was a good cover for a new Queen of New Alderaan to travel under the guise of a commoner. She didn't want to draw too much attention—it was already hard enough being the oldest Padawan in Jedi history! Despite the challenge, learning from her brother about tapping into the Force through meditation was the most peaceful part of her day. Every day her telepathic and telekinetic skills grew stronger—she'd even managed to lift R2-D2 two feet off the ground yesterday! Ok, so she was no Master Yoda, but she was on her way.

Leia quietly rose from her bed and got dressed. She pulled her hair back into a hefty bun and made her way to the nursery to check on the twins, Jaina and Jacen. She leaned over to kiss the sleeping infants. Jaina smiled in her slumber with a cherubic glow, but Jacen balled his tiny fists and slept fitfully, tossing and turning with his little brow furrowed. "What could be troubling such a young mind?" Leia wondered.

She suddenly heard a low growl and felt the floor vibrate beneath her feet. "Damn it!" she whispered out loud while shaking her head. "How does anyone sleep through that Wookiee's snoring?"

Leia loved Chewbacca just as much as her husband did... well, almost. Their little bromance was a bit much. Living with the seven-foot-three furball was no picnic, what with the snoring that sounded like the Millennium Falcon was landing in his bedroom and the never-ending hairballs that she would find in every corner of the house.

But cleaning up Chewie's messes was a small price to pay for such a loyal addition to the family. Even Jaina and Jacen loved him. Despite his overwhelming mane, long claws, and guttural utterings in Thykarann, he was a source of joy for the little ones. Some of their best naps happened in his big furry arms.

As Leia tucked her blue saber into her utility belt and boarded the elevator, she smiled knowing that all was right in her little corner of the galaxy.

MY ABDUCTION

AMANDA BERLIN

Learning to deal with anxiety and depression can feel like being thrown into a new world, one you hadn't intended to explore. However, in a new place you get to be a new person, and it's up to you who that person is.

 Gomez, p. 214

 p. 33

I pack my carabineer and my climbing rope, my harness, and the shoes that have the extra grips, designed specifically for this kind of trek. In January of 2012, they cut the rope that had me tethered to the corporate ladder I never had any desire to climb. I didn't have my equipment with me at the time, but I knew what I needed. And I was ready.

I got my stuff together and moved over to another peak, one that promised fulfillment, great views, and an element of choose-your-own-adventure, at least according to the guidebooks. It was green and lush and the trail was lined with tall grass, swaying in a breeze that brought with it hints of lavender and pine.

When I started walking, I listened for my footfalls and I gave thanks for the new earth beneath my feet. I was jittery with excitement. I could extend my arms and open my heart and let this new world in. It welcomed me. As I climbed, though, the air got thin.

The walk got harder as the fraternal twins, anxiety and depression, wrapped their arms around my neck. All limbs and thick in the middle, they scurried their way up my back. Using all their might to pull me from the path, I lose my footing and they drag me to the edge of the trail. The beautiful landscape morphs into a craggy moonscape, barren and threatening. Someplace that might starve me and rob me of breath.

My feet scrape the earth searching for footing. But all I do is loosen black pebbles, making it even harder for me to regain a stance. The harder I try, the further off course they lead me, dragging me behind them like a criminal fighting against her executioners. Finally, I let myself collapse under their weight. They each put a foot on my chest, claiming victory, pumping long arms over their heads. The twins begin jumping up and down on what they believe is my lifeless corpse, like flying monkeys eviscerating the scarecrow.

I play dead until they get distracted. Then, I carefully raise myself from the scarred earth and make my way back to the path, the original one that beckons, the one I know I should be on. I look back and see the twins scurrying to reclaim me. All arms and legs, hooting and hollering.

Instead of quickening my pace and dealing with another death-grip tackle and abduction, I entertain the idea of inviting them along. They catch up, one on either side of me. They each sling a long ape-like limb through mine, walking beside me. My journey into this world would be better without them. But when we arrive back to the place where I left all my gear, I clip in and pray the ropes and harnesses can accommodate the extra weight.

STEPHANIE HUANCAS, MENTEE 2006-2007

At the young and chaotic age of fifteen, writing was my only means to escape reality into a world more optimistic and full of hope. It helped me assume the mantle of an artist, and I felt proud of being a creator of worlds happier than my life.

workshops
BEHIND THE SCENES

All writing is exploration. From the most expansive travel journal to the smallest self-examination, we write to discover what we think and feel about the world. Thoughtful exploration gives us the power to choose how we live our lives.

With that in mind, we created this year's curriculum around the theme *New Worlds*. We wanted to encourage our community to grapple with the idea of exploration through our six workshops—poetry, fiction, memoir, journalism, play- or screenwriting, and a "wildcard" to end the year—from perspectives as broad as seeing another country for the first time and as specific as arriving at a new understanding of the world from a single experience.

Each workshop is itself an exercise in exploration. We start with an opening exercise and build on it throughout the day, and we focus each workshop on a particular writing skill. We created poetry that was epic, traveled to Civil War-era Brooklyn through historical fiction, journeyed inward in our Family Memoir Workshop, learned about travel writing in journalism, and experienced how locations influence drama in site-specific theater. For this year's wildcard, we chose fan fiction, culminating our year of exploration either by taking characters we knew and dropping them into brand new worlds of our own invention, or by inventing new characters to exist in fictional worlds.

In this chapter, you'll meet the mentors who help produce our curriculum, the esteemed guest authors who deliver craft talks, and the mentors and mentees who build their portfolios and their writing identities with each workshop. Take a peek behind the scenes.

JULIE POLK
CURRICULUM CO-CHAIR

POETRY WORKSHOP: NARRATIVE POETRY

OCTOBER 2012

As we trickled into the Girls Write Now headquarters on Saturday morning, there was an unspoken magnetic buzz in the air. The lights were off, but the sun was doing a remarkable job of seeping through the big windows and giving the room that subtle autumn glow that makes mornings so special.

That day at the workshop, mentees and mentors were introduced to narrative poetry. Rather than jumping straight into writing a poem, the pairs constructed a poem from the ground up. We began by brainstorming characters, adding a scenario, and writing a story.

With help from our special guest poets, Dorothea Lasky and Camille Rankine, we considered what defines poetry. We observed its rhythm, breaks, language, look, and the feelings evoked by reading it.

We then turned our stories into poems by deleting words, inverting sentences, and adding more descriptions while maintaining the element of storytelling. To switch things up a bit, we also took each other's characters and scenarios and made narrative poems out of these new prompts.

JOANN DELUNA, MENTOR LEADER

GUEST AUTHORS

DOROTHEA LASKY is the author of three full-length collections of poetry: *Thunderbird, Black Life,* and *AWE.*

CAMILLE RANKINE is the author of *Slow Dance with Trip Wire*, selected by Cornelius Eady for the Poetry Society of America's 2010 New York Chapbook Fellowship.

FROM THE WORKSHOP

By the end of the session, sitting in my pink notebook were two narrative poems I could proudly call my own, all because of the guidance given to me throughout the workshop. With this being my first year in Girls Write Now, I am so happy to be a part of this vibrant community that I can call home.

MAYA LASHLEY, MENTEE

I can't even imagine how empowered I would feel right now if I had an experience like Girls Write Now growing up. The girls there are lucky to have such a tremendous group of mentors to learn and draw from. But we are also lucky to have these girls, because they are going to grow up strong, brave, and poised to change literature for the better.
DOROTHEA LASKY, GUEST AUTHOR

As if he
Himself
Had melted the gold in his own pot
And dipped the very paintbrush inside
As if he, himself
Brushed over everything
She loved.

And it was only to make him stop, she
gently
Touched the tips of her fingers
To his shoulder
So lightly, even she
Could not feel his warmth under her
But instead of him stopping, she was

Running across a river of
Golden syrup, engulfing her,
Everything slowing down,

And suddenly, she was
Stopping.
KIARA KERINA-RENDINA, MENTEE

FICTION WORKSHOP: HISTORICAL FICTION

NOVEMBER 2012

We are asked to step into a time machine—to fiddle with bright dials, tinker with metal gearshifts, set the clock backward to the period that most inspires us. The past is a world we'll attempt to pin down by means of recording new sights, sounds, and smells.

Guest author Zetta Elliott, a vibrant, engaging speaker and the author of

A Wish After Midnight, reads an excerpt from her work. Times have changed for women and minorities in this country, but her protagonist fears "ghetto" is stamped onto her skin just as boldly as "slave" might have been 150 years ago. Elliott speaks passionately of sankofa, the notion of "go back and fetch it"; we learn that there is no shame in going back to retrieve something of value you left in a darker time.

Jennifer Epstein, author of *The Painter from Shanghai*, describes world-building as a sensory experience, not a march of dry historical facts. Next in the process comes character, followed by conflict, which propels the story forward. Human beings don't differ significantly today from our ancestors, and ultimately the tale we want to tell is about struggles that resonate in the present day.

We choose a point of conflict—money, poisoned water, a baby, a murder; any charged incident will do—and use it to introduce chaos into our orderly historical world. Whether we use meticulous research or create wild alternate histories, whether our books are based on vintage news articles or on the imagined history of Grandma's favorite hatpin, we are stirring the pot, adding drama to our already-foreign and fascinating scene.

As I leave the workshop, inspired by the company of so many female writers of all ages and backgrounds, I find myself dwelling on Elliott's talk of magic doors. "The Door of No Return" is both a real historical aspect of the slave trade and an imagined rabbit hole, a tunnel through which our characters plummet, leaving the present behind to explore the wonders of the past.

LYNDSAY FAYE, MENTOR

GUEST AUTHORS

ZETTA ELLIOTT is a poet, playwright, essayist, and novelist. Her latest novel, *Ship of Souls*, was published in 2012 and named one of *Booklist's* Top Ten Sci-fi/Fantasy Titles for Youth.

HILLARY JORDAN is the author the novels *Mudbound* and *When She Woke*. Her books have been translated into ten languages, including French, Turkish, Brazilian Portuguese, and Chinese.

FROM THE WORKSHOP

I work with rather fast-paced, ephemeral material, as I'm a professional blogger-Tweeter-Facebooker, but I also love writing about life in the pre-

Internet, pre-texting era, which fostered a quieter state of mind. Yet the world I conjured in the workshop had just as much intrigue, romance, and conflict as my own does today. I imagined my grandparents as they first met in the 1930s, and had a lot of fun with two characters who were too shy to even say hello. (Spoiler alert: someone did.)
KRISTEN DEMALINE, MENTOR (*See the finished piece on p. 176*)

I remember walking down the broken road with my brown leather suitcase in one hand and my father's business bag in the other. Pieces of glass, pebbles, broken items and drugs of every kind were crushing and lingering under the soles of my black military boots, custom made by the most famous and #1 designer in Afghanistan. After a few more steps, Babu and I turned back around to look one last time at what was left of our beautiful mansion, and the greatest piece of land in all the country. But now, our life had completely changed.
BUSHRA MIAH, MENTEE

MEMOIR WORKSHOP: FAMILY MEMOIR

DECEMBER 2012

Everyone has family stories. But which ones do you want to tell? Which ones can you tell? The Family Memoir Workshop asked mentors and mentees to transform their families into compelling characters while still writing truthful portraits of them.

We began by sketching a memorable moment, which became the foundation for another exercise: building a scene enlivened by details and dialogue, aiming to capture unique quirks and habits. Then the group was asked to take a step back and explain why the moment was important, adding reflection and perspective. What made this a story worth telling versus just a fond memory?

Guest authors Patricia Bosworth and Susan Morse entertained and inspired us with their insights into the delicate process of transforming memory into material that has the narrative force of fiction and the resonance of true stories bravely told.

As we listened to one another's memories—of closeness and estrangement,

sorrow and happiness—the group gained understanding of the craft and courage it takes to honor our family stories through the art of memoir.

JULIE SALAMON, MENTOR LEADER

GUEST AUTHORS

PATRICIA BOSWORTH is the author of several biographies, including *Jane Fonda: The Private Life of a Public Woman*, and *Anything Your Little Heart Desires: An American Family Story*, a memoir about her relationship with her father.

SUSAN MORSE is the author of *The Habit*, an account of her experience with her mother's journey into old age.

FROM THE WORKSHOP

I'm excited to try my hand at memoir, but truthfully I don't know if I have enough memories yet—if I've lived enough. One thing I am going to do is follow a piece of advice Patricia Bosworth gave us: keep a journal to record the experiences, impressions, and characters of my life. By the time I accumulate my book of memories, I hope to have the tools to turn them into a story.
NINA AGRAWAL, MENTOR

I gave a five-minute reading to demonstrate how and when a writer can get away with misquoting and satirizing the villain in a true story. Then we discussed why I might have wanted to do this (for revenge, of course) and finished up with a rousing Q&A. Here's a standout question they threw at me: Which do you consider yourself first, a writer or a family member? Fantastic question for a memoirist. Girls Write Now rocks.
SUSAN MORSE, GUEST AUTHOR

His kindergarten teacher would never hear the end of this. How had she sent a five-year-old to sit outside of her classroom without supervision as punishment for being a disruption? She said he'd been Hurricane Connor—loud and jumpy and ignoring class rules, rolling around like a bowling ball, taking Legos and crayons and playing with them for seconds before bouncing off to do something else. I knew exactly what she was talking about.
BRIANNA MARIE MARINI, MENTEE

JOURNALISM WORKSHOP: TRAVEL WRITING

MARCH 2013

The Journalism Workshop invited us to take each other on a journey. We learned how to truly transport a reader by focusing on setting: the smells, tastes, sounds, sights, and feel of a place.

First we considered a new and exciting place we've been to recently, or a familiar place that really lights us up. Then we answered a series of questions that helped us get in touch with the concrete details about the place, or the journey to get there, as well as the intangible energy of the experience.

Guest journalists Lauren Mechling and Heidi Mitchell led us through the process of idea conception, the dos and don'ts of finding an angle, pitching an idea, editing a piece, and finally presenting it to the reading public. We dissected differences in tone, types of information, and the experience of the reader. The workshops also covered other journalism nuances, like how to write a lede or make a pitch, and working with an editor.

By the end of the workshop, we had crafted our own reviews, distilled them down to a lede, listened and reviewed like editors, and presented our work as we would in the professional world of journalism.

AMANDA BERLIN, MENTOR LEADER

GUEST AUTHORS

LAUREN MECHLING is editor-at-large of the *Wall Street Journal's* Off Duty section. She has been published in *The Wall Street Journal, The New York Times, New York Magazine, The New York Sun*, and *Marie Claire,* among others. Lauren has written or co-written six young adult books.

HEIDI MITCHELL is a journalist and editor based in New York. She has contributed to *Town & Country, Town & Country Weddings, Town & Country Travel, Travel + Leisure, The Financial Times, The Wall Street Journal, Architectural Digest*, and *Newsweek.*

FROM THE WORKSHOP

I learned how to describe the space and places around me in a way that would intrigue others. Not only was the guest speaker, Heidi Mitchell, attention-grabbing and funny, she also taught me a lot about travel writing and

journalism. I've never before given much thought or time to the travel articles I've seen in magazines and in papers, but now I'm really intrigued.
KATHERINE MARTINEZ, MENTEE

Our guest author started the workshop with one of her own pieces, a story about her learning how to ride a galloping horse in Argentina. It reminded me of the fact that there is a personal touch in everything we write—in Mitchell's case, the gallop took her back to her Midwestern roots. Her story highlighted the importance of personal experience and taking notes while things are fresh in your mind. Both make a story that can transport the reader from feeling the metallic background of a New York City subway to the hot, sweet sun of Argentina.
RACHEL ZHAO, MENTEE

PLAYWRITING WORKSHOP: SITE-SPECIFIC PLAYS

APRIL 2013

This workshop may live in infamy as the first (and almost certainly last!) time that a workshop leader was attacked with a trash can. Well, almost attacked. It was for educational purposes!

Our playwriting team and guest authors, Jessica Blank and Erika Sheffer, used the innovative genre of site-specific theatre to dig into what gives a great play its heartbeat, no matter where it's being performed: the dialogue. We investigated how the characters' interactions with one another are influenced by where they are. Two people breaking up during yoga class, whispering between poses, would probably have very different dialogue than they would if they were breaking up at a construction site and screaming over the power tools. Right?

Of course, no Playwriting Workshop would be complete without getting some of our mentors and mentees up on stage! We asked groups to think about how the dialogue in the scenes they'd written earlier in the day might change if they were set somewhere completely different, and the results were so much fun for our performers and workshop partipants alike. Everyone left empowered to unleash their works of theater on the world, wherever they may find a stage. Or abandoned hospital. Or boardwalk. Or park bench. Or subway car.

CHRISTINA BROSMAN, MENTOR LEADER

GUEST AUTHORS

JESSICA BLANK is the co-author of *The Exonerated*, a play based on interviews conducted with over 40 exonerated death row inmates. The play has been nominated for five Ovation Awards, three NAACP Awards, and won the Ovation for Best World Premiere Play.

ERIKA SHEFFER is the current recipient of The Vineyard Theater's Paula Vogel Playwriting Award, and her playwriting debut, *Russian Transport*, received its world premiere at The New Group in January 2012.

FROM THE WORKSHOP

Later in the workshop, we took our newfound knowledge about site-specific conflict and broke into small groups, where we co-wrote a skit and performed it for our fellow mentees and mentors. Suddenly, I was transported back to those high school performances I had long since tucked away in my memories: the giddy energy of creating a believable performance with peers, and the joy of performing, no matter how small the role. It turns out that the stage door is always open—no matter how long you thought it was closed.
AMY FLYNTZ, MENTOR

I felt nervous about sharing our writing through acting. Much to my surprise though, when our turn to perform came, I had a lot of fun seeing the words we had written on our pages transformed into a living, breathing, in-person experience. It turns out writing doesn't have to be so far removed from the stage after all.
NINA AGRAWAL, MENTOR

WILDCARD WORKSHOP: FAN FICTION

MAY 2013

This year's workshops explored new worlds —of writing, self, and circumstance. Each month we honed our skills to create richer settings, build greater suspense, craft realistic dialogue, and develop dynamic characters. The Fan Fiction Workshop was the capstone of our curriculum, where we explored the concept of worldbuilding—creating an imaginary world complete with culture, custom, history, and geography.

Guest author Racheline Maltese, a dynamic performer and storyteller, inspired us to write our own stories about the worlds we've come to love through others' writing. Assured that the desire to write about our favorite literary worlds was both legitimate and writerly, we immediately became fan fiction writers.

The first step is to ask oneself, "What if?" What if Alice wasn't dreaming? What if Harry was You-Know-Who? What if we knew what happened after the story ended, or what transpired before it began? What if our favorite characters could transport from one work to another and have new adventures in alternate worlds, and what if we had the power to make that happen? Turns out, we do.

ALLISON YARROW, CURRICULUM CO-CHAIR

GUEST AUTHOR

RACHELINE MALTESE is a performer and storyteller. Her fiction, non-fiction and poetry has appeared in numerous outlets, and she is a regular speaker on pop culture topics at fan and academic conferences. Racheline is also a co-founder of the musical theater production company Treble Entendre.

FROM THE WORKSHOP

I looked out at the sea of victims waiting to see who would be called to compete in the Quarter Quell alongside my sister. The theme of this Quell was gender. The last victor of each district would be sent into the Hunger Games with a person of the same gender. There was no emotion on the faces of these girls, not even fear. There were dark circles under their eyes and they hadn't even bothered to brush their hair.

LAWRENCIA TERRIS, MENTEE

Hermione, with her bushy hair pinned into a messy excuse for a bun, glanced at the great clock levitating above her head. It was nearly midnight, she determined, as she slammed her potions book shut with excessive anxiety. "Am I really doing this again?" she rhetorically asked herself, her cheeks flushing a lively red as she raced past the staircase to Gryffindor's common room. The grounds were off-limits for students after dark, and even dangerous. Yet, Hermione proceeded with a racing heart, only remembering Draco's face last night, as he reached out and kissed her lips.

SARA REKA, MENTEE

BRITTANY BARKER, MENTEE 2008-2011

It's been two years since I graduated from Girls Write Now and I still carry the knowledge and confidence they gave me. After two years in the program, I recognized the power of voice, and the power of individualism through narrative. Though I obtained many of these opportunities on my own, Girls Write Now is one of the most prominent catalysts behind my desire to take advantage of them, and why I believe in myself as a respectable writer. I am a spoken word poet. I am a voice for and of Girls Write Now.

BOARD OF DIRECTORS Kamy Wicoff, *Board Chair;* Chelsea Rao, *Vice Chair;* Lisa Chai, *Treasurer;* Nancy K. Miller, *Secretary;* Unyi Agba, Sandra Bang, Carol Blum, Lee Clifford, Sang Lee, Justine Lelchuk, Maya Nussbaum, Ellen Sweet

PROGRAM ADVISORY COMMITTEE Maria T. Romano, *Program Advisory Committee Chair;* Julie Polk, *Curriculum Co-Chair;* Allison Yarrow, *Curriculum Co-Chair;* Demetria Irwin, *Mentor Enrollment Chair;* Rachel Cohen, *Mentee Enrollment Chair;* Heather Smith, *Mentor Community Chair;* Erin Baer, *Pair Support Co-Chair;* Alissa Riccardelli, *Pair Support Co-Chair;* Hilary Leichter, *Readings Co-Chair;* Ilana Manaster, *Readings Co-Chair*

YOUTH BOARD Ximena Castillo, *Youth Board Chair;* Christina Butan, Taysha Clark, Rocio Cuevas, Shannon Daniels, Teamaré Gaston, Sussy Liz, Amanda Day McCullough, Ava Nadel, Emely Paulino, Idamaris Perez, Yolandri Vargas, Samantha White, Xiao Hong Zhang

STAFF Maya Nussbaum, *Founder & Executive Director;* Jessica Wells-Hasan, *Director of Development & External Affairs;* Tiffany Stevens, *Director of Operations;* Laura Stenson Wynne, *Director of Programs;* Laura Cheung, *Communications Coordinator;* Anusha Mehar, *Senior Program Coordinator;* Rebecca Haverson, *Program Coordinator;* Emily Coppel, *Digital Program Manager;* Meghan McNamara, *Program Advisor;* Julia Vallera, *Digital Media Arts Consultant*

INTERNS Louise Albano-Hurley, Gabrielle Barnes, Monica Carr, Natalia Fadul, Jessica Figueroa, Nora Hennick, Kathryn Jagai, Josie Orsini

POETRY AMBASSADORS Mariah Teresa Aviles, Christina Butan, Priscilla Guo, Joanne Lin, Bre'Ann Newsome, Tema Regist, Najaya Royal

WORKSHOP TEAMS

POETRY: Anna Bradfield, Amy Choi, JoAnn Deluna, Jessi Hempel, Leora Morinis, Jodi Narde

FICTION: Allie Alberts, Jennifer Epstein, Christy Pottroff, Hanna Pylväinen, Kate Trebuss, Alyssa Vine

MEMOIR: Savannah Ashour, Pam Bayless, Linda Corman, Sara Lippmann, Julie Salamon, My-Thuan Tran

JOURNALISM: Nina Agrawal, Amanda Berlin, Amy DiLuna, Rachel Krantz, Lynn Lurie, Claudia Parsons, Ingrid Skjong

PLAYWRITING: Christina Brosman, Mary Pat Kane, Heather Kristin, Katherine Nero, Annie Reuter, Juliet Werner

FAN FICTION: Lyndsay Faye, Kate Jacobs, Kathryn O'Dell Hurdman, Gillian Reagan, Rory Satran, Kathleen Scheiner

READINGS COMMITTEE Sherry Amatenstein, Alex Berg, Siobhan Burke, Alice Canick, Amy Flyntz, Jess Pastore, Jeanine Poggi, Hadia Sheerazi

MENTOR ENROLLMENT COMMITTEE Jalylah Burrell, Robin Marantz Henig, Nancy Hooper, LaToya Jordan, Joanna Laufer, Luciana Lopez, Heidi Overbeck

MENTEE ENROLLMENT COMMITTEE Meg Cassidy, Mayuri Chandra, Ehmonie Hainey, Judy Roland

THERAPY PANEL Kristin Long, *Therapy Panel Coordinator;* Julie May, *Therapy Panel Coordinator;* Betty Bederson, Simone Bloch, Jason Conover, Judi Evans, Cora Goldfarb, Peggy Horowitz, Judi Levy, Nancy Long, Stephanie Vanden Bos, Eva Young

COLLEGE PREP PANEL Andrea Gabbidon-Levene, *College Prep Co-Chair;* Moira Taylor, *College Prep Co-Chair*

MARKETING COMMITTEE Ellen Sweet, *Acting Marketing Chair;* Unyi Agba, Morgan Baden, Lizz Carroll, Ashley Howard, Vicki Jacobs, Anuja Madar, Susan Oehrig, Tracy Perez

FUNDRAISING COMMITTEE Chelsea Rao, *Fundraising Chair*; Elaine Stuart-Shah, *Mentor Fundraising Chair;* Unyi Agba, Carol Blum, Samantha Carlin, Lee Clifford, Anne Feigus, Madelyne Zollo

FINANCE & AUDIT COMMITTEE Lisa Chai, *Finance & Audit Chair;* Carol Blum, Sang Lee, Julia Monteith Semrai, Erica Mui